Excel 2007 for Starters

THE MISSING MANUAL

D1366019

Excel 2007 for Starters

THE MISSING MANUAL

Your best friend for answers

Matthew MacDonald

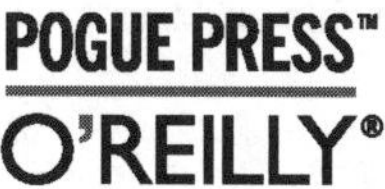

Beijing • Cambridge • Farnham • Köln • Paris • Sebastopol • Taipei • Tokyo

Excel 2007 for Starters: THE MISSING MANUAL

by Matthew MacDonald

Copyright © 2007 O'Reilly Media, Inc. All rights reserved.
Printed in the United States of America.

Published by O'Reilly Media, Inc., 1005 Gravenstein Highway North, Sebastopol, CA 95472.

O'Reilly books may be purchased for educational, business, or sales promotional use. Online editions are also available for most titles (*safari.oreilly.com*). For more information, contact our corporate/institutional sales department: (800) 998-9938 or *corporate@oreilly.com*.

Printing History:
January 2007: First Edition.

Nutshell Handbook, the Nutshell Handbook logo, and the O'Reilly logo are registered trademarks of O'Reilly Media, Inc. *Excel 2007 for Starters: The Missing Manual*, The Missing Manual logo, Pogue Press, the Pogue Press logo, For Starters, and "Your best friend for answers" are trademarks of O'Reilly Media, Inc.

Many of the designations used by manufacturers and sellers to distinguish their products are claimed as trademarks. Where those designations appear in this book, and O'Reilly Media, Inc. was aware of a trademark claim, the designations have been printed in caps or initial caps.

While every precaution has been taken in the preparation of this book, the publisher and author assume no responsibility for errors or omissions, or for damages resulting from the use of the information contained herein.

This book uses RepKover™, a durable and flexible lay-flat binding.

ISBN-10: 0-596-52832-9
ISBN-13: 978-0-596-52832-4
[M]

TABLE OF CONTENTS

PART TWO: WORKSHEET POWER

THE MISSING CREDITS

About the Author

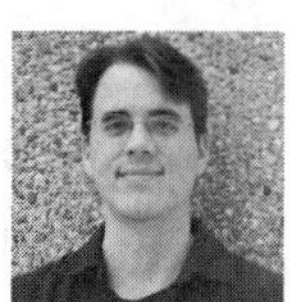

Matthew MacDonald is an author and programmer extraordinaire. He's the author of *Access 2007: The Missing Manual, Creating Web Sites: The Missing Manual,* and over a dozen books about programming with the Microsoft .NET Framework. In a dimly remembered past life, he studied English literature and theoretical physics.

About the Creative Team

Peter Meyers (editor) works as an editor at O'Reilly Media on the Missing Manual series. He lives with his wife and cats in New York City. Email: *peter.meyers@gmail.com.*

Rhea Howard (technical reviewer) works in the Operations department at O'Reilly Media and is an avid Excel user. She currently splits her time between Sebastopol and San Francisco, CA.

Zack Barresse (technical reviewer) started teaching himself Excel in 2003 and fast became an addict. In October 2005, he was awarded the Microsoft MVP award for Excel. Along with Jake Hilderbrand, he owns *www.VBAeXpress.com*, a site dedicated to VBA. His full-time gig is as an ambulance EMT. Zack's a family man and a volunteer lieutenant with his local fire department.

Sohaila Abdulali (copy editor) is a freelance writer and editor. She has published a novel, several children's books, and numerous short stories and articles. She lives in New York City with her husband, Tom, and their small but larger-than-life daughter, Samara. She can be reached through her web site at *www.sohailaink.com.*

Acknowledgements

Writing a book about a program as sprawling and complex as Excel is a labor of love (love of pain, that is). I'm deeply indebted to a whole host of people, including those who helped me track down all the neat and nifty things you can do with the latest version of Office (including bloggers extraordinaire David Gainer and Jensen Harris), those who kept the book clear, concise, and technically accurate (Peter Meyers, Sarah Milstein, Zack Barresse, and Rhea Howard), and those who put up with me while I wrote it (more on that in a moment). I also owe thanks to many people who worked to get this book formatted, indexed, and printed.

Completing this book required a few sleepless nights (and many sleep-deprived days). I extend my love and thanks to my daughter, Maya, who put up with it without crying most of the time; my dear wife Faria, who mostly did the same; and our moms and dads (Nora, Razia, Paul, and Hamid), who contributed hours of babysitting, tasty meals, and general help around the house that kept this book on track. So thanks everyone—without you, half of the book would still be trapped inside my brain!

The Missing Manual Series

Missing Manuals are witty, superbly written guides to computer products that don't come with printed manuals (which is just about all of them). Each book features a handcrafted index and RepKover, a detached-spine binding that lets the book lie perfectly flat without the assistance of weights or cinder blocks.

Recent and upcoming titles include:

Access 2003 for Starters: The Missing Manual by Kate Chase and Scott Palmer

Access 2007 for Starters: The Missing Manual by Matthew MacDonald

Access 2007: The Missing Manual by Matthew MacDonald

Digital Photography: The Missing Manual by Chris Grover and Barbara Brundage

Excel 2003 for Starters: The Missing Manual by Matthew MacDonald

Excel 2003: The Missing Manual by Matthew MacDonald

Excel 2007: The Missing Manual by Matthew MacDonald

Google: The Missing Manual, Second Edition by Sarah Milstein, J.D. Biersdorfer, and Matthew MacDonald

iMovie 6 & iDVD: The Missing Manual by David Pogue

iPhoto 6: The Missing Manual by David Pogue

iPod: The Missing Manual, Fifth Edition by J.D. Biersdorfer

PCs: The Missing Manual by Andy Rathbone

Photoshop Elements 5: The Missing Manual by Barbara Brundage

PowerPoint 2007 for Starters: The Missing Manual by E.A. Vander Veer

PowerPoint 2007: The Missing Manual by E.A. Vander Veer

Quicken for Starters: The Missing Manual by Bonnie Biafore

The Internet: The Missing Manual by David Pogue and J.D. Biersdorfer

Windows XP for Starters: The Missing Manual by David Pogue

Windows XP Home Edition: The Missing Manual, Second Edition by David Pogue

Windows XP Pro: The Missing Manual, Second Edition by David Pogue, Craig Zacker, and Linda Zacker

Windows Vista: The Missing Manual by David Pogue

Windows Vista for Starters: The Missing Manual by David Pogue

Word 2007 for Starters: The Missing Manual by Chris Grover

Word 2007: The Missing Manual by Chris Grover

INTRODUCTION

- What You Can Do with Excel
- Excel's New Face
- Excel's New Features
- About This Book

MOST PEOPLE DON'T NEED MUCH CONVINCING TO USE EXCEL, Microsoft's premier spreadsheet software. In fact, the program comes *preinstalled* on a lot of computers, making it the obvious choice for millions of number crunchers. Despite its wide use, however, few people know where to find Excel's most impressive features or why they'd want to use them in the first place. *Excel 2007 for Starters: The Missing Manual* fills that void, explaining everything from basic Excel concepts to time- and frustration-saving shortcuts.

This book teaches you not only how the program works, but it helps you steer clear of obscure options that aren't worth the trouble to learn. Meanwhile, you'll learn how to home in on the hidden gems that'll win you the undying adoration of your coworkers, family, and friends—or at least your accountant.

NOTE

This book is written with Microsoft's latest and greatest release in mind: Excel 2007. This book won't help you if you're using an earlier version of Excel, because Microsoft has dramatically changed Excel's user interface (the "look and feel" of the program). However, if you're an unredeemed Excel 2003 or Excel 2002 fanatic, you can get help from the previous edition of this book, which is simply named *Excel 2003 for Starters: The Missing Manual*. The Mac version of Excel is covered in *Office 2004 for Macintosh: The Missing Manual*.

What You Can Do with Excel

Excel and Word are the two powerhouses of the Microsoft Office family. While Word lets you create and edit documents, Excel specializes in letting you create, edit, and analyze *data* that's organized into lists or tables. This grid-like arrangement of information is called a *spreadsheet*. Figure I-1 shows an example.

TIP

Excel shines when it comes to *numerical* data, but the program doesn't limit you to calculations. While it has the computing muscle to analyze stacks of numbers, it's equally useful for keeping track of the DVDs in your personal movie collection.

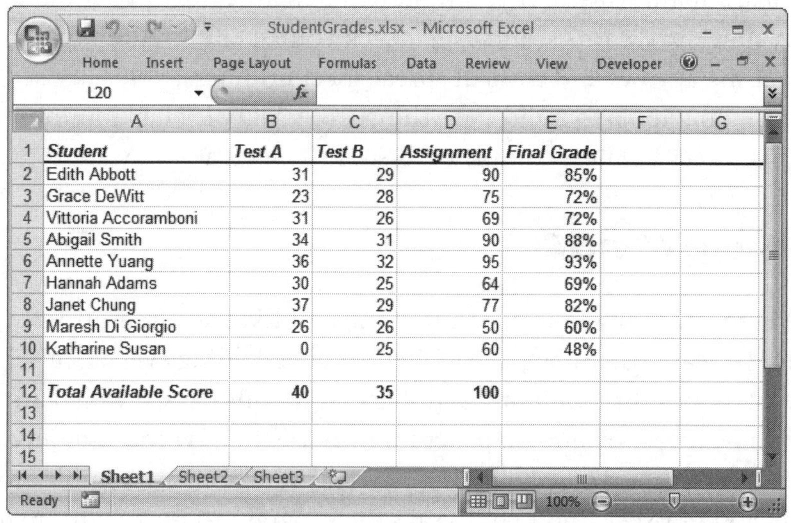

	A	B	C	D	E	F	G
1	*Student*	*Test A*	*Test B*	*Assignment*	*Final Grade*		
2	Edith Abbott	31	29	90	85%		
3	Grace DeWitt	23	28	75	72%		
4	Vittoria Accoramboni	31	26	69	72%		
5	Abigail Smith	34	31	90	88%		
6	Annette Yuang	36	32	95	93%		
7	Hannah Adams	30	25	64	69%		
8	Janet Chung	37	29	77	82%		
9	Maresh Di Giorgio	26	26	50	60%		
10	Katharine Susan	0	25	60	48%		
11							
12	***Total Available Score***	**40**	**35**	**100**			
13							
14							
15							

Figure I-1. This spreadsheet lists nine students, each of whom has two test scores and an assignment grade. Using Excel formulas, it's easy to calculate the final grade for each student.

Some common spreadsheets include:

- **Business documents** like financial statements, invoices, expense reports, and earnings statements.
- **Personal documents** like weekly budgets, catalogs of your *Star Wars* action figures, exercise logs, and shopping lists.
- **Scientific data** like experimental observations, models, and medical charts.

These examples just scratch the surface. Resourceful spreadsheet gurus use Excel to build everything from cross-country trip itineraries to logs of every Kevin Bacon movie they've ever seen.

Note

Keen eyes will notice that Figure I-1 doesn't include the omnipresent Excel ribbon, which usually sits atop the window, stacked with buttons. That's because it's been collapsed neatly out of the way to let you focus on the spreadsheet. You'll learn how to use this trick yourself on page 37.

Excel's not just a math wizard. If you want to add a little life to your data, you can inject color, apply exotic fonts, and even check your spelling. And if you're bleary-eyed from staring at rows and rows of spreadsheet numbers, you can use Excel's many chart-making tools to build everything from 3-D pie charts to more exotic scatter graphs. Excel can be as simple or as sophisticated as you want it to be.

Excel's New Face

Although Microsoft's reluctant to admit it, most of Excel's core features were completed nearly 10 years ago. So what has Microsoft been doing ever since? The answer, at least in part, is spending millions of dollars on usability tests, which are aimed at figuring out how easy—or not—a program is to use. In a typical usability test, Microsoft gathers a group of spreadsheet novices, watches them fumble around with the latest version of Excel, and then tweaks the program to make it more intuitive.

After producing Excel 2003, Microsoft finally decided that minor tune-ups couldn't fix Excel's overly complex, button-heavy toolbars. So they decided to start over. The result is a radically redesigned user interface that actually makes sense. The centerpiece of this redesign is the super-toolbar called the *ribbon*.

The Ribbon

Everything you'll ever want to do in Excel—from picking a fancy background color to prepping your spreadsheet for printing—is packed into the ribbon. To accommodate all these buttons without becoming an over-stuffed turkey, the ribbon uses *tabs*. Excel starts out with seven tabs in the ribbon. When you click one of these tabs, you see a whole new collection of buttons (Figure I-2).

TIP

Wondering what each tab holds? You'll take a tab tour in Chapter 1.

The ribbon is the best thing to hit the Excel scene in years. The ribbon makes it easier to find features and remember where they are, because each feature is grouped into a logically related tab. Even better, once you find the button you need you can often find other, associated commands by looking at the section where the button is placed. In other words, the ribbon isn't just a convenient tool—it's also a great way to explore Excel.

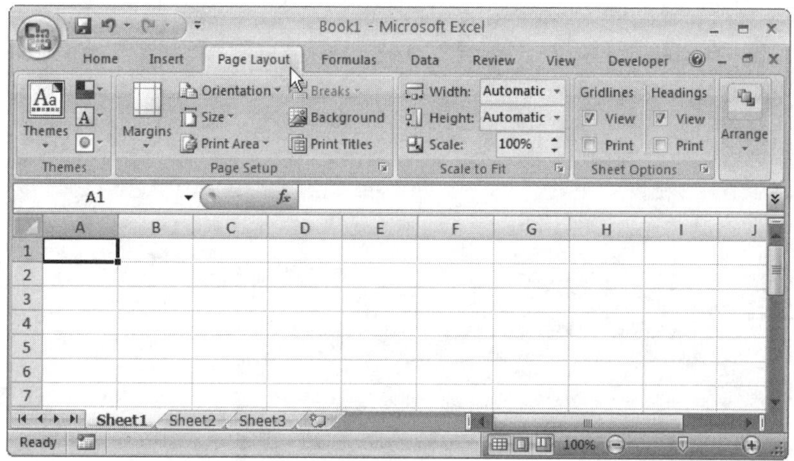

Figure I-2. When you launch Excel you start at the Home tab, but here's what happens when you click the Page Layout tab. Now, you have a slew of options for tasks like adjusting paper size and making a decent printout. The buttons in a tab are grouped into smaller boxes for clearer organization.

The ribbon is full of craftsmanship-like detail. For example, when you hover over a button, you don't see a paltry two- or three-word description in a yellow box. Instead, you see a friendly pop-up box with a complete mini-description and a shortcut that lets you trigger this command from the keyboard. Another nice detail is the way the way you can jump through the tabs at high velocity by positioning the mouse pointer over the ribbon and rolling the scroll wheel (if your mouse has a scroll wheel). And you're sure to notice the way the ribbon rearranges itself to fit the available space in the Excel window (see Figure I-3).

Using the Ribbon with the Keyboard

If you're an unredeemed keyboard lover, you'll be happy to hear that you can trigger ribbon commands with the keyboard. The trick is using *keyboard accelerators*, a series of keystrokes that starts with the Alt key (the same key you used to use to get to a menu). When using a keyboard accelerator, you *don't* hold down all the keys at the same time. (As you'll soon see, some of these keystrokes contain so many letters that you'd be playing Finger Twister if you tried holding them all down simultaneously.) Instead, you hit the keys one after the other.

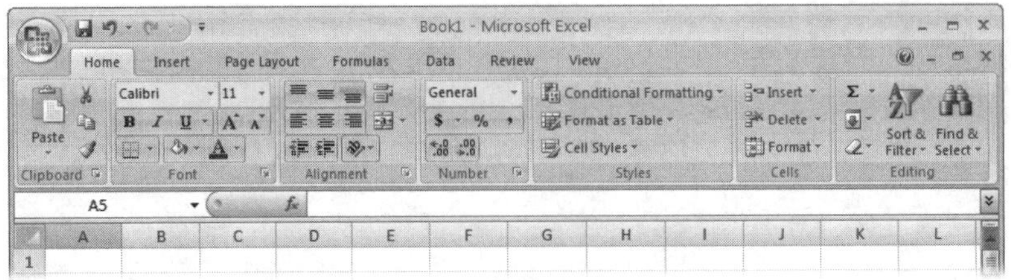

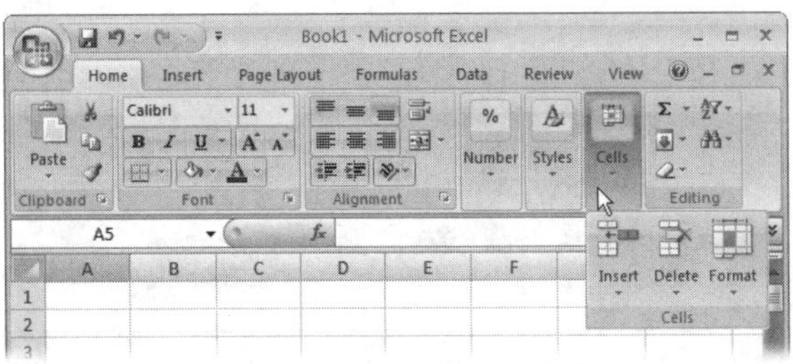

Figure I-3. Top: A large Excel window gives you plenty of room to play. The ribbon uses the space effectively, making the most important buttons bigger.

Bottom: When you shrink the Excel window, the ribbon rearranges its buttons and makes some smaller (by shrinking the button's icon or leaving out the title). Shrink small enough, and you might run out of space for a section altogether. In that case, you get a single button (like the Number, Styles, and Cells sections in this example) for an entire section. Click this button and the missing commands appear in a drop-down panel.

The trick to using keyboard accelerators is to understand that once you hit the Alt key, there are two things you do, in this order:

1. **Pick the ribbon tab you want.**
2. **Choose a command in that tab.**

Before you can trigger a specific command, you *must* select the correct tab (even if it's already displayed). Every accelerator requires at least two key presses after you hit the Alt key. You need even more if you need to dig through a submenu.

By now, this whole process probably seems hopelessly impractical. Are you really expected to memorize dozens of different accelerator key combinations?

Fortunately, Excel is ready to help you out with a new feature called *KeyTips*. Here's how it works. Once you press the Alt key, letters magically appear over every tab in the ribbon (Figure I-4). Once you hit a key to pick a tab, letters appear over every button in that tab. You can then press the corresponding key to trigger the command (Figure I-5).

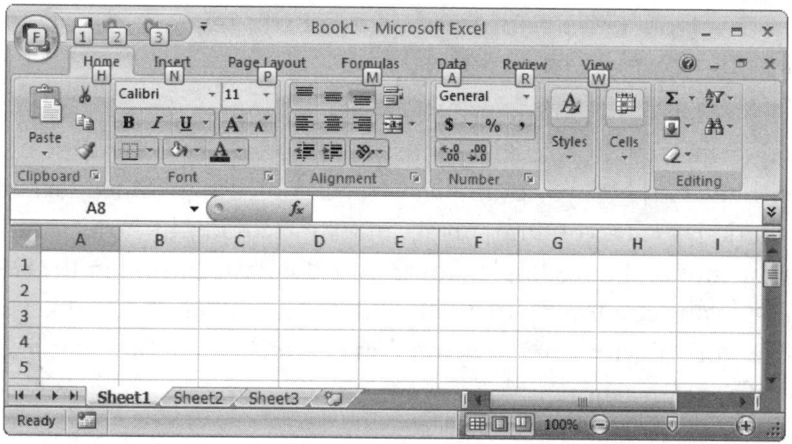

Figure I-4. When you press Alt, Excel helps you out with KeyTips next to every tab. If you follow up with M (for the Formulas tab), you'll see letters next to every command in that tab, as shown in Figure I-5.

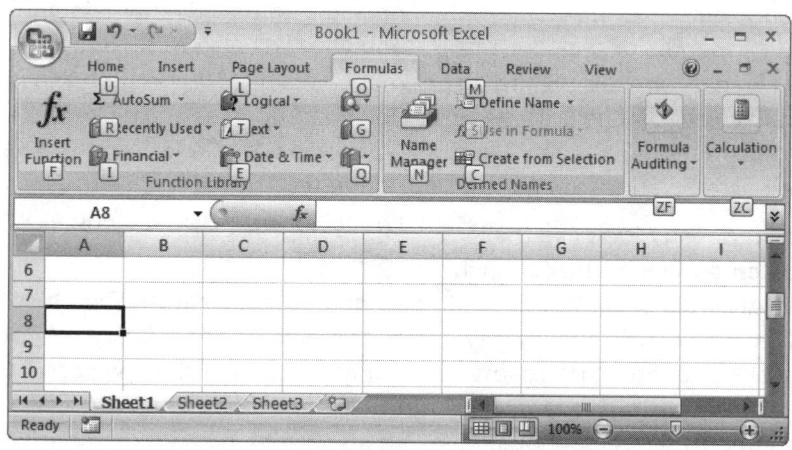

Figure I-5. You can now follow up with F to trigger the Insert Function button, U to get to the AutoSum feature, and so on. Don't bother trying to match letters with tab or button names—there are so many features packed into the ribbon that in many cases the letters don't mean anything at all.

In some cases, a command might have two letters, in which case you need to press both keys, one after the other. (For example, the Find & Select button on the Home tab has the letters FD. To trigger it, press Alt, then H, then F, and then D.)

TIP

You can back out of KeyTips mode without triggering a command at any time by pressing the Alt key again.

There are other shortcut keys that don't use the ribbon. These are key combinations that start with the Ctrl key. For example, Ctrl+C copies highlighted text and Ctrl+S saves your work. Usually, you find out about a shortcut key by hovering over a command with the mouse. For example, hover over the Paste button in the ribbon's Home tab, and you see a tooltip that tells you its timesaving shortcut key is Ctrl+V. And if you've worked with a previous version of Excel, you'll find that Excel 2007 keeps most of the same shortcut keys.

NOSTALGIA CORNER

Excel 2003 Menu Shortcuts

If you've worked with a previous version of Excel, you might have trained yourself to use menu shortcuts—key combinations that open a menu and pick out the command you want. For example, if you press Alt+E in Excel 2003, the Edit menu pops open. You can then press the S key to choose the Paste Special command.

At first glance, it doesn't look like these keyboard shortcuts will amount to much in Excel 2007. After all, Excel 2007 doesn't even have a corresponding series of menus! Fortunately, Microsoft went to a little extra trouble to make life easier for longtime Excel aficionados. The result is that you can still use your menu shortcuts, but they work in a slightly different way.

When you hit Alt+E in Excel 2007, you see a tooltip appear over the top of the ribbon (Figure I-6) that lets you know you've started to enter an Excel 2003 menu shortcut. If you go on to press S, you wind up at the familiar Paste Special dialog box, because Excel knows what you're trying to do. It's almost as though Excel has an invisible menu at work behind the scenes.

Of course, this feature can't help you out all the time. It doesn't work if you're trying to use one of the few commands that doesn't exist any longer. And if you need to see the menu to remember what key to press next, you're out of luck. All Excel gives you is the tooltip.

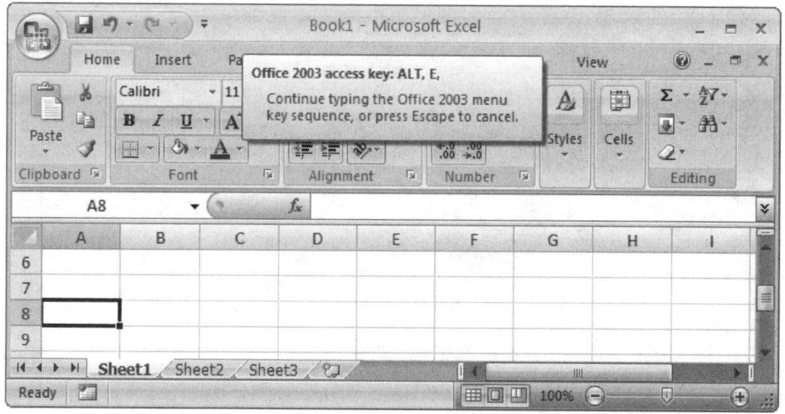

Figure I-6. By pressing Alt+E, you've triggered the "imaginary" Edit menu from Excel 2003, and earlier versions. You can't actually see it (because in Excel 2007 this menu doesn't exist). However, the tooltip lets you know that Excel is paying attention. You can now complete your action by pressing the next key for the menu command you're nostalgic for.

The Office Menu

There's still one small part of the traditional Excel menu system left in Excel 2007—sort of. The traditional File menu that lets you open, save, and print files has been transformed into the *Office menu*. You get there using the Office button, which is the big round logo in the top-left corner of the window (Figure I-7).

The Office menu is generally used for three things:

- Working with files (creating, opening, closing, and saving them). You'll do plenty of this in Chapter 1.
- Printing your work (Chapter 6).
- Configuring how Excel behaves. Choose Excel Options at the bottom of the menu to get to the Excel Options dialog box, an all-in-one place for configuring Excel.

There's one menu quirk that takes a bit of getting used to. Some menu commands hide submenus that have more commands. Take for instance the Print command. From the Office menu, you can choose Print to fire off a quick printout of your work. But if you click the right-pointing arrow at the edge of the Print command (or if you hover over it for a moment), you see a submenu with more options, as shown in Figure I-8.

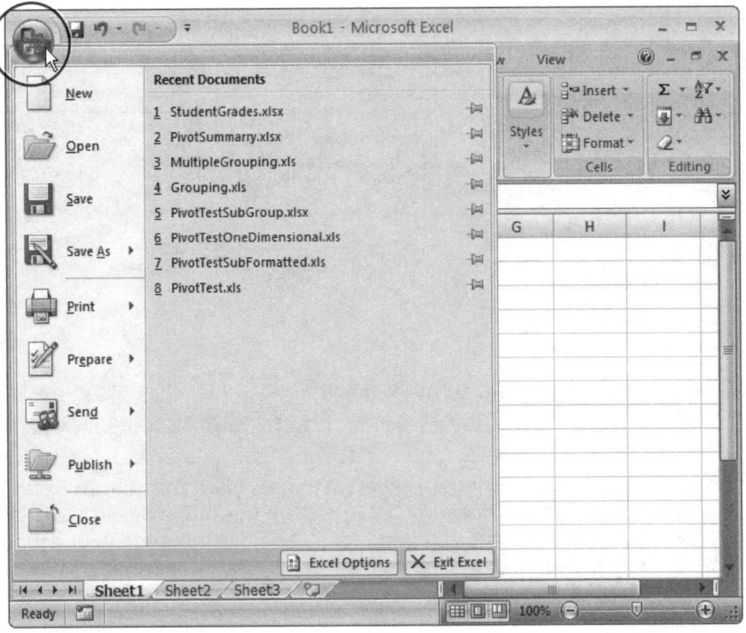

Figure I-7. The Office menu is bigger and easier to read than a traditional menu. It also has a list of the documents you used recently on the right side. (You'll learn about this handy feature on page 54.)

The Quick Access Toolbar

Keen eyes will have noticed the tiny bit of screen real estate that sits on the right side of the Office button, just above the ribbon (Figure I-9). It holds a series of tiny icons, like the toolbars in older versions of Excel. This is the Quick Access toolbar (or QAT to Excel nerds).

If the Quick Access toolbar was nothing but a specialized shortcut for three commands, it wouldn't be worth the bother. However, the nifty thing about the Quick Access toolbar is that you can customize it. In other words, you can remove commands you don't use and add your own favorites; the Appendix shows you how.

Microsoft has deliberately kept the Quick Access toolbar very small. It's designed to provide a carefully controlled outlet for those customization urges. Even if you go wild stocking the Quick Access toolbar with your own commands, the rest of the ribbon remains unchanged. (And that means a coworker or spouse can still use your computer without suffering a migraine.)

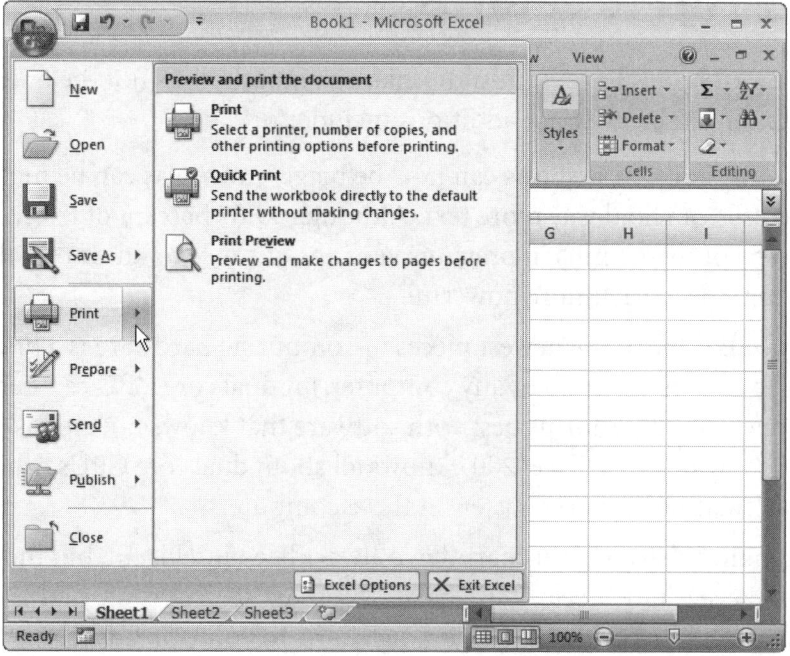

Figure I-8. Print is both a clickable menu command and holder of a submenu. To see the submenu, you need to hover over Print (without clicking) or click the arrow at the right edge (shown here). The ribbon also has a few buttons that work this way.

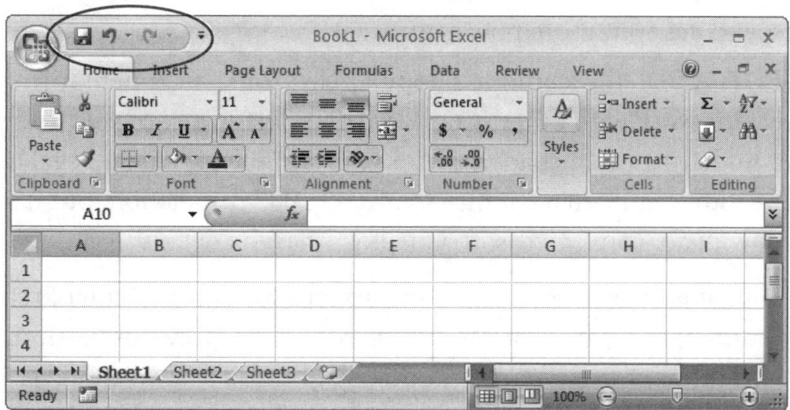

Figure I-9. The Quick Access toolbar puts the Save, Undo, and Redo command right at your fingertips. These commands are singled out because most people use them more frequently than any other commands. But as you'll learn in the Appendix, you can add anything you want here.

Excel's New Features

The slick new ribbon is Excel's most dramatic change, but it's not the only new feature in Excel 2007. Other hot additions include:

- **Fewer limits.** Excel worksheets can now be bigger, formulas can be more complex, and cells can hold way more text. Although 99.87 percent of Excel fans never ran into any of these limits in previous versions, it's nice to know that the Excel engine continues to get more powerful.
- **Faster speeds.** One of the newest pieces of computing hardware is a *dual core CPU*. (The CPU is the brain of any computer.) A dual core CPU can perform two tasks at once, but it performs best with software that knows how to take advantage of the way it works. Excel 2007 knows all about dual core CPUs, which means intense calculations are even faster on these computers.
- **Better-looking charts.** Excel charts have always been intelligent, but they've never made good eye candy. Excel 2007 shakes things up with a whole new graphics engine that lets you add fantastic looking charts to your spreadsheets.
- **Formula AutoComplete.** The latest in a whole bunch of auto-do-something features, formula AutoComplete just might be the most helpful innovation yet. It prompts you with possible values when you type in complex formulas.
- **Tables.** When Microsoft created Excel 2003, they added a wildly popular *list* feature that helped people manage lists of information. In Excel 2007, lists morph into *tables* and get even more powerful.
- **Save-as-PDF.** A PDF file is Adobe's popular electronic document format that lets you share your work with other people, without losing any of your formatting (and without letting them change any of your numbers). Due to legal headaches, this feature didn't quite make it into the Excel 2007 installation, but it's available as a free download from Microsoft. Chapter 1 has the details.

Of course, this list is by no means complete. Excel 2007 is chock-full of refinements, tweaks, and tune-ups that make it easier to use than any previous version. You'll learn all the best tricks throughout this book. And if you've used a previous version of Excel, look for the "Nostalgia Corner" boxes, which tell how things have changed.

About This Book

Despite the many improvements in software over the years, one feature hasn't improved a bit: Microsoft's documentation. In fact, with Office 2007, you get no printed user guide at all. To learn about the thousands of features included in this software collection, Microsoft expects you to read the online help.

Occasionally, the online help is actually helpful, like when you're looking for a quick description explaining a mysterious new function. On the other hand, if you're trying to learn how to, say, create an attractive chart, you'll find nothing better than terse and occasionally cryptic instructions.

The purpose of this book, then, is to serve as the manual that should have accompanied Excel 2007. In these pages, you'll find step-by-step instructions and tips for using Excel's most popular features, including those you may not even know exist.

NOTE

This book is based on *Excel 2007: The Missing Manual* (O'Reilly). That book is a truly complete reference for Excel 2007, covering every feature, including geeky stuff like XML, VBA, ERROR.TYPE( ) functions, and other things you'll probably never encounter—or even want to. But if you get really deep into Excel and want to learn more, *Excel 2007: The Missing Manual* can be your trusted guide.

About the Outline

This book is divided into two parts, each containing several chapters.

- **Part 1: Worksheet Basics.** In this part, you'll get acquainted with Excel's interface and learn the basic techniques for creating spreadsheets and entering and organizing data. You'll also learn how to format your work to make it more presentable and how to create slick printouts.
- **Part 2: Worksheet Power.** This part introduces you to Excel's most important feature—formulas. You'll learn how to perform calculations and create formulas using Excel's built-in functions. You'll also learn how to search, sort, and filter large amounts of information using tables. And to top things off, you'll learn about the wide range of different chart types available and when it makes sense to use each one.

About → These → Arrows

Throughout this book, you'll find sentences like this one: "Choose Insert → Illustrations → Picture." This a shorthand way of telling you how to find a feature in the Excel ribbon. It translates to the following instructions: "Click the **Insert** tab of the toolbar. On the tab, look for the **Illustrations** section. In the Illustrations box, click the **Picture** button." Figure I-10 shows the button you want.

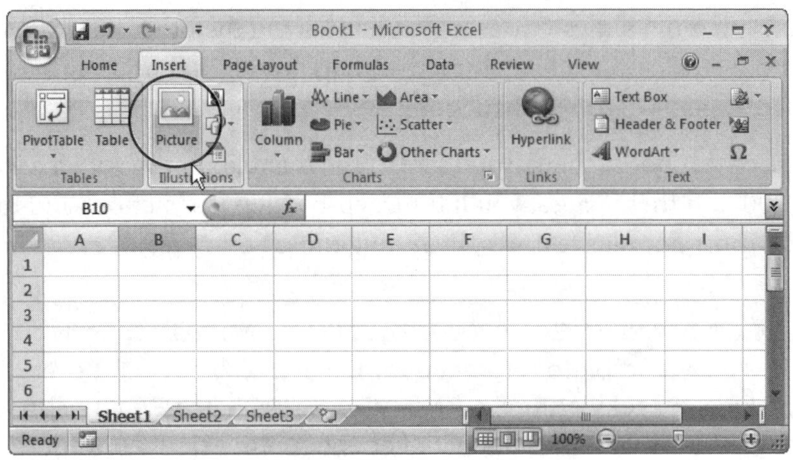

Figure I-10. In this book, arrow notations help to simplify ribbon commands. For example, "Choose Insert → Illustrations → Picture" leads to the highlighted button shown here.

NOTE

As you saw back in Figure I-3, the ribbon adapts itself to different screen sizes. Depending on the size of your Excel window, it's possible that the button you need to click won't include any text. Instead, it shows up as a small icon. In this situation, you can hover over the mystery button to see its name before deciding whether to click it.

Contextual tabs

There are some tabs that only appear in the ribbon when you're working on specific tasks. For example, when you create a chart, a Chart Tools section appears with three new tabs (see Figure I-11).

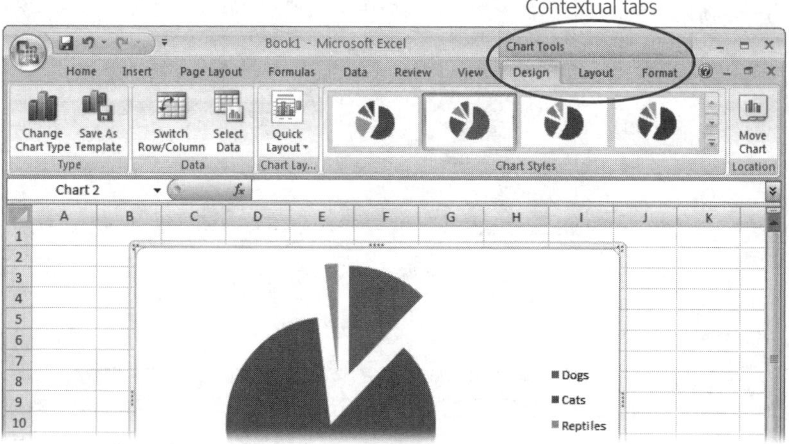

Figure I-11. Excel doesn't bother to show these three tabs unless you're working on a chart, because it's frustrating to look at a bunch of buttons you can't use. This sort of tab, which appears only when needed, is called a contextual tab.

When dealing with contextual tabs, the instructions in this book always include the title of the tab section (it's Chart Tools in Figure I-11). Here's an example: "Choose Chart Tools | Design → Type → Change Chart Type." Notice that the first part of this instruction includes the tab section title (Chart Tools) and the tab name (Design), separated by the | character. That way, you can't mistake the Chart Tools | Design tab for a Design tab in some other group of contextual tabs.

Drop-down buttons

From time-to-time you'll encounter buttons in the ribbon that have short menus attached to them. Depending on the button, this menu might appear as soon as you click the button, or it might appear only if you click the button's drop-down arrow, as shown in Figure I-12.

When dealing with this sort of button, the last step of the instructions in this book tells you what to choose from the drop-down menu. For example, say you're directed to "Home → Clipboard → Paste → Paste Special." That tells you to select the Home tab, look for the Clipboard section, click the drop-down part of the Paste button (to reveal the menu with extra options), and then choose Paste Special from the menu.

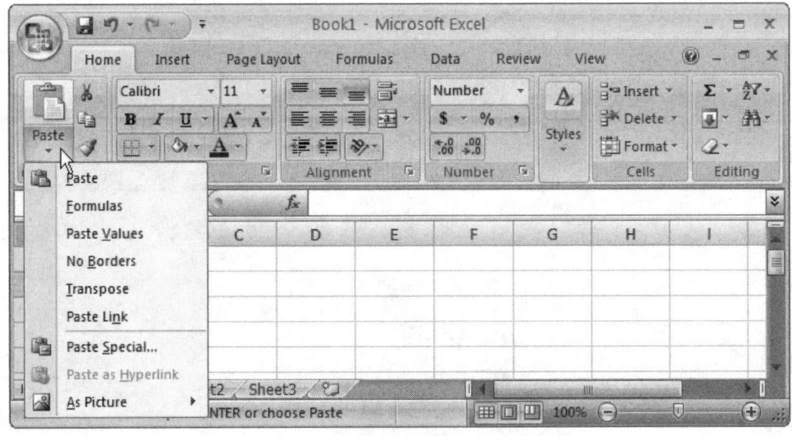

Figure I-12. Excel gives you several options for pasting text from the clipboard. Click the top part of the Paste button to perform a plain-vanilla paste (with all the standard settings), or click the bottom part to see the menu of choices shown here.

NOTE

Be on the lookout for drop-down arrows in the ribbon—they're tricky at first. You need to click the *arrow* part of the button to see the full list of options. When you click the other part of the button, you don't see the list. Instead, Excel fires off the standard command (the one Excel thinks is the most common choice) or the command you used most recently.

Dialog box launchers

As powerful as the ribbon is, you can't do everything using the buttons it provides. Sometimes you need to use a good ol' fashioned dialog box. (A *dialog box* is a term used in the Windows world to describe a small window with a limited number of options. Usually, dialog boxes are designed for one task and they aren't resizable, although software companies like Microsoft break these rules all the time.)

There are two ways to get to a dialog box in Excel 2007. First, some ribbon buttons take you there straight away. For example, if you choose Home → Clipboard → Paste → Paste Special, you always get a dialog box. There's no way around it.

The second way to get to a dialog box is through something called a *dialog box launcher*, which is just a nerdified name for the tiny square-with-arrow icon that sometimes appears in the bottom-right corner of a section of the ribbon. The easiest way to learn how to spot a dialog box launcher is to look at Figure I-13.

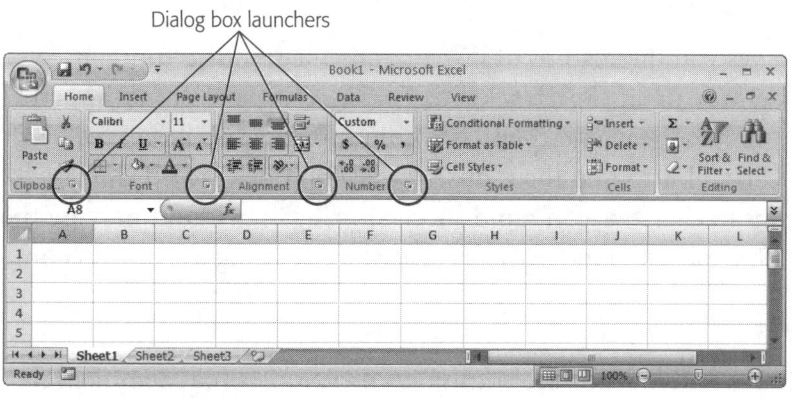

Figure I-13. As you can see here, the Clipboard, Font, Alignment, and Number sections all have dialog box launchers. The Styles, Cells, and Editing sections don't.

When you click a dialog box launcher, the related dialog box appears. For example, click the dialog box launcher for the Font section and you get a full Font dialog box that lets you scroll through all the typefaces on your computer, choose the size and color, and so on.

In this book, there's no special code word that tells you to use a dialog box launcher. Instead, you'll see an instruction like this: "To see more font options, look at the Home → Font section and click the dialog box launcher (the small icon in the bottom-right corner)." Now that you know what a dialog box launcher is, that makes perfect sense.

About Shortcut Keys

Every time you take your hand off the keyboard to move the mouse, you lose a few microseconds. That's why many experienced computer fans use keystroke combinations instead of toolbars and menus wherever possible. Ctrl+S, for example, is a keyboard shortcut that saves your current work in Excel (and most other programs).

When you see a shortcut like Ctrl+S in this book, it's telling you to hold down the Ctrl key, and, while it's down, press the letter S, and then release both keys. Similarly, the finger-tangling shortcut Ctrl+Alt+S means hold down Ctrl, and then press and hold Alt, and then press S (so that all three keys are held down at once).

About Clicking

This book gives you three kinds of instructions that require you to use your computer's mouse or laptop's trackpad. To *click* means to point the arrow cursor at something on the screen, and then—without moving the cursor at all—press and release the clicker button on the mouse (or laptop trackpad). To *double-click*, of course, means to click twice in rapid succession, again without moving the cursor at all. And to *drag* means to move the cursor while pressing the button continuously.

Examples

As you read this book, you'll see a number of examples that demonstrate Excel features and techniques for building good spreadsheets. Many of these examples are available as Excel workbook files in a separate download. Just surf to *www.missingmanuals.com*, click the link for this book, and then click the "Missing CD" to visit a page where you can download a zip file that includes the examples, organized by chapter.

About MissingManuals.com

At *www.missingmanuals.com*, you'll find news, articles, and updates to the books in the Missing Manual series.

But the Web site also offers corrections and updates to this book (to see them, click the book's title, and then click Errata). In fact, you're invited and encouraged to submit such corrections and updates yourself. In an effort to keep the book as up-to-date and accurate as possible, each time we print more copies of this book, we'll make any confirmed corrections you've suggested. We'll also note such changes on the Web site, so that you can mark important corrections in your own copy of the book.

In the meantime, we'd love to hear your own suggestions for new books in the Missing Manual series. There's a place for that on the Web site, too, as well as a place to sign up for free email notification of new titles in the series.

Safari® Enabled

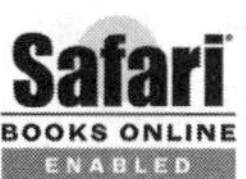

When you see a Safari® Enabled icon on the cover of your favorite technology book, that means the book is available online through the O'Reilly Network Safari Bookshelf.

Safari offers a solution that's better than e-books. It's a virtual library that lets you easily search thousands of top tech books, cut and paste code samples, download chapters, and find quick answers when you need the most accurate, current information. Try it for free at *http://safari.oreilly.com*.

PART ONE: WORKSHEET BASICS

CREATING AND NAVIGATING WORKSHEETS

1

- Creating a Basic Worksheet
- Editing Data
- Navigating in Excel
- Saving Files
- Opening Files

EVERY EXCEL GRANDMASTER NEEDS TO START SOMEWHERE. In this chapter, you'll create your first spreadsheet. You'll learn to move around in it, enter basic information, and save it for posterity. Along the way, you'll take a quick tour of the Excel window, and stop to meet the different tabs in the ribbon, the status bar, and the formula bar.

Creating a Basic Worksheet

When you first launch Excel, it starts you off with a new, blank *worksheet*, as shown in Figure 1-1. A worksheet is the grid of cells where you type your information and formulas; it takes up most of the window. This grid is the most important part of the Excel window. It's where you'll perform all your work, such as entering data, writing formulas, and reviewing the results.

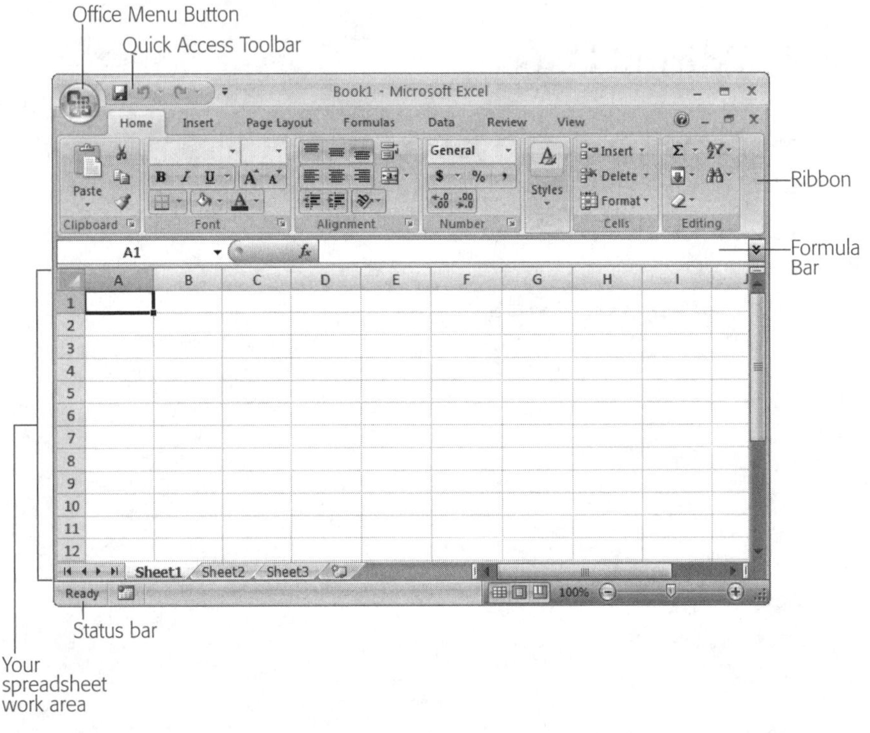

Figure 1-1. The largest part of the Excel window is the worksheet grid where you type in your information.

Here are a few basics about Excel's grid:

- **The grid divides your worksheet into rows and columns.** Columns are identified with letters (A, B, C ...), while rows are identified with numbers (1, 2, 3 ...).
- **The smallest unit in your worksheet is the *cell*.** Cells are identified by column and row. For example, C6 is the address of a cell in column C (the third column), and row 6 (the sixth row). Figure 1-2 shows this cell, which looks like a rectangular box. Incidentally, an Excel cell can hold up to 32,000 characters.

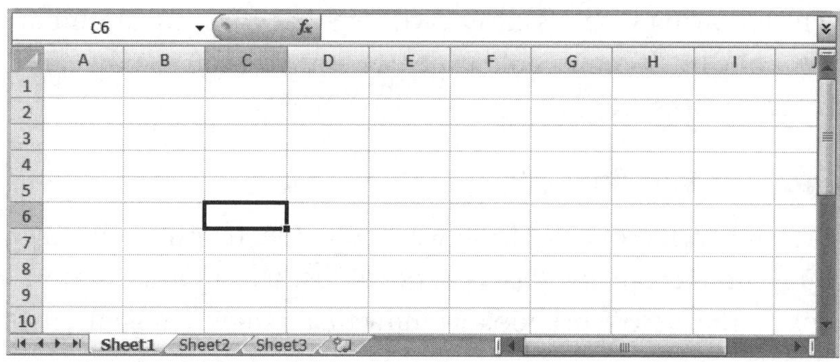

Figure 1-2. Here, the current cell is C6. You can recognize the current (or active) cell based on its heavy black border. You'll also notice that the corresponding column letter (C) and row number (6) are highlighted at the edges of the worksheet. Just above the worksheet, on the left side of the window, the formula bar tells you the active cell address.

- **A worksheet can span an eye-popping 16,000 columns and 1 million rows.** In the unlikely case that you want to go beyond those limits—say you're tracking blades of grass on the White House lawn—you'll need to create a new worksheet. Every spreadsheet file can hold a virtually unlimited number of worksheets, as you'll learn in Chapter 4.
- **When you enter information, you enter it one cell at a time.** However, you don't have to follow any set order. For example, you can start by typing information into cell A40 without worrying about filling any data in the cells that appear in the earlier rows.

NOTE

Obviously, once you go beyond 26 columns, you run out of letters. Excel handles this by doubling up (and then tripling up) letters. For example, column Z is followed by column AA, then AB, then AC, all the way to AZ and then BA, BB, BC—you get the picture. And if you create a ridiculously large worksheet, you'll find that column ZZ is followed by AAA, AAB, AAC, and so on.

The best way to get a feel for Excel is to dive right in and start putting together a worksheet. The following sections cover each step that goes into assembling a simple worksheet. This one tracks household expenses, but you can use the same approach to create any basic worksheet.

Starting a New Workbook

When you fire up Excel, it opens a fresh workbook file. If you've already got Excel open and you want to create *another* workbook, just select Office button → New. This step pops up the New Workbook window that's shown in Figure 1-3.

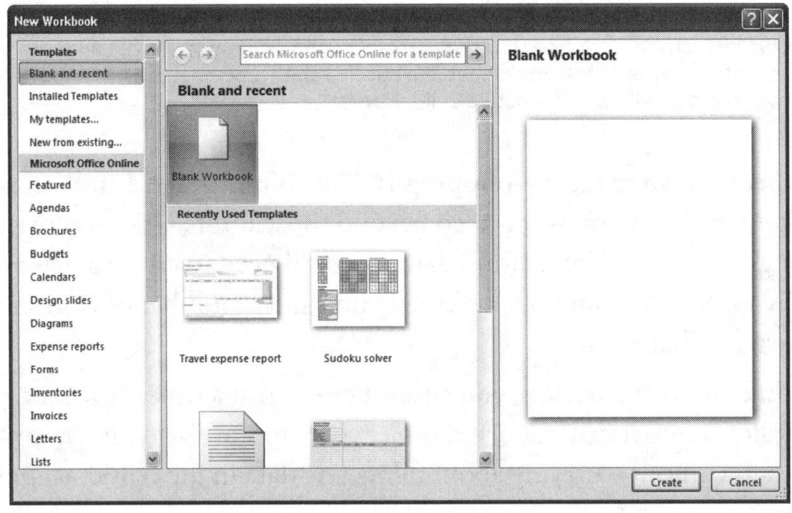

Figure 1-3. The New Workbook window lets you create a new, blank workbook. Choose Blank Workbook (in the window's middle section), and then click Create to get started with an empty canvas.

NOTE

A *workbook* is a collection of one or more *worksheets*. That distinction isn't terribly important now because you're using only a single worksheet in each workbook you create. But in Chapter 4, you'll learn how to use several worksheets in the same workbook to track related collections of data.

For now, all you need to know is that the worksheet is the grid of cells where you place your data, and the workbook is the spreadsheet file that you save on your computer.

You don't need to pick the file name for your workbook when you first create it. Instead, that decision happens later, when you *save* your workbook (page 44). For now, you start with a blank canvas that's ready to receive your numerical insights.

NOTE

Creating new workbooks doesn't disturb what you've already done. Whatever workbook you were using remains open in another window. You can use the Windows taskbar to move from one workbook to the other. Page 55 shows the taskbar close up.

Adding the Column Titles

The most straightforward way to create a worksheet is to design it as a table with headings for each column. It's important to remember that even for the simplest worksheet, the decisions you make about what's going to go in each column can have a big effect on how easy it is to manipulate your information.

For example, in a worksheet that stores a mailing list, you *could* have two columns: one for names and another for addresses. But if you create more than two columns, your life will probably be easier since you can separate first names from street addresses from Zip codes, and so on. Figure 1-4 shows the difference.

You can, of course, always add or remove columns later. But you can avoid getting gray hairs by starting a worksheet with all the columns you think you'll need.

The first step in creating your worksheet is to add your headings in the row of cells at the top of the worksheet (row 1). Technically, you don't need to start right in the

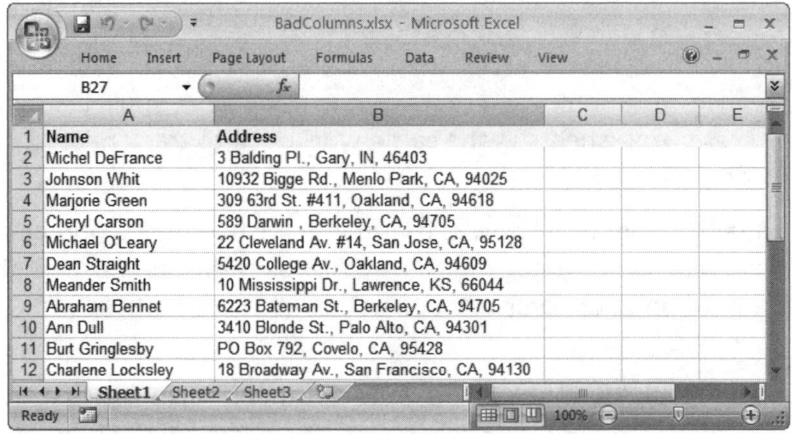

	A	B
1	**Name**	**Address**
2	Michel DeFrance	3 Balding Pl., Gary, IN, 46403
3	Johnson Whit	10932 Bigge Rd., Menlo Park, CA, 94025
4	Marjorie Green	309 63rd St. #411, Oakland, CA, 94618
5	Cheryl Carson	589 Darwin , Berkeley, CA, 94705
6	Michael O'Leary	22 Cleveland Av. #14, San Jose, CA, 95128
7	Dean Straight	5420 College Av., Oakland, CA, 94609
8	Meander Smith	10 Mississippi Dr., Lawrence, KS, 66044
9	Abraham Bennet	6223 Bateman St., Berkeley, CA, 94705
10	Ann Dull	3410 Blonde St., Palo Alto, CA, 94301
11	Burt Gringlesby	PO Box 792, Covelo, CA, 95428
12	Charlene Locksley	18 Broadway Av., San Francisco, CA, 94130

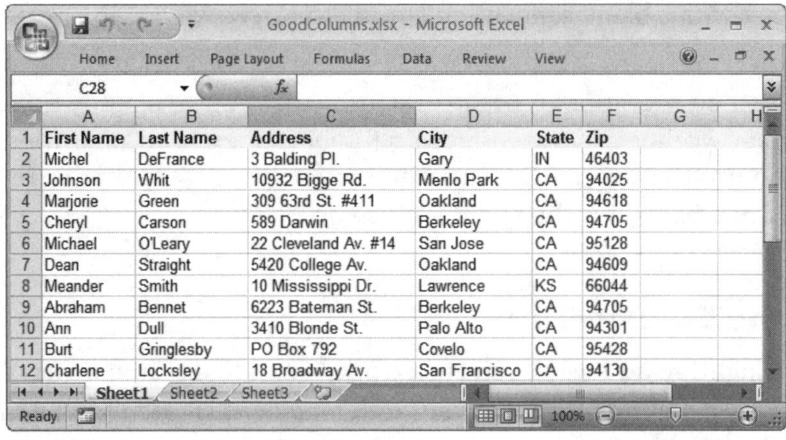

	A	B	C	D	E	F
1	**First Name**	**Last Name**	**Address**	**City**	**State**	**Zip**
2	Michel	DeFrance	3 Balding Pl.	Gary	IN	46403
3	Johnson	Whit	10932 Bigge Rd.	Menlo Park	CA	94025
4	Marjorie	Green	309 63rd St. #411	Oakland	CA	94618
5	Cheryl	Carson	589 Darwin	Berkeley	CA	94705
6	Michael	O'Leary	22 Cleveland Av. #14	San Jose	CA	95128
7	Dean	Straight	5420 College Av.	Oakland	CA	94609
8	Meander	Smith	10 Mississippi Dr.	Lawrence	KS	66044
9	Abraham	Bennet	6223 Bateman St.	Berkeley	CA	94705
10	Ann	Dull	3410 Blonde St.	Palo Alto	CA	94301
11	Burt	Gringlesby	PO Box 792	Covelo	CA	95428
12	Charlene	Locksley	18 Broadway Av.	San Francisco	CA	94130

Figure 1-4. Top: If you enter the first and last names together in one column, Excel can sort only by the first names. And if you clump the addresses and Zip codes together, you give Excel no way to count how many people live in a certain town or neighborhood because Excel can't extract the Zip codes.

Bottom: The benefit of a six-column table is significant: it lets you sort (reorganize) your list according to people's last names or where they live.

first row, but unless you want to add more information before your table—like a title for the chart or today's date—there's no point in wasting the space. Adding information is easy—just click the cell you want and start typing. When you're finished, hit Tab to complete your entry and move to the next cell to the right (or Enter to head to the cell just underneath).

NOTE

The information you put in an Excel worksheet doesn't need to be in neat, ordered columns. Nothing stops you from scattering numbers and text in random cells. However, most Excel worksheets resemble some sort of table, because that's the easiest and most effective way to deal with large amounts of structured information.

For a simple expense worksheet designed to keep a record of your most prudent and extravagant purchases, try the following three headings:

- **Date Purchased** stores the date when you spent the money.
- **Item** stores the name of the product that you bought.
- **Price** records how much it cost.

Right away, you face your first glitch: awkwardly crowded text. Figure 1-5 shows how you can adjust column width for proper breathing room.

Adding Data

You can now begin adding your data: simply fill in the rows under the column titles. Each row in the expense worksheet represents a separate purchase that you've made. (If you're familiar with databases, you can think of each row as a separate record.)

As Figure 1-6 shows, the first column is for dates, the second column is for text, and the third column holds numbers. Keep in mind that Excel doesn't impose any rules on what you type, so you're free to put text in the Price column. But if you don't keep a consistent kind of data in each column, you won't be able to easily analyze (or understand) your information later.

That's it. You've created a living, breathing worksheet. The next two sections explain how to edit data and move around the grid.

Editing Data

Every time you start typing in a cell, Excel erases any existing content in that cell. (You can also quickly remove the contents of a cell by just moving to it and pressing Delete.)

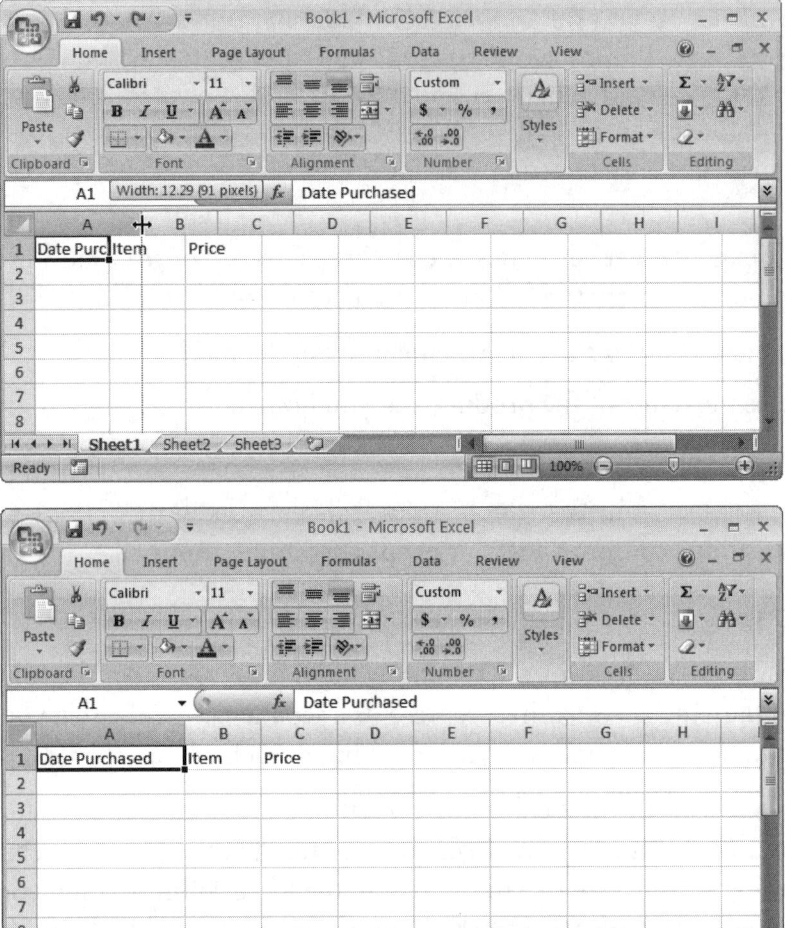

Figure 1-5. Top: The standard width of an Excel column is 8.43 characters, which hardly allows you to get a word in edgewise. To solve this problem, position your mouse on the right border of the column header you want to expand so that the mouse pointer changes to the resize icon (it looks like a double-headed arrow). Now drag the column border to the right as far as you want.

Bottom: When you release the mouse, the entire column of cells is resized to the new size.

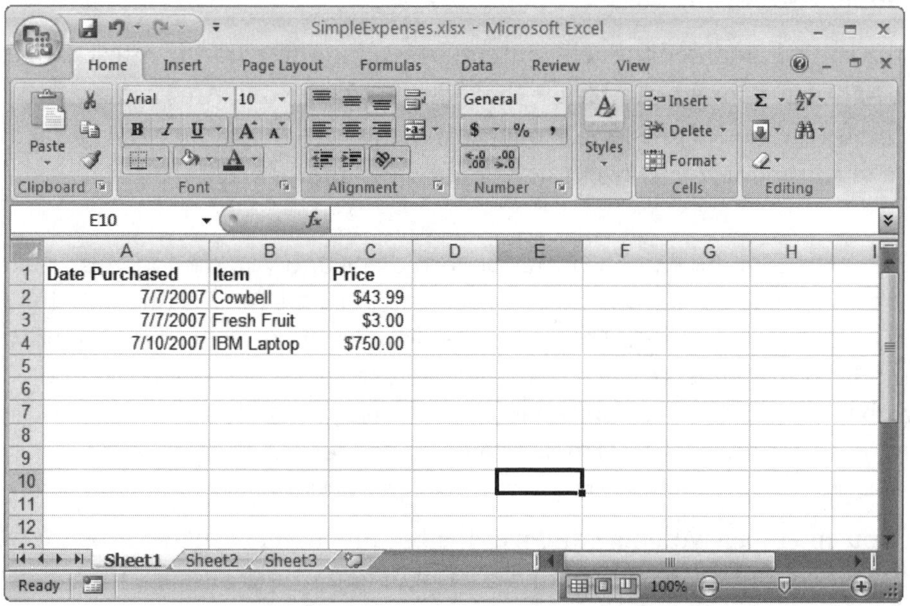

Figure 1-6. This rudimentary expense list has three items (in rows 2, 3, and 4). The alignment of each column reflects the data type (by default, numbers and dates are right-aligned, while text is left-aligned), indicating that Excel understands your date and price information.

If you want to edit cell data instead of replacing it, you need to put the cell in *edit mode*, like this:

1. **Move to the cell you want to edit.**

   Use the mouse or the arrow keys to get to the correct cell.

2. **Put the cell in edit mode by pressing F2.**

   Edit mode looks almost the same as ordinary text entry mode. The only difference is that you can use the arrow keys to move through the text you're typing and make changes. (When you aren't in edit mode, pressing these keys just moves you to another cell.)

   If you don't want to use F2, you can also get a cell into edit mode by double-clicking it.

3. **Complete your edit.**

   Once you've modified the cell content, press Enter to commit your change or Esc to cancel your edit and leave the old value in the cell. Alternatively, you can turn off edit mode (press F2 again), and then move to a new cell. As long as you stay in edit mode, Excel won't let you move to another cell.

TIP

If you start typing new information into a cell and you decide you want to move to an earlier position in your entry (to make an alteration, for instance), just press F2. The cell box still looks the same, but you're now in edit mode, which means that you can use the arrow keys to move within the cell (instead of moving from cell to cell). You can press F2 again to return to the normal data entry mode.

As you enter data, you may discover the Bigtime Excel Display Problem: cells in adjacent columns can overlap one another. Figure 1-7 shows the problem. One way to fix this problem is to manually resize the column, as shown in Figure 1-5. Another option is to use *wrapping* to fit multiple lines of text in a single cell, as described on page 150.

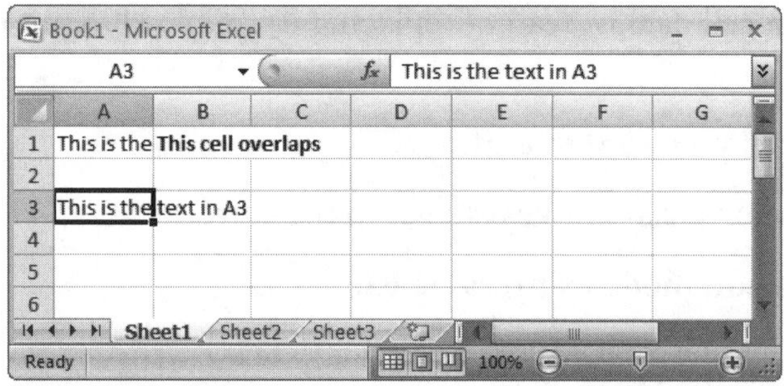

Figure 1-7. Overlapping cells can create big headaches. For example, if you type a large amount of text into A1, and then you type some text into B1, you see only part of the data in A1 on your worksheet (as shown here). The rest is hidden from view. But if, say, A3 contains a large amount of text and B3 is empty, the content in A3 is displayed over both columns, and you don't have a problem.

Navigating in Excel

Learning how to move around the Excel grid quickly and confidently is an indispensable skill. To move from cell to cell, you have two basic choices:

- **Use the arrow keys on the keyboard.** Keystrokes move you one cell at a time in any direction.
- **Click the cell with the mouse.** A mouse click jumps you directly to the cell you've clicked.

As you move from cell to cell, you see the black focus box move to highlight the currently active cell. In some cases, you might want to cover ground a little quicker. You can use any of the shortcut keys listed in Table 1-1. The most useful shortcut keys include the Home key combinations, which bring you back to the beginning of a row or the top of your worksheet.

Table 1-1. Shortcut Keys for Moving Around a Worksheet

Key Combination	Result
→ (or Tab)	Moves one cell to the right.
← (or Shift+Tab)	Moves one cell to the left.
↑	Moves one cell up.
↓ (or Enter)	Moves one cell down.
Page Up	Moves up one screen. Thus, if the grid shows 10 cells at a time, this key moves to a cell in the same column, 10 rows up (unless you are already at the top of the worksheet).
Page Down	Moves down one screen. Thus, if the grid shows 10 cells at a time, this key moves to a cell in the same column, 10 rows down.
Home	Moves to the first cell (column A) of the current row.
Ctrl+Home	Moves to the first cell in the top row, which is A1.
Ctrl+End (or End, Home)	Moves to the last column of the last occupied row. This cell is at the bottom-right edge of your data.

NOTE

Shortcut key combinations that use the + sign must be entered together. For example, "Ctrl+Home" means you hold down Ctrl and press Home at the same time. Key combinations with a comma work in sequence. For example, the key combination "End, Home" means press End first, release it, and then press Home.

Excel also lets you cross great distances in a single bound using a *Ctrl+arrow key* combination. These key combinations jump to the *edges* of your data. Edge cells include cells that are next to other blank cells. For example, if you press Ctrl+→ while you're inside a group of cells with information in them, you'll skip to the right, over all filled cells, and stop just before the next blank cell. If you press Ctrl+→ again, you'll skip over all the nearby blank cells and land in the next cell to the right that has information in it. If there aren't any more cells with data on the right, you'll wind up on the very edge of your worksheet.

The *Ctrl+arrow key* combinations are useful if you have more than one table of data in the same worksheet. For example, imagine you have two tables of data, one at the top of a worksheet and one at the bottom. If you are at the top of the first table, you can use Ctrl+↓ to jump to the bottom of the first table, skipping all the rows in between. Press Ctrl+↓ again, and you leap over all the blank rows, winding up at the beginning of the second table.

TIP

You can also scroll off into the uncharted regions of the spreadsheet with the help of the scrollbars at the bottom and on the right side of the worksheet.

Finding your way around a worksheet is a fundamental part of mastering Excel. Knowing your way around the larger program window is no less important. The next few sections help you get oriented, pointing out the important stuff and letting you know what you can ignore altogether.

GEM IN THE ROUGH

Getting Somewhere in a Hurry

If you're fortunate enough to know exactly where you need to go, you can use the Go To feature to make the jump. Go To moves to the cell address you specify. It comes in useful in extremely large spreadsheets, where just scrolling through the worksheet takes half a day.

To bring up the Go To dialog box (shown in Figure 1-8), choose Home → Editing → Find & Select → Go To. Or you can do yourself a favor and just press Ctrl+G. Enter the cell address (such as C32), and then click OK.

The Go To feature becomes more useful the more you use it. That's because the Go To window maintains a list of the most recent cell addresses that you've entered. In addition, every time you open the Go To window, Excel automatically adds the current cell to the list. This feature makes it easy to jump to a far-off cell and quickly return to your starting location by selecting the last entry in the list.

The Go To window isn't your only option for leaping through a worksheet in a single bound. If you look at the Home → Editing → Find & Select menu, you'll find more specialized commands that let you jump straight to cells that contains formulas, comments, conditional formatting, and other advanced Excel ingredients that you haven't learned about yet. And if you want to hunt down cells that have specific text, you need the popular Find command (Home → Editing → Find & Select → Find), which is covered on page 115.

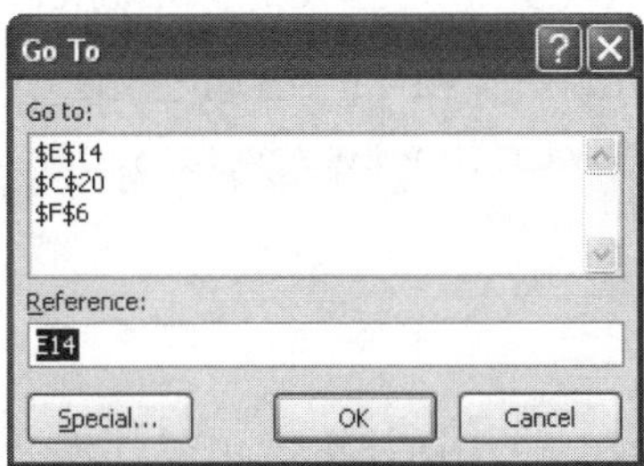

Figure 1-8. You'll notice that in the Go To list, cell addresses are written a little differently than the format you use when you type them in. Namely, dollar signs are added before the row number and column letter. Thus, C32 becomes $C$32, which is simply the convention that Excel uses for fixed cell references. (You'll learn much more about the different types of cell references in Chapter 7.)

The Tabs of the Ribbon

In the introduction you learned about the ribbon, the super-toolbar that offers one-stop shopping for all of Excel's features. All the most important Office applications—including Word, Access, PowerPoint, and Excel—use the new ribbon. However, each program has a different set of tabs and buttons.

Throughout this book, you'll dig through the different tabs of the ribbon to find important features. But before you start your journey, it's nice to get a quick overview of what each tab provides. Here's the lowdown:

- **Home** includes some of the most commonly used buttons, like those for cutting and pasting information, formatting your data, and hunting down important bits of information with search tools.
- **Insert** lets you add special ingredients like tables, graphics, charts, and hyperlinks.
- **Page Layout** is all about getting your worksheet ready for the printer. You can tweak margins, paper orientation, and other page settings.
- **Formulas** are mathematical instructions that you use to perform calculations. This tab helps you build super-smart formulas and resolve mind-bending errors.
- **Data** lets you get information from an outside data source (like a heavy-duty database) so you can analyze it in Excel. It also includes tools for dealing with large amounts of information, like sorting, filtering, and subgrouping.
- **Review** includes the familiar Office proofing tools (like the spell checker). It also has buttons that let you add comments to a worksheet and manage revisions.
- **View** lets you switch on and off a variety of viewing options. It also lets you pull off a few fancy tricks if you want to view several separate Excel spreadsheet files at the same time.

The Formula Bar

The *formula bar* appears above the worksheet grid but below the ribbon (Figure 1-10). It displays the address of the active cell (like A1) on the left edge, and it also shows you the current cell's contents.

GEM IN THE ROUGH

Collapsing the Ribbon

Most people are happy to have the ribbon sit at the top of the Excel window, with all its buttons on hand. However, serious number crunchers demand maximum space for their data. They'd rather look at another row of numbers than a pumped-up toolbar. If this describes you, then you'll be happy to find out you can *collapse* the ribbon, which shrinks it down to a single row of tab titles, as shown in Figure 1-9. To collapse it, just double-click any tab title.

Even when the ribbon's collapsed, you can still use all its features. All you need to do is click a tab. For example, if you click Home, the Home tab pops up over your worksheet. As soon as you click the button you want in the Home tab (or click a cell in your worksheet), the ribbon collapses itself again. The same trick works if you trigger a command in the ribbon using the keyboard, as described on page 7.

If you use the ribbon only occasionally, or if you prefer to use keyboard shortcuts, it makes sense to collapse the ribbon. Even when collapsed, the ribbon commands are available—it just takes an extra click to open the tab. On the other hand, if you make frequent trips to the ribbon, or you're learning about Excel and you like to browse the ribbon to see what features are available, don't bother collapsing it. The two or three rows that you'll lose are well worth keeping.

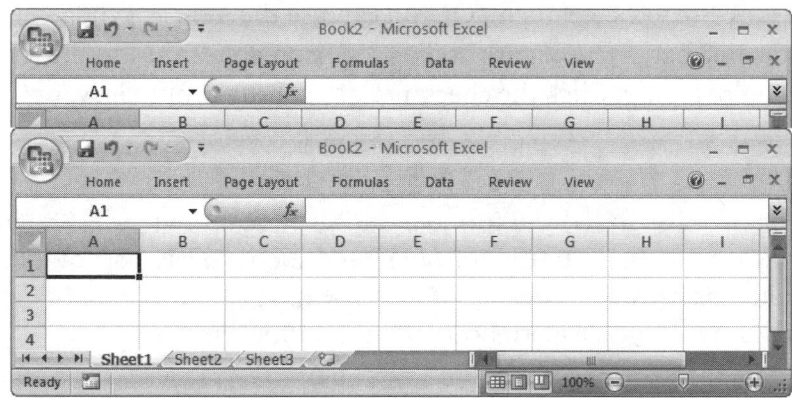

Figure 1-9. Do you want to use every square inch of screen space for your cells? You can collapse the ribbon (as shown here) by double-clicking any tab. Click a tab to pop it open temporarily, or double-click a tab to bring the ribbon back for good. And if you want to perform the same trick without raising your fingers from the keyboard, you can use the shortcut key Ctrl+F1.

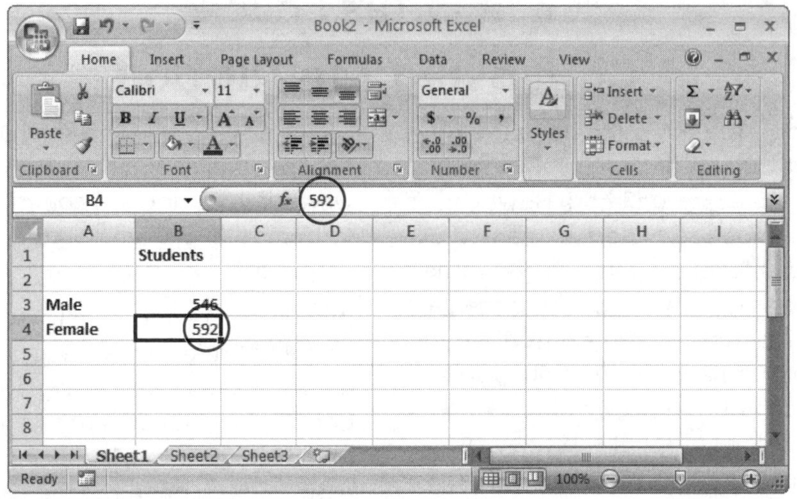

Figure 1-10. The formula bar (just above the grid) shows information about the active cell. In this example, the formula bar shows that the current cell is B4 and that it contains the number 592. Instead of editing this value in the worksheet, you can click anywhere in the formula bar and make your changes there.

You can use the formula bar to enter and edit data, instead of editing directly in your worksheet. This approach is particularly useful when a cell contains a formula or a large amount of information. That's because the formula bar gives you more work room than a typical cell. Just as with in-cell edits, you press Enter to confirm your changes or Esc to cancel them. Or you can use the mouse: When you start typing in the formula bar, a checkmark and an "X" icon appear just to the left of the box where you're typing. Click the checkmark to confirm your entry, or "X" to roll it back.

Note

You can hide (or show) the formula bar by choosing View → Show/Hide → Formula Bar. But the formula bar's such a basic part of Excel that you'd be unwise to get rid of it. Instead, keep it around until Chapter 7, when you'll learn how to build formulas.

Ordinarily, the formula bar is a single line. If you have a *really* long entry in a cell (like a paragraph's worth of text), you need to scroll from one side to the other.

However, there's another option—you can resize the formula bar so it fits more information, as shown in Figure 1-11.

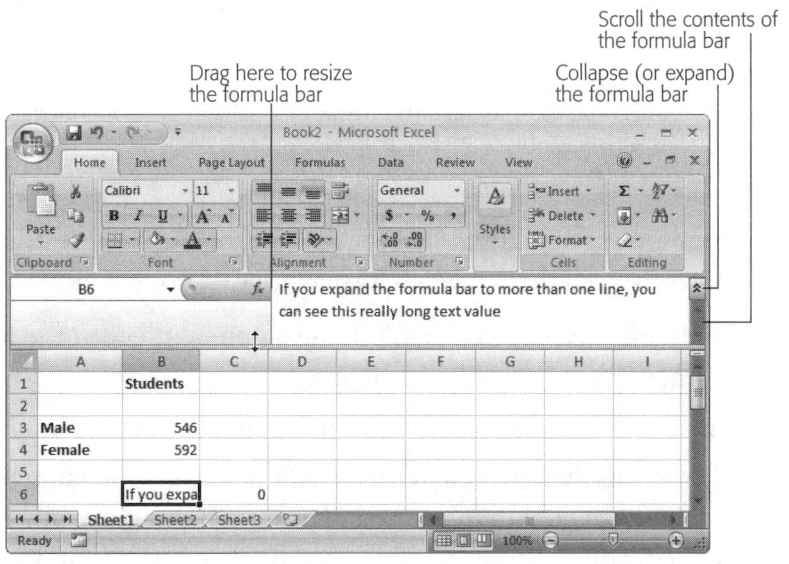

Figure 1-11. To enlarge the formula bar, click the bottom edge and pull down. You can make it two, three, four, or many more lines large. Best of all, once you get the size you want, you can use the expand/collapse button on the right side of the formula bar to quickly expand it to your preferred size and collapse it back to the single-line view.

The Status Bar

Though people often overlook it, the status bar (Figure 1-12) is a good way to keep on top of Excel's current state. For example, if you save or print a document, the status bar shows the progress of the printing process. If you're performing a quick action, the progress indicator may disappear before you have a chance to even notice it. But if you're performing a time-consuming operation—say, printing out an 87-page table of the airline silverware you happen to own—you can look to the status bar to see how things are coming along.

TIP

To hide or show the status bar, choose View → Show/Hide → Status Bar.

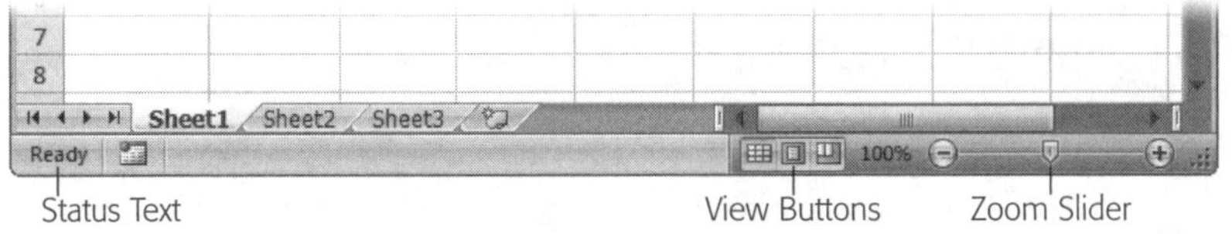

Figure 1-12. In the status bar, you can see the basic status text (which just says "Ready" in this example), the view buttons (which are useful when you're preparing a spreadsheet for printing), and the zoom slider bar (which lets you enlarge or shrink the current worksheet view).

The status bar combines several different types of information. The leftmost part of the status bar shows the Cell Mode, which displays one of three indicators.

- The word "Ready" means that Excel isn't doing anything much at the moment, other than waiting for you to take some action.
- The word "Enter" appears when you start typing a new value into a cell.
- The word "Edit" means the cell is currently in edit mode, and pressing the left and right arrow keys moves through the cell data, instead of moving from cell to cell. As discussed earlier, you can place a cell in edit mode or take it out of edit mode by pressing F2.

Farther to the right on the status bar are the view buttons, which let you switch to Page Layout View or Page Break Preview. These different views help you see what your worksheet will look like when you print it. They're covered in Chapter 6.

The zoom slider is next to the view buttons, at the far right edge of the status bar. You can slide it to the left to zoom out (which fits more information into your Excel window at once) or slide it to the right to zoom in (and take a closer look at fewer cells). You can learn more about zooming on page 176.

In addition, the status bar displays other miscellaneous indicators. For example, if you press the Scroll Lock key, a Scroll Lock indicator appears on the status bar (next to the "Ready" text). This indicator tells you that you're in *scroll mode*. In scroll mode, the arrow keys don't move you from one cell to another; instead, they scroll the entire worksheet up, down, or to the side. Scroll mode is a great way to check out another part of your spreadsheet without leaving your current position.

You can control what indicators appear in the status bar by configuring it. To see a full list of possibilities, right-click the status bar. A huge list of options appears, as shown in Figure 1-13. Table 1-2 describes the most useful status bar options.

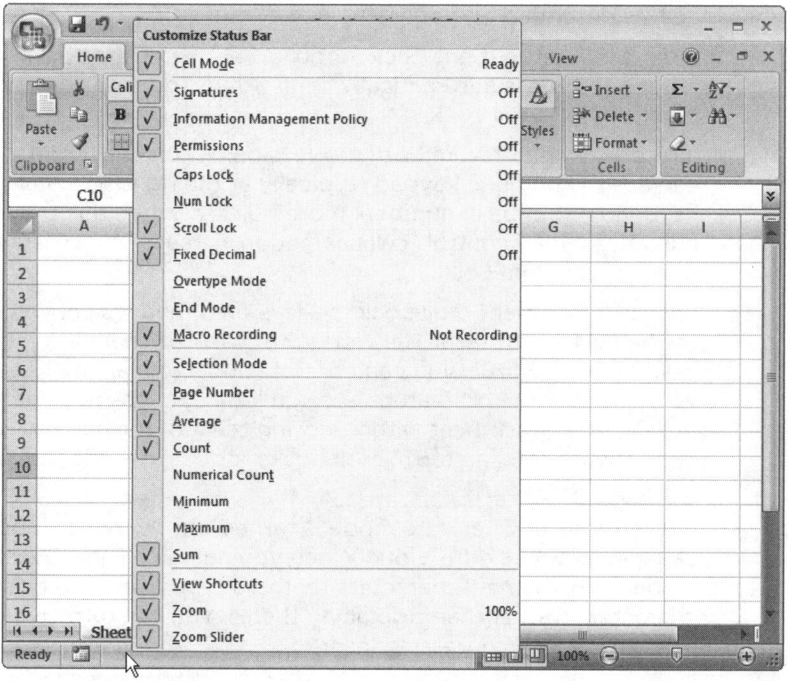

Figure 1-13. Every item that has a checkmark appears in the status bar when you need it. For example, if you choose Caps Lock, the text "Caps Lock" appears in the status bar whenever you hit the Caps Lock key to switch to all-capital typing.

NOTE

The Caps Lock indicator doesn't determine whether or not you can use the Caps Lock key—that feature always works. The Caps Lock indicator just lets you know when Caps Lock mode is on. That way you won't be surprised by an accidental keystroke that turns your next data entry INTO ALL CAPITALS.

Table 1-2. Status Bar Indicators

Indicator	Meaning
Cell Mode	Shows Ready, Edit, or Enter depending on the state of the current cell, as described on page 40.
Caps Lock	Indicates whether Caps Lock mode is on. When Caps Lock is on, every letter you type is automatically capitalized. To turn Caps Lock mode on or off, hit Caps Lock.
Num Lock	Indicates whether Num Lock mode is on. When this mode is on, you can use the numeric keypad (typically at the right side of your keyboard) to type in numbers more quickly. When this sign's off, the numeric keypad controls cell navigation instead. To turn Num Lock on or off, press Num Lock.
Scroll Lock	Indicates whether Scroll Lock mode is on. When it's on, you can use the arrow keys to scroll the worksheet without changing the active cell. (In other words, you can control your scrollbars by just using your keyboard.) This feature lets you look at all the information you have in your worksheet without losing track of the cell you're currently in. You can turn Scroll Lock mode on or off by pressing Scroll Lock.
Overtype Mode	Indicates when Overwrite mode is turned on. Overwrite mode changes how cell edits work. When you edit a cell and Overwrite mode is on, the new characters that you type overwrite existing characters (rather than displacing them). You can turn Overwrite mode on or off by pressing Insert.
End Mode	Indicates that you've pressed End, which is the first key in many two-key combinations; the next key determines what happens. For example, hit End and then Home to move to the bottom-right cell in your worksheet. See Table 1-1 for a list of key combinations, some of which use End.
Selection Mode	Indicates the current Selection mode. You have two options: normal mode and *extended selection*. When you press the arrows keys and extended selection is on, Excel automatically selects all the rows and columns you cross. Extended selection is a useful keyboard alternative to dragging your mouse to select swaths of the grid. To turn extended selection on or off, press F8. You'll learn more about selecting cells and moving them around in Chapter 3.
Page Number	Shows the current page and the total number of pages (as in "Page 1 of 4"). This indicator appears only in Page Layout view (as described on page 195).

Table 1-2. Status Bar Indicators (continued)

Indicator	Meaning
Average, Count, Numerical Count, Minimum, Maximum, Sum	Show the result of a calculation on the selected cells. For example, the Sum indicator shows the total of all the numeric cells that are currently selected. You'll take a closer look at this handy trick on page 87.
View Shortcuts	Shows the three view buttons that let you switch between Normal view, Page Layout View, and Page Break Preview (as described on page 209).
Zoom	Shows the current zoom percentage (like 100 percent for a normal-sized spreadsheet, and 200 percent for a spreadsheet that's blown up to twice the magnification).
Zoom Slider	Shows a slider that lets you zoom in closer (by sliding it to the right) or out to see more information at once (by sliding it to the left).

Excel Options

You might have already seen the Excel Options window, which provides a central hub where you can adjust how Excel looks, behaves, and calculates (see Figure 1-14). To get to this window, click the Office button, and then choose Excel Options on the bottom-right edge.

The top five sections in the Excel Options window let you tweak a wide variety of different details. Some of these details are truly handy, like the options for opening and saving files (which are described at the end of this chapter). Others are seldom-used holdovers from the past, like the option that lets Excel act like Lotus—an ancient piece of spreadsheet software—when you hit the "/" key.

TIP

Some important options have a small i-in-a-circle icon next to them, which stands for "information." Hover over this icon and you see a tooltip that gives you a brief description about that setting.

Beneath the top five sections are four more specialized sections:

- **Customize** lets you put your favorite commands on the Quick Access toolbar, a maneuver you can learn more about in the Appendix.
- **Add-Ins** lets you configure other utilities (mini-programs) that work with Excel and enhance its powers.

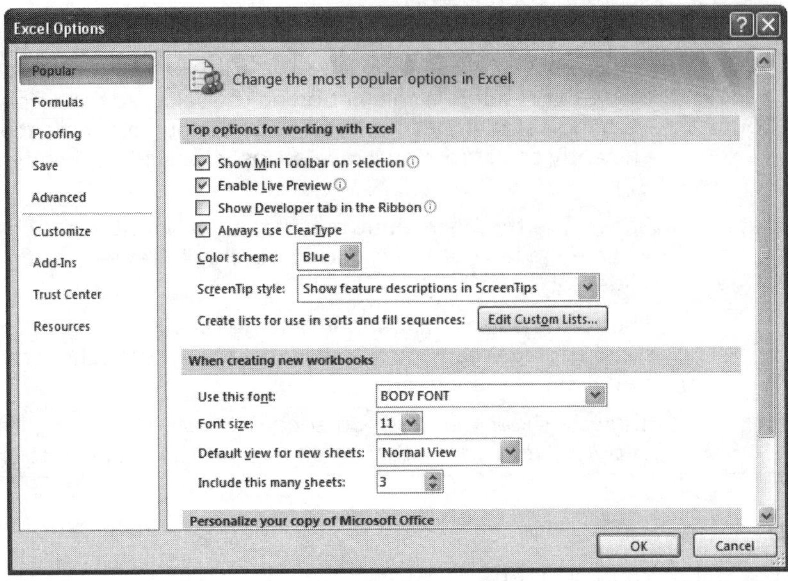

Figure 1-14. The Excel Options window is divided into nine sections. To pick which section to look at, choose an entry from the list on the left. In this example, you're looking at the Popular settings group. In each section, the settings are further subdivided into titled groups. You may need to scroll down to find the setting you want.

- **Trust Center** lets you tweak Excel's security settings that safeguard against dangerous actions (think: viruses).
- **Resources** provides a few buttons that let you get extra diagnostic information, activate your copy of Office (which you've no doubt done already), and get freebies and updates on the Web.

While you're getting to know Excel, you can comfortably ignore most of what's in the Excel Options window. But you'll return here many times throughout this book to adjust settings and fine-tune the way Excel works.

Saving Files

As everyone who's been alive for at least three days knows, you should save your work early and often. Excel is no exception. You have two choices for saving a spreadsheet file:

- **Save As.** This choice allows you to save your spreadsheet file with a new name. You can use Save As the first time you save a new spreadsheet, or you can use it to save a copy of your current spreadsheet with a new name, in a new folder, or as a different file type. (Alternate file formats are discussed on page 47.) To use Save As, select Office button → Save As, or press F12. Figure 1-15 shows you the Save As dialog box as it appears on a Windows XP computer. (The Windows Vista version of the Save As dialog box has all the same features, but way more style.)

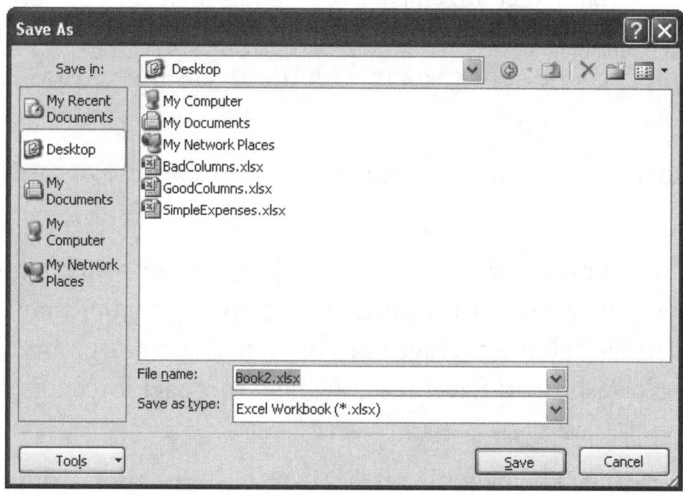

Figure 1-15. The Save As dialog box lets you jump to common folders using the big buttons on the left, or you can browse a folder tree using the drop-down "Save in" menu. Once you've found the folder you want, type the file name at the bottom of the window, and then pick the file type. Finally, click Save to finish the job.

- **Save.** This option updates the spreadsheet file with your most recent changes. If you use Save on a new file that hasn't been saved before, it has the same effect as Save As: Excel prompts you to choose a folder and file name. To use Save, select Office button → Save, or press Ctrl+S. Or, look up at the top of the Excel window in the Quick Access toolbar for the tiny Save button, which looks like an old-style diskette.

TIP

Resaving a spreadsheet is an almost instantaneous operation, and you should get used to doing it all the time. After you've made any significant change, just hit Ctrl+S to make sure you've stored the latest version of your data.

The Excel 2007 File Format

Since time immemorial, Excel fans have been saving their lovingly crafted spreadsheets in *.xls* files (as in AirlineSilverware.xls). Excel 2007 changes all that. In fact, it introduces a completely new file format, with the extension *.xlsx* (as in AirlineSilverware.xlsx).

At first glance, this seems a tad over the top. But the new file format has some real advantages:

- **It's compact.** The new Excel file format uses Zip file compression, so spreadsheet files are smaller—way smaller (as much as 75 percent smaller than their original sizes). And even though the average hard drive is already large enough to swallow thousands of old-fashioned Excel files, the new compact format is easier to email around.
- **It's less error-prone.** The new file format carefully separates ordinary content, pictures, and macro code into separate sections. (Macros are automated routines that perform a specific task in a spreadsheet.) Microsoft claims that this change makes for tougher files. Now, if a part of your Excel file is damaged (for example, due to a faulty hard drive), there's a much better chance that you can still retrieve the rest of the information. (You'll learn about Excel disaster recovery on page 51.)
- **It's extensible.** The new file format uses XML (the eXtensible Markup Language), which is a standardized way to store information. XML storage doesn't benefit the average person, but it's sure to earn a lot of love from companies that plan to build custom software that uses Excel documents. As long as Excel documents are stored in XML, these companies can create automated programs that pull the information they need straight out of a spreadsheet, without going through Excel. These programs can also generate made-to-measure Excel documents all on their own.

For all these reasons, .xlsx is the format of choice for Excel 2007. However, Microsoft prefers to give people all the choices they could ever need (rather than make life really simple), and Excel file formats are no exception. Along with the standard .xlsx, there's the closely related .xls*m* cousin, which adds the ability to store macro code. If you've added any macros to your spreadsheet, Excel prompts you to use this file type when you save your spreadsheet.

Saving Your Spreadsheet in Older Formats

Most of the time, you don't need to think about Excel's file format—you can just create your spreadsheets, save them, and let Excel take care of the rest. The only time you need to stop and think twice is when you need to share your work with other, less fortunate people who have older versions of Excel.

When you find yourself in this situation, you have two choices:

- **Save your spreadsheet in the old format.** You can save a copy of your spreadsheet in the traditional .xls Excel standard that's been supported since Excel 97. To do so, choose Office button → Save As → Excel 97-2003 Format.
- **Use a free add-in for older versions of Excel.** People who are stuck with Excel 2000, Excel 2002, or Excel 2003 *can* read your Excel 2007 files—they just need a free add-in that's provided by Microsoft. This is a good solution because it's doesn't require any work on your part. People with past-its-prime versions of Excel can find the add-in they need by surfing to *www.microsoft.com/downloads* and searching for "compatibility pack file formats" (or use the secret shortcut URL *http://tinyurl.com/y5w78r*).

Often, the best thing you can do is keep your spreadsheet in the newer format and save a *copy* in the older format (using Office button → Save As → Excel 97-2003 Format). You can then hand that copy out to your backward friends.

Some eccentric individuals have even older or stranger spreadsheet software on their computers. If you want to save a copy of your spreadsheet in a more exotic file type, you can choose Office button → Save As, and then find the desired format in the "Save as type" drop-down list (Figure 1-16). Excel lets you save your spreadsheet using a variety of different formats, including the classic Excel 95 format from a decade ago. If you're looking to view your spreadsheet using a mystery program, use the CSV file type, which produces a comma-delimited text file that almost all spreadsheet applications on any operating system can read (comma-delimited means the information has commas separating each cell).

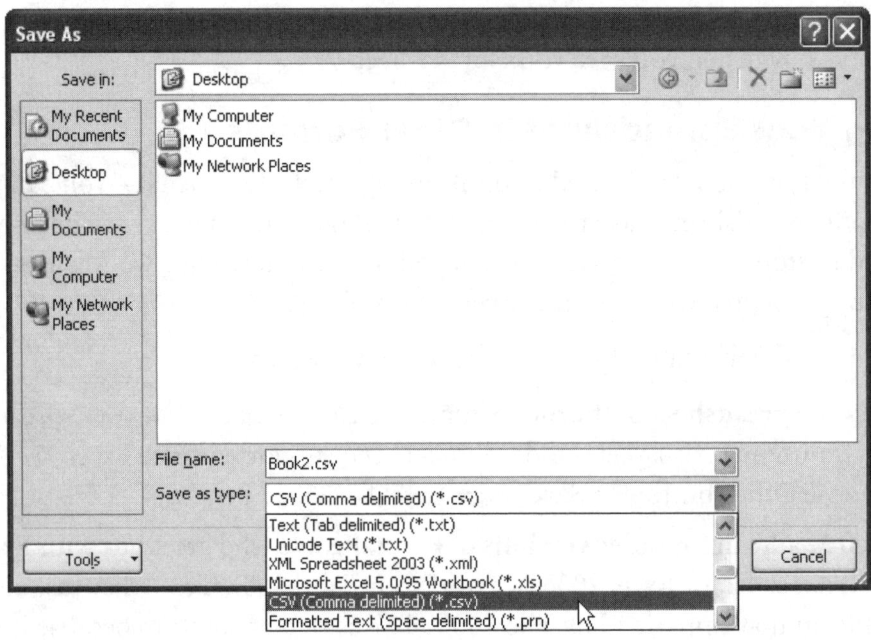

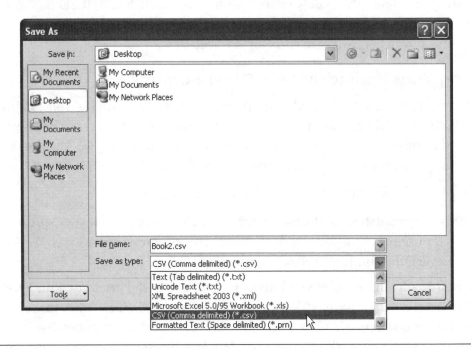

Figure 1-16. Excel offers a few useful file type options in the "Save as type" list. CSV format is the best choice for compatibility with truly old software (or when nothing else seems to work). If you're a longtime Excel fan, you'll notice that the list has been slimmed down a bit—for example, there's no option to use the old dBase and Lotus formats from the DOS world.

TIP

When you save your Excel spreadsheet in another format, make sure you keep a copy in the standard .xlsx format. Why bother? Because other formats aren't guaranteed to retain all your information, particularly if you choose a format that doesn't support some of Excel's newer features.

Saving Your Spreadsheet As a PDF

Sometimes you want to save a copy of your spreadsheet so that people can read it even if they don't have Excel (and even if they're running a different operating system, like Linux or Apple's OS X). In this situation, you have several choices:

- **Use the Excel Viewer.** Even if you don't have Excel, you can install a separate tool called the Excel Viewer, which is available from Microsoft's Web site (search for "Excel Viewer" at *www.microsoft.com/downloads*). However, few people have the viewer, and even though it's free, few want to bother installing it. And it doesn't work on non-Windows computers.
- **Save your workbook as an HTML Web page.** That way, all you need to view the workbook is a Web browser (and who doesn't have one of those?). The only disadvantage is that you could lose complex formatting. Some worksheets may make the transition to HTML gracefully, while others don't look very good when they're squashed into a browser window. And if you're planning to let other people print the exported worksheet, the results might be unsatisfactory.
- **Save your workbook as a PDF file.** This gets you the best of both worlds—you keep all the rich formatting (so your workbook can be printed), and you let people who don't have Excel (and possibly don't even have Windows) view your workbook. The only disadvantage is that this feature isn't included in the basic Excel package. Instead, you need to install a free add-in to get it.

To get the Save As PDF add-in, surf to *www.microsoft.com/downloads* and search for "PDF." The links lead you to a page where you can download the add-in and install it with just a couple of clicks.

Once you install the Save As PDF add-in, all your Office applications have the ability to save their documents in PDF format. In Excel, you work this magic by choosing Office button → Save As → PDF, which brings up the "Publish as PDF" dialog box (Figure 1-17).

When you save a PDF file, you get a few extra options in the Save As dialog box. PDF files can be saved with different resolution and quality settings (which mostly affect any graphical objects that you've placed in your workbook, like pictures and charts).

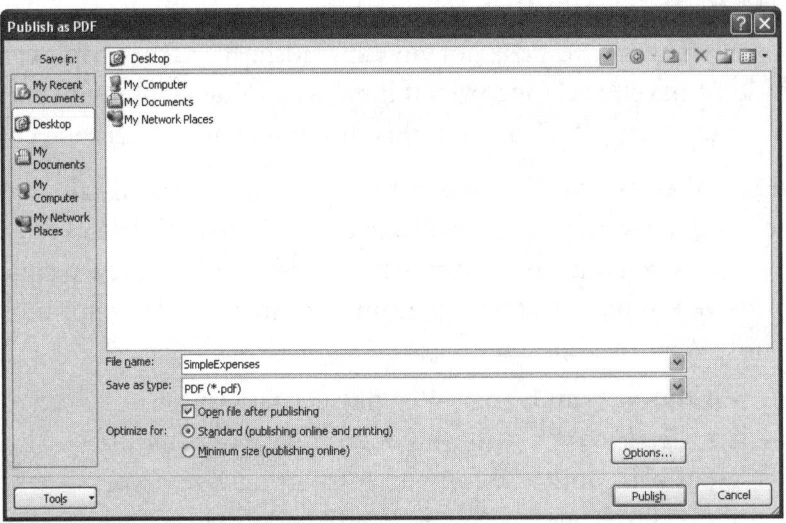

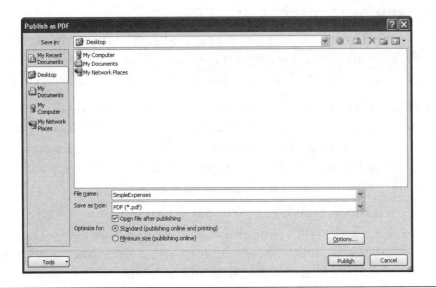

Figure 1-17. The "Publish as PDF" dialog box looks a lot like the Save As dialog box, except it has a Publish button instead of a Save button. You can switch on the "Open file after publishing" setting to tell Excel to open the PDF file in Adobe Reader (assuming you have it installed) after the publishing process is complete, so you can check the result.

Normally, you use higher quality settings if you're planning to print your PDF file, because printers use higher resolutions than computer monitors.

The "Publish as PDF" dialog box gives you some control over the quality settings with the "Optimize for" options. If you're just saving a PDF copy so other people can *view* the information in your workbook, choose "Minimum size (publishing online)" to save some space. On the other hand, if there's a possibility that the people reading your PDF might want to print it out, choose "Standard (publishing online and printing)" to save a slightly larger PDF that makes for a better printout.

Finally, if you want to publish only a portion of your spreadsheet as a PDF file, click the Options button to open a dialog box with even more settings. You can choose to publish just a fixed number of pages, just the selected cells, and so on. These options mirror the choices you get when sending a spreadsheet to the printer. You also see a few more cryptic options, most of which you can safely ignore. (They're intended for PDF nerds.) One exception is the "Document properties" option—turn this off if you don't want the PDF to keep track of certain information that identifies you, like your name.

TIP

Getting the Save As PDF add-in is a bit of a hassle, but it's well worth the effort. In previous versions of Excel, people who wanted to create PDFs file had to get another add-in or buy the expensive full version of the Adobe Acrobat software. The Save As PDF feature was originally slated for inclusion in Excel (with no add-in required), but anti-trust concerns caused ultra-cautious Microsoft to leave it out.

Disaster Recovery

The corollary to the edict "Save your data early and often" is the truism "Sometimes things fall apart quickly…before you've even had a chance to back up." Fortunately, Excel includes an invaluable safety net called AutoRecover.

AutoRecover periodically saves backup copies of your spreadsheet while you work. If you suffer a system crash, you can retrieve the last AutoRecover backup even if you never managed to save the file yourself. Of course, even the AutoRecover backup won't necessarily have *all* the information you entered in your spreadsheet before the problem occurred. But if AutoRecover saves a backup every 10 minutes (the standard), at most you'll lose 10 minutes of work.

AutoRecover comes switched on when you install Excel, but you can tweak its settings. Select Office → Excel Options, and then choose the Save section. Under the "Save workbooks" section, make sure that "Save AutoRecover information" is turned on. You can also make a few other changes to AutoRecover settings:

- You can also adjust the backup frequency in minutes. Figure 1-18 has some tips on timing.
- You can choose the folder where you'd like Excel to save backup files. (The standard folder works fine for most people, but feel free to pick some other place.) Unfortunately, there's no handy Browse button to help you find the folder, so you need to find the folder you want in advance (using a tool like Windows Explorer), write it down somewhere, and then copy the full folder path into this dialog box.
- Under the "AutoRecover exceptions" heading, you can tell Excel not to bother saving a backup of a specific spreadsheet. Pick the spreadsheet name from the list (which shows all the currently open spreadsheet files), and then turn on the

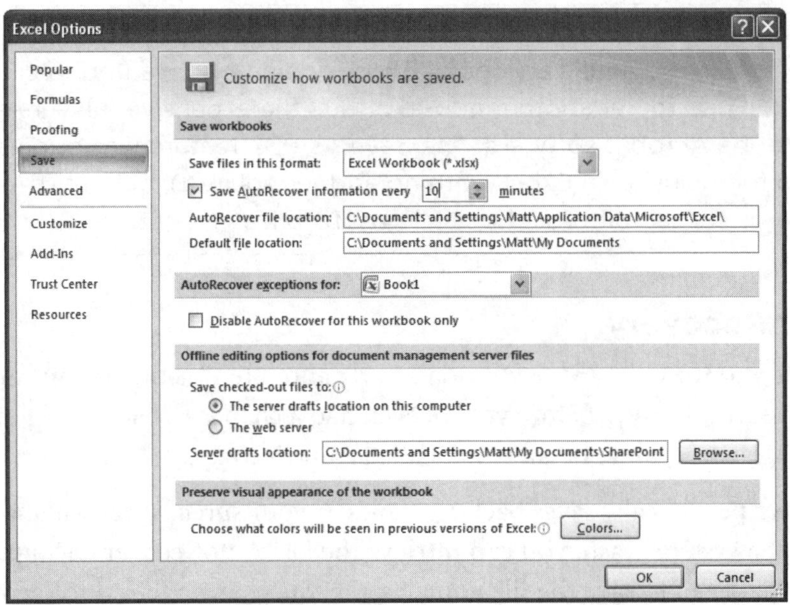

Figure 1-18. You can configure how often AutoRecover saves backups. There's really no danger in being too frequent. Unless you work with extremely complex or large spreadsheets—which might suck up a lot of computing power and take a long time to save—you can set Excel to save the document every five minutes with no appreciable slowdown.

"Disable AutoRecover for this workbook only" setting. This setting is exceedingly uncommon, but you might use it if you have a gargantuan spreadsheet full of data that doesn't need to be backed up.

If your computer does crash, when you get it running again, you can easily retrieve your last AutoRecover backup. In fact, the next time you launch Excel, it automatically checks the backup folder, and, if it finds a backup, it opens a Document Recovery panel on the left of the Excel window.

If your computer crashes in mid-edit, the next time you open Excel you'll probably see the same file listed twice in the Document Recovery window, as shown in Figure 1-19. The difference is the status. The status [AutoSaved] indicates the most recent backup created by Excel. The status [Original] indicates the last version of the file that *you* saved (which is safely stored on your hard drive, right where you expect it).

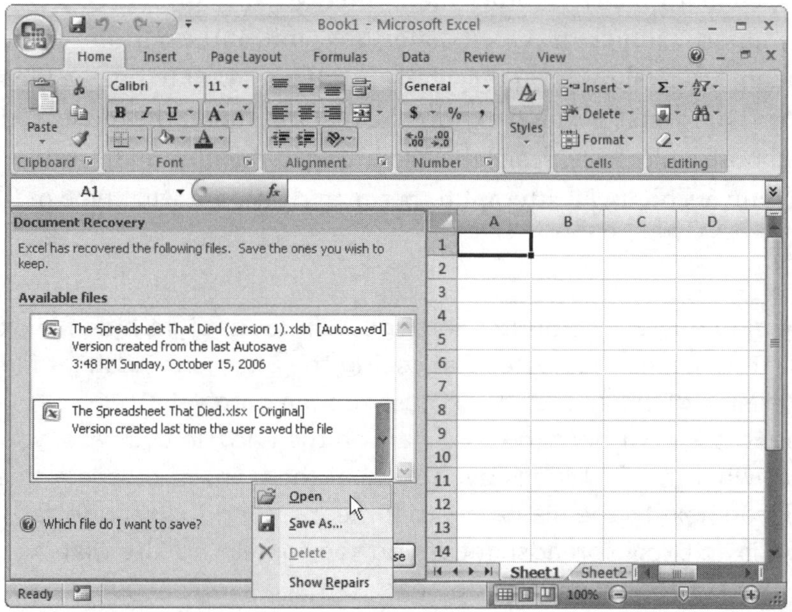

Figure 1-19. You can save or open an AutoRecover backup just as you would an ordinary Excel file; simply click the item in the list. Once you've dealt with all the backup files, close the Document Recovery window by clicking the Close button. If you haven't saved your backup, Excel asks you at this point whether you want to save it permanently or delete the backup.

To open a file that's in the Document Recovery window, just click it. You can also use a drop-down menu with additional options (Figure 1-19). Make sure you save the file before you leave Excel. After all, it's just a temporary backup.

If you attempt to open a backup file that's somehow been scrambled (technically known as *corrupted*), Excel automatically attempts to repair it. You can choose Show Repairs to display a list of any changes Excel had to make to recover the file.

Opening Files

Opening existing files in Excel works much the same as it does in any Windows program. To get to the standard Open dialog box, choose Office button → Open. Using the Open dialog box, you can browse to find the spreadsheet file you want, and then click Open to load it into Excel.

Excel can open many file types other than its native .xlsx format. To learn the other formats it supports, launch the Open dialog box, and, at the bottom, open the "Files of type" menu, which shows you the whole list. If you want to open a file but you don't know what format it's in, try using the first option on the menu, "All Files." Once you choose a file, Excel scans the beginning of the file and informs you about the type of conversion it will attempt to perform (based on what type of file Excel thinks it is).

Note

Depending on your computer settings, Windows might hide file extensions. That means that instead of seeing the Excel spreadsheet file MyCoalMiningFortune.xlsx, you'll just see the name MyCoalMiningFortune (without the .xlsx part on the end). In this case, you can still tell what the file type is by looking at the icon. If you see a small Excel icon next to the file name, that means Windows recognizes that the file is an Excel spreadsheet. If you see something else (like a tiny paint palette, for example), you need to make a logical guess about what type of file it is.

Plan to take another crack at a recent spreadsheet? You can find the most recently opened documents in Excel's Recent Documents list. To see this list, just open the Office button—it appears as a separate column on the right. The best part about the Recent Documents list is the way you can *pin* a document there so it stays forever, as shown in Figure 1-20.

Opening Multiple Spreadsheets at Once

As you open multiple spreadsheets, Excel creates a new window for each one. You can easily jump from one spreadsheet to another by clicking the appropriate spreadsheet button in the Windows taskbar at the bottom of your screen.

If you have *taskbar grouping* switched on, you'll find that your computer has an odd habit of spontaneously bunching together taskbar buttons. For example, shortly after you open four Excel files, you might find them in one taskbar button (see Figure 1-21). Taskbar grouping does save screen space, but it also makes it a little

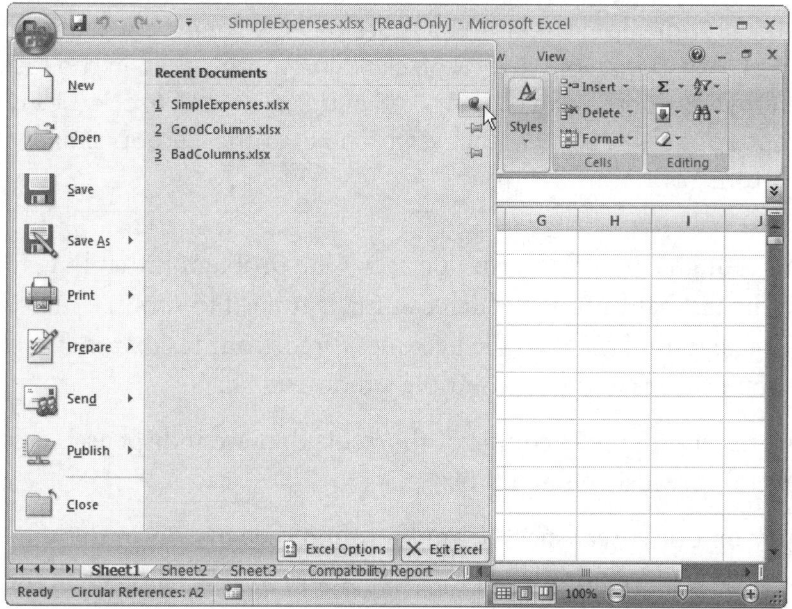

Figure 1-20. To keep a spreadsheet around on the Recent Documents list, click the thumbtack on the right. It becomes green, and is now pinned in place. That means it won't ever leave the list, no matter how many documents you open. If you decide to stop working with it later on, just click the thumbtack again to release it. Pinning is a great trick for keeping your most important files at your fingertips.

more awkward to get to the Excel spreadsheet you want. You now need two mouse clicks instead of one—the first to click the taskbar button, and the second to choose the window you want from the group.

Figure 1-21. Similar taskbar buttons sometimes get bunched into groups. You can tell that a button contains a group of files when a drop-down arrow appears on the right side of the button, and a number appears on the left side. The number indicates how many buttons Windows has grouped together.

TIP

If the taskbar grouping seems like more trouble than it's worth, you can switch off this behavior. Just right-click an empty space in the taskbar and choose Properties. In the Taskbar and Start Menu Properties dialog box that appears, clear the checkmark next to the "Group similar taskbar buttons" option.

The taskbar, though convenient, isn't perfect. One problem is that long file names don't fit on the taskbar buttons, which can make it hard to spot the files you need. And the struggle to find an open file becomes dire if your taskbar is also cluttered with other applications and *their* multiple windows.

Fortunately, Excel provides a couple of shortcuts that are indispensable when dealing with several spreadsheets at a time:

- To jump from one spreadsheet to another, find the window in the View → Window → Switch Windows list, which includes the file name of all the currently open spreadsheets (Figure 1-22).

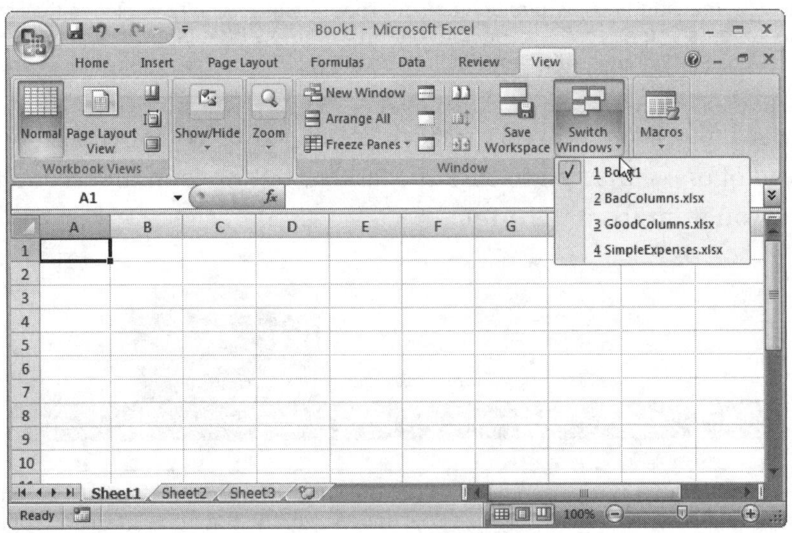

Figure 1-22. When you have multiple spreadsheets open at the same time, you can easily move from one to the other using the Switch Windows list.

- To move to the next spreadsheet, use the keyboard shortcut Ctrl+Tab or Ctrl+F6.
- To move to the previous spreadsheet, use the shortcut key Ctrl+Shift+Tab or Ctrl+Shift+F6.

When you have multiple spreadsheets open at the same time, you need to take a little more care when closing a window so you don't accidentally close the entire Excel application—unless you want to. Here are your choices:

- **You can close all the spreadsheets at once.** To do so, you need to close the Excel window. Select Office button → Exit Excel from any active spreadsheet, or just click the close icon (the infamous X button) in the top-righthand corner.
- **You can close a single spreadsheet.** To do so, right-click the spreadsheet on the taskbar, and click Close. Or, switch to the spreadsheet you want to close (by clicking the matching taskbar button) and then choose Office button → Close.

NOTE

One of the weirdest limitations in Excel occurs if you try to open more than one file with the same name. No matter what steps you take, you can't coax Excel to open both of them at once. It doesn't matter if the files have different content or if they're in different folders or even different drives. When you try to open a file that has the same name as a file that's already open, Excel displays an error message and refuses to go any further. Sadly, the only solution is to open the files one at a time, or rename one of them.

ADDING INFORMATION TO WORKSHEETS

2

- Adding Different Types of Data
- Quick Ways to Add Data

NOW THAT YOU'VE CREATED A BASIC WORKSHEET, and you're acquainted with Excel and its spiffy new interface, it's time to get down and dirty adding data. Whether you want to plan your household budget, build a sales invoice, or graph your soaring (or plunging) net worth, you first need to understand how Excel interprets the information you put in your worksheet.

Depending on what kind of data you type into a cell, Excel classifies it as a date, a number, or a piece of text. In this chapter, you'll learn how Excel makes up its mind, and how you can make sure it makes the right decision. You'll also learn how to use Excel's best timesavers, including the indispensable Undo feature.

Adding Different Types of Data

One of Excel's most important features is its ability to distinguish between different types of information. A typical worksheet contains both text and numbers. There isn't a lot you can do in Excel with ordinary text (other than alphabetize a list, perform a simple spell check, and apply some basic formatting). On the other hand, Excel gives you a wide range of options for numeric data. For example, you can string your numbers together into complex calculations and formulas, or you can graph them on a chart. Programs that don't try to separate text and numbers—like Microsoft Word, for example—can't provide these features.

Most of the time, when you enter information in Excel, you don't explicitly indicate the type of data. Instead, Excel examines the information you've typed in, and, based on your formatting and other clues, classifies it automatically. Excel distinguishes between four core data types:

- **Ordinary text.** Column headings, descriptions, and any content that Excel can't identify as one of the other data types.
- **Numbers.** Prices, integers, fractions, percentages, and every other type of numeric data. Numbers are the basic ingredient of most Excel worksheets.
- **Dates and times.** Dates (like Oct 3, 2007), times (like 4:30 p.m.), and combined date and time information (like Oct 3, 2007, 4:30 p.m.). You can enter date and time information in a variety of formats.

- **True or false values.** This data type (known in geekdom as a *Boolean* value) can contain one of two things: TRUE or FALSE (displayed in all capitals). You don't need Boolean data types in most worksheets, but they're useful for programmer types and power users who want to create complex formulas.

One useful way to tell how Excel is interpreting your data is to look at cell alignment, as explained in Figure 2-1.

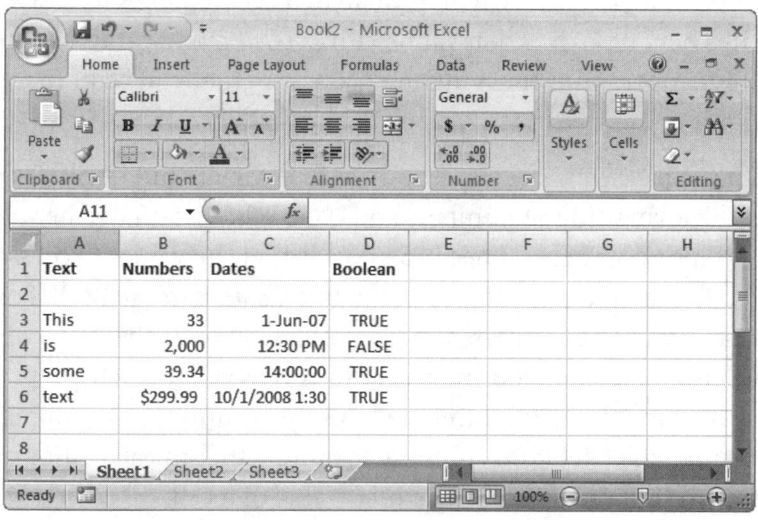

Figure 2-1. Unless you explicitly change the alignment, Excel always left-aligns text (that is, it lines it up against the left edge of a cell), as in column A. On the other hand, it always right-aligns numbers and dates, as in columns B and C. And it centers Boolean values, as in column D.

Note

The standard alignment of text and numbers doesn't just represent the whims of Excel—it also matches the behavior you want most of the time. For example, when you type in text, you usually want to start at the left edge so that subsequent entries in a column line up. But when entering numbers, you usually want them to line up on the *decimal point* so that it's easier to scan a list of numbers and quickly spot small and large values. Of course, if you don't like Excel's standard formatting, you're free to change it, as you'll see in Chapter 5.

As Figure 2-1 shows, Excel can display numbers and dates in several different ways. For example, some of the numbers include decimal places, one uses a comma, and one has a currency symbol. Similarly, one of the time values uses the 12-hour clock while another uses the 24-hour clock. Other entries include only date information or both date and time information. You might assume that when you type in a number, it will appear in the cell exactly the way you typed it. For example, when you type 3-comma-0-0-0 you expect to see 3,000. However, that doesn't always happen. To see the problem in action, try typing *3,000* in a cell. It shows up exactly the way you entered it. Then, type over that value with *2000*. The new number appears as 2,000. Excel remembers your first entry, and assumes that you want to use thousand separators in this cell *all the time*.

These differences may seem like a spreadsheet free-for-all, but don't despair—you can easily set the formatting of numbers and dates. (In fact, that's the subject of Chapter 5.) At this point, all you need to know is that the values Excel *stores* in each cell don't need to match exactly the values that it *displays* in each cell. For example, the number 4300 could be formatted as plain old 4300 or as the dollar amount $4,300. Excel lets you format your numbers so you have exactly the representation you want. At the same time, Excel treats all numbers equivalently, no matter how they're formatted, which lets you combine them together in calculations. Figure 2-2 shows you how to find the underlying stored value of a cell.

NOTE

Excel assigns data types to each cell in your worksheet, and you can't mix more than one data type in the same cell. For example, when you type in *44 fat cats*, Excel interprets the whole thing as text because it contains letters. If you want to treat 44 as a number (so that you can perform calculations with it, say), then you need to split this content into two cells—one that contains the number 44 and one that contains the remaining text.

Controlling Your Data Types

By looking at cell alignment, you can easily tell how Excel is interpreting your data. That's helpful. But what happens when Excel's interpretation is at odds with your wishes? For example, what if you type in something you consider a *number* but Excel

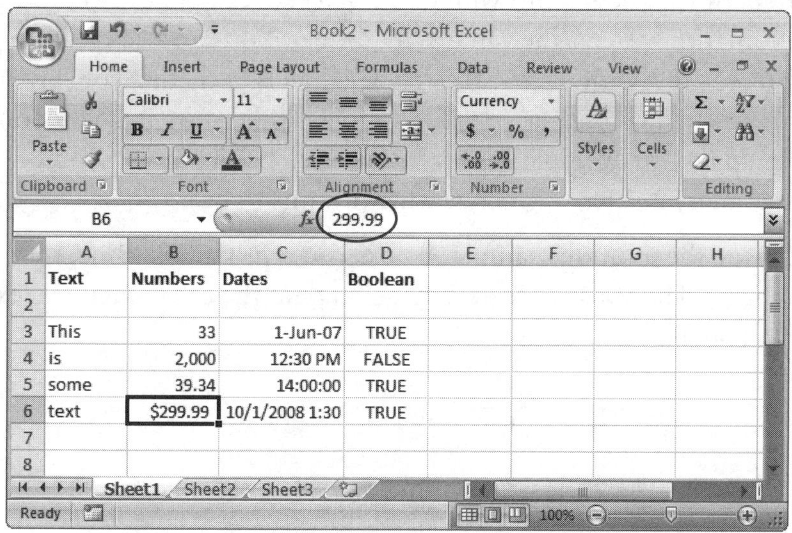

Figure 2-2. You can see the underlying value that Excel is storing for a cell by selecting the cell and then glancing at the formula bar. In this sheet, you can see that the value $299.99 is actually stored without the dollar currency symbol, which Excel applied only as part of the display format. Similarly, Excel stores the number 2,000 without the comma; it stores the date 1-Jun-07 as 6/1/2007; the time 12:30 p.m. as 12:30:00 PM, and the time 14:00:00 as 2:00:00 PM.

freakishly treats it as *text*, or vice versa? The first step to solving this problem is grasping the logic behind Excel's automatic decision-making process.

How Excel decides your data is text

If your cell meets any of the following criteria, Excel automatically treats the content as ordinary *text*:

- **It contains any letters.** Thus, C123 is text, not a number.
- **It contains any punctuation that Excel can't interpret numerically.** Punctuation allowed in numbers and dates includes the comma (,), the decimal point (.), and the forward slash (/) or dash (-) for dates. When you type in any other punctuation, Excel treats the cell as text. Thus, 14! is text, not a number.

Occasionally, Excel reads your data the wrong way. For example, you may have a value—like a social security number or a credit card number—that's made up entirely of numeric characters but that you want to treat like text because you don't ever want to perform calculations with it. But Excel doesn't know what you're up to, and so it automatically treats the value as a number. You can also run into problems when you precede text with the equal sign (which tells Excel that you have a formula in progress), or when you use a series of numbers and dashes that you don't intend to be part of a date (for example, you want to enter 1-2-3 but you don't want Excel to read it as January 2, 2003—which is what it wants to do).

In all these cases, the solution's simple. Before you type the cell value, start by typing an apostrophe ('). The apostrophe tells Excel to treat the cell content as text. Figure 2-3 shows you how it works.

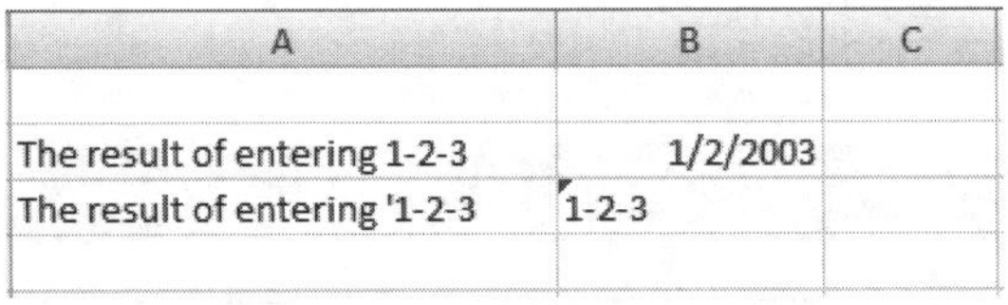

A	B	C
The result of entering 1-2-3	1/2/2003	
The result of entering '1-2-3	1-2-3	

Figure 2-3. To have Excel treat any number, date, or time as text, just precede the value with an apostrophe (you can see the apostrophe in the formula bar, but not in the cell). This worksheet shows the result of typing 1-2-3, both with and without the initial apostrophe.

When you precede a numeric value with an apostrophe, Excel checks out the cell to see what's going on. When Excel determines that it can represent the content as a number, it places a green triangle in the top left corner of the cell and gives you a few options for dealing with the cell, as shown in Figure 2-4.

NOTE

When you type in either *false* or *true* (using any capitalization you like), Excel automatically recognizes the data type as Boolean value instead of text, converts it to the uppercase word FALSE or TRUE, and centers it in the cell. If you want to make a cell that contains *false* or *true* as text and *not* as Boolean data, start by typing an apostrophe (') at the beginning of the cell.

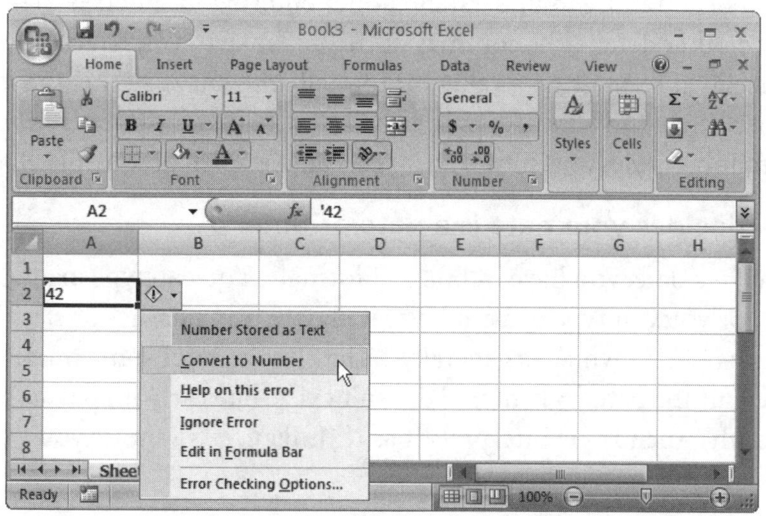

Figure 2-4. In this worksheet, the number 42 is stored as text, thanks to the apostrophe that precedes it. Excel notices the apostrophe, wonders if it's an unintentional error, and flags the cell by putting a tiny green triangle in the top-left corner. If you move to the cell, an exclamation mark icon appears, and, if you click that, a menu appears, letting you choose to convert the number or ignore the issue for this cell.

How Excel decides your data is numeric

Excel automatically interprets any cell that contains only numeric characters as a number. In addition, you can add the following non-numeric characters to a number without causing a problem:

- One decimal point (but not two). For example, 42.1 is a number, but 42.1.1 is text.
- One or more commas, provided you use them to separate groups of three numbers (like thousands, millions, and so on). Thus 1,200,200 is a valid number, but 1,200,20 is text.
- A currency sign ($ for U.S. dollars), provided it's at the beginning of the number.
- A percent symbol at the beginning or end of the number (but not both).
- A plus (+) or minus (–) sign before the number. You can also create a negative number by putting it in parentheses. In other words, entering (33) is the same as entering –33.
- An equal sign at the start of the cell.

The most important thing to understand about entering numbers is that when you choose to add other details like commas or the dollar sign, you're actually doing two things at once: you're entering a value for the cell *and* you're setting the format for the cell, which affects how Excel displays the cell. Chapter 5 provides more information about number styles and shows how you can completely control cell formatting.

How Excel decides your data is a date or time

When typing in a date, you have a choice of formats. You can type in a full date (like *July 4, 2007*) or you can type in an abbreviated date using dashes or slashes (like *7-4-2007* or *7/4/2007*), which is generally easier. If you enter some numbers formatted as a date, but the date you entered doesn't exist (like the 30th day in February or the 13th month), then Excel interprets it as text. Figure 2-5 shows you the options.

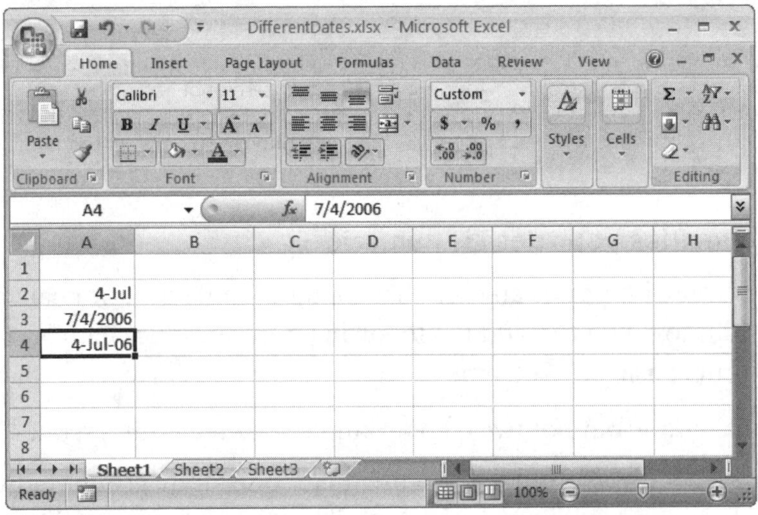

Figure 2-5. Whichever way you type in the date in a cell, it always appears the same on the formula bar (the specific formula bar display depends on the regional settings on your computer, explained next).

Because you can represent dates a few different ways, working with them can be tricky, and you're likely to encounter some unexpected behavior from Excel. Here are some tips for using dates, trouble-free:

- **Instead of using a number for the month, you can use a three-letter month abbreviation, but you must put the month in the middle.** In other words, you can use *7/4/2007* and *4/Jul/2007* interchangeably.
- **When you use a two-digit year as part of a date, Excel tries to guess whether the first two digits of the year should be 20 or 19.** When the two-digit year is from 00 to 29, Excel assumes it belongs to the 21st century. If the year is from 30 to 99, Excel plants it in the 1900s. In other words, Excel translates 7/4/29 into 7/4/2029, while 7/4/30 becomes 7/4/1930.

TIP

If you're a mere mortal and you forget where the cutoff point is, enter the year as a four-digit number, which prevents any confusion.

- **If you don't type in any year at all, Excel automatically assumes you mean the current year.** For example, when you enter 7/4, Excel inserts the date 7/4/2007 (assuming it's currently 2007 on your computer's internal clock). When you enter a date this way, the year component doesn't show up in the cell, but it's still stored in the worksheet (and visible on the formula bar).
- **Excel understands and displays dates differently depending on the regional settings on your computer.** Windows has a setting that determines how your computer interprets dates (see the box on page 69.) On the U.S. system, Month-Day-Year is the standard progression. But on the UK system, Day-Month-Year is the deal. For example, in the U.S., either 11-7-08 or 11/7/08 is shorthand for November 7, 2008. In the UK, the same notations refer to July 11, 2008.

  Thus, if your computer has U.S. regional settings turned on, and you type in *11/7/08*, then Excel understands it as November 7, 2008, and the formula bar displays 11/7/08.

NOTE

The way Excel *recognizes* and *displays* dates varies according to the regional settings on your computer, but the way Excel *stores* dates does not. This feature comes in handy when you save a worksheet on one computer and then open it on another computer with different regional settings. Because Excel stores every date the same way, the date information remains accurate on the new computer, and Excel can display it according to the new regional settings.

Typing in times is more straightforward than typing in dates. You simply use numbers, separated by a colon (:). You need to include an hour and minute component at minimum (as in 7:30), but you can also add seconds, milliseconds, and more (as in 7:30:10.10). You can use values from 1 to 24 for the hour part, though if your system is set to use a 12-hour clock, Excel converts the time accordingly (in other words, 19:30 becomes 7:30 PM). If you want to use the 12-hour clock when you type in a time, follow your time with a space and the letters P or PM (or A or AM).

Finally, you can create cells that have both date and time information. To do so, just type the date portion first, followed by a space, and then the time portion. For example, Excel happily accepts this combo: 7/4/2008 1:30 PM.

Behind the scenes, Excel stores dates as *serial numbers*. It considers the date January 1, 1900 to be day 1. January 2, 1900 is day 2, and so on, up through the year 9999. This system is quite nifty because if you use Excel to subtract one date from another, then you actually end up calculating the difference in days, which is exactly what you want. On the other hand, it means you can't enter a date in Excel that's earlier than January 1, 1900 (if you do, Excel treats your date like text).

Similarly, Excel stores times as fractional numbers from 0 to 1. The number 0 represents 12:00 a.m. (the start of the day) and 0.999 represents 11:59:59 p.m. (the end of the day). As with dates, this system allows you to subtract one time value from another.

Quick Ways to Add Data

Some of Excel's timesaving frills can make your life easier when you're entering data in a worksheet. This section covers four such features: AutoComplete, AutoCorrect, AutoFill, and AutoFit, along with Excel's top candidates for the Lifetime Most Useful Achievement award: Undo and Redo.

UP TO SPEED

Regional Dating

Windows has regional settings for your computer, which affect the way Microsoft programs understand things like dates and currency. You can change the settings, and they don't have to correspond to where you live—you can set them for your company headquarters on another continent, for instance. But keep in mind that these affect all the programs on your computer.

To make a switch, go to the Start menu in Windows and choose Settings → Control Panel, and then double-click Regional and Language Options, which brings up a dialog box. The Regional Options tab has the settings you want. The most important setting is in the first box, which has a drop-down list you can use to pick the region you want, like English (United States) or Swedish (Finland).

You can fine-tune the settings in your region, too. This makes sense only if you have particular preferences about how dates should be formatted that don't match the standard options. Click the Customize button next to the region box to bring up a new dialog box, and then click the Date tab (shown in Figure 2-6).

No matter what the regional settings are, you can always use the international date standard, which is Year/Month/Day, though you must supply a four-digit year (as in 2008/7/4). When you use a two-digit year, Excel assumes you're trying to use the Month-Day-Year or Day-Month-Year pattern.

Note

Excel really has two types of automatic features. First off, there are features that do things to your spreadsheets *automatically*, namely AutoComplete and AutoCorrect. Sometimes that's cool and convenient, but other times it can send you running for the old manual typewriter. Fortunately, you can turn off both. Excel also has "auto" features that really aren't that automatic. These include AutoFill and AutoFit, which never run on their own.

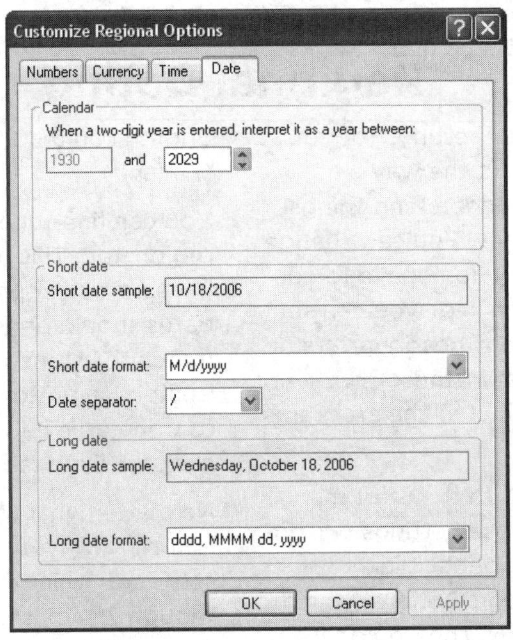

Figure 2-6. Tweaking the regional settings on your computer gives you complete control over how Excel recognizes dates. Use the pull-down menus to specify the date separator, order of month, day, and year components in a date, and how Excel should interpret two-digit years.

AutoComplete

Some worksheets require that you type in the same information row after row. For example, if you're creating a table to track the value of all your *Sesame Street* collectibles, you can type in *Kermit* only so many times before you start turning green. Excel tries to help you out with its AutoComplete feature, which examines what you type, compares it against previous entries in the same column, and, if it recognizes the beginning of an existing word, fills it in.

For instance, in your *Sesame Street* worksheet, if you already have Kermit in the Characters column, when you start typing a new entry in that column beginning with the letter K, Excel automatically fills in the whole word Kermit. Excel then selects the letters that it's added (in this case, *ermit*). You now have two options:

- **If you want to accept the AutoComplete text, move to another cell.** For example, when you hit the right arrow key or press Enter to move down, Excel leaves the word Kermit behind.
- **If you want to blow off Excel's suggestion, just keep typing.** Because Excel automatically selects the AutoComplete portion of the word (*ermit*), your next keystrokes overtype that text. Or, if you find the AutoComplete text is distracting, then press Delete to remove it right away.

TIP

When you want to use the AutoComplete text but change it slightly, turn on edit mode for the cell by pressing F2. Once you enter edit mode, you can use the arrow keys to move through the cell and make modifications. Press Enter or F2 to switch out of edit mode when you're finished.

AutoComplete has a few limitations. It works only with text entries, ignoring numbers and dates. It also doesn't pay any attention to the entries you've placed in other columns. And finally, it takes a stab at providing you with a suggestion only if the text you've typed in matches another column entry *unambiguously*. This means that when your column contains two words that start with K, like Kermit and kerplop, Excel doesn't make any suggestion when you type *K* into a new cell, because it can't tell which option is the most similar. But when you type *Kerm*, Excel realizes that kerplop isn't a candidate, and it supplies the AutoComplete suggestion Kermit.

If you find AutoComplete annoying, you can get it out of your face with a mere click of the mouse. Just select Office button → Excel Options, choose the Advanced section, and look under the "Editing options" heading for the "Enable AutoComplete for cell values" setting. Turn this setting off to banish AutoComplete from your spreadsheet.

AutoCorrect

As you type text in a cell, AutoCorrect cleans up behind you—correcting things like wrongly capitalized letters and common misspellings. AutoCorrect is subtle enough that you may not even realize it's monitoring your every move. To get a taste of its magic, look for behaviors like these:

- If you type *HEllo*, AutoCorrect changes it to *Hello*.
- If you type *friday*, AutoCorrect changes it to *Friday*.
- If you start a sentence with a lowercase letter, AutoCorrect uppercases it.
- If you scramble the letters of a common word (for example, typing *thsi* instead of *this*, or *teh* instead of *the*), AutoCorrect replaces the word with the proper spelling.
- If you accidentally hit Caps Lock key, and then type *jOHN sMITH* when you really wanted to type *John Smith*, Excel not only fixes the mistake, it also switches off the Caps Lock key.

NOTE

AutoCorrect doesn't correct most misspelled words, just common typos. To correct other mistakes, use the spell checker described on page 126.

For the most part, AutoCorrect is harmless and even occasionally useful, as it can spare you from delivering minor typos in a major report. But if you need to type irregularly capitalized words, or if you have a garden-variety desire to rebel against standard English, then you can turn off some or all of the AutoCorrect actions.

To reach the AutoCorrect settings, select Office button → Excel Options. Choose the Proofing section, and then click the AutoCorrect Options button. (All Auto-Correct options are language specific, and the title of the dialog box that opens indicates the language you're currently using.) Most of the actions are self-explanatory, and you can turn them off by turning off their checkboxes. Figure 2-7 explains the "Replace text as you type" option, which isn't just for errors.

TIP

For really advanced AutoCorrect settings, you can use the Exceptions button to define cases where Excel *won't* use AutoCorrect. When you click this button, the AutoCorrect Exceptions dialog box appears with a list of exceptions. For example, this list includes abbreviations that include the period but shouldn't be capitalized (like pp.) and words where mixed capitalization is allowed (like WordPerfect).

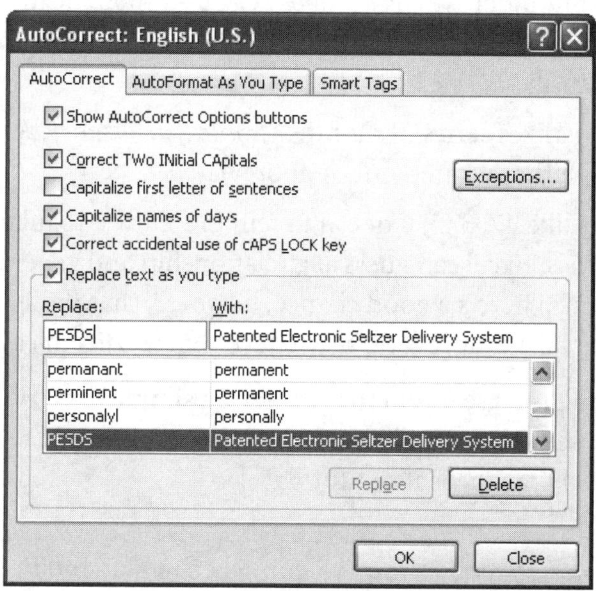

Figure 2-7. Under "Replace text as you type" is a long list of symbols and commonly misspelled words (the column on the left) that Excel automatically replaces with something else (the column on the right). But what if you want the copyright symbol to appear as a C in parentheses? You can remove individual corrections (select one, and then click Delete); or you can change the replacement text. And you can add your own rules. For example, you might want to be able to type PESDS and have Excel insert Patented Electronic Seltzer Delivery System. Simply type in the "Replace" and "With" text, as shown here, and then click OK.

AutoFill

AutoFill is a quirky yet useful feature that lets you create a whole column or row of values based on just one or two cells that Excel can extrapolate into a series. Put another way, AutoFill looks at the cells you've already filled in a column or row, and then makes a reasonable guess about the additional cells you'll want to add. People commonly use AutoFill for sequential numbers, months, or days.

Here are a few examples of lists that AutoFill can and can't work with:

- The series 1, 2, 3, 4 is easy for Excel to interpret—it's a list of steadily increasing numbers. The series 5, 10, 15 (numbers increasing by five) is just as easy. Both of these are great AutoFill candidates.

- The series of part numbers CMP-40-0001, CMP-40-0002, CMP-40-0003 may seem more complicated because it mingles text and numbers. But clever Excel can spot the pattern easily.
- Excel readily recognizes series of months (*January, February, March*) and days (*Sun, Mon, Tue*), either written out or abbreviated.
- A list of numbers like 47, 345, 6 doesn't seem to follow a regular pattern. But by doing some analysis, Excel can guess at a relationship and generate more numbers that fit the pattern. There's a good chance, however, that these won't be the numbers you want, so take a close look at whatever Excel adds in cases like these.

Bottom line: AutoFill is a great tool for generating simple lists. When you're working with a complex sequence of values, it's no help—unless you're willing to create a custom list (page 74) that spells it out for Excel.

TIP

AutoFill doubles as a quick way to *copy* a cell value multiple times. For example, if you select a cell in which you've typed *Cookie Monster*, you can use the AutoFill technique described below to fill every cell in that row or column with the same text.

To use AutoFill, follow these steps:

1. **Fill in a couple of cells in a row or column to start off the series.**

   Technically, you can use AutoFill if you fill in only one cell, although this approach gives Excel more room to make a mistake if you're trying to generate a series. Of course, when you want to copy only a single cell several times, one cell is a sufficient start.

2. **Select the cells you've entered so far. Then click (and hold) the small black square at the bottom-right corner of the selected box.**

   You can tell that your mouse is in the correct place when the mouse pointer changes to a plus symbol (+).

3. **Drag the border down (if you're filling a column of items) or to the right (if you're filling a row of items).**

   As you drag, a tooltip appears, showing the text that Excel is generating for each cell.

   While you're dragging, you can hold down Ctrl to affect the way that Excel fills a list. When you've already filled in at least *two* cells, Ctrl tells Excel to just copy the list multiple times, rather than look for a pattern. When you want to expand a range based on just *one* cell, Ctrl does the opposite: It tells Excel to try to predict a pattern, rather than just copy it.

   When you release the mouse, Excel automatically fills in the additional cells, and a special AutoFill icon appears next to the last cell in the series, as shown in Figure 2-8.

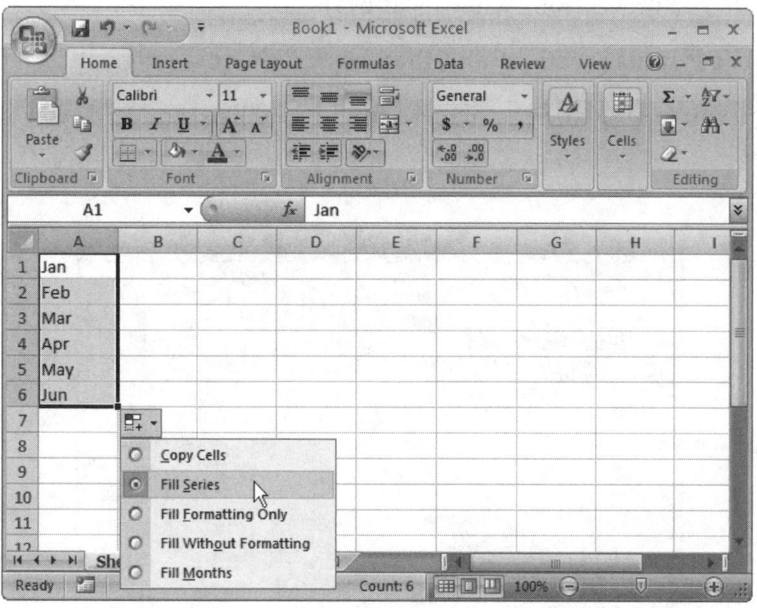

Figure 2-8. After AutoFill does its magic, Excel displays a menu that lets you fill the series without copying the formatting, or copy the formatting without filling the series. You can also choose to copy values instead of generating a list. For example, if you choose to copy values—or Copy Cells, as Excel calls it—then in the two-item series Jan, Feb, you end up with Jan, Feb, Jan, Feb, rather than Jan, Feb, Mar, Apr.

Custom AutoFill lists

Excel stores a collection of AutoFill lists that it refers to every time you use the feature. You can add your own lists to the collection, which extends the series AutoFill recognizes. For example, Excel doesn't come set to understand Kermit, Cookie Monster, Grover, Big Bird, Oscar, and Snuffleupagus as a series, but you can add it to the mix.

But why bother to add custom lists to Excel's collection? After all, if you need to type in the whole list before you use it, is AutoFill really saving you any work? The benefit occurs when you need to create the same list in *multiple* worksheets, in which case you can type it in just once and then use AutoFill to recreate it as often as you'd like.

To create a custom list, follow these steps:

1. **Choose Office button → Excel Options.**

   The familiar Excel Options window appears.

2. **Choose the Popular section, and then click Edit Custom Lists.**

   Here, you can take a gander at Excel's predefined lists, and add your own (Figure 2-9).

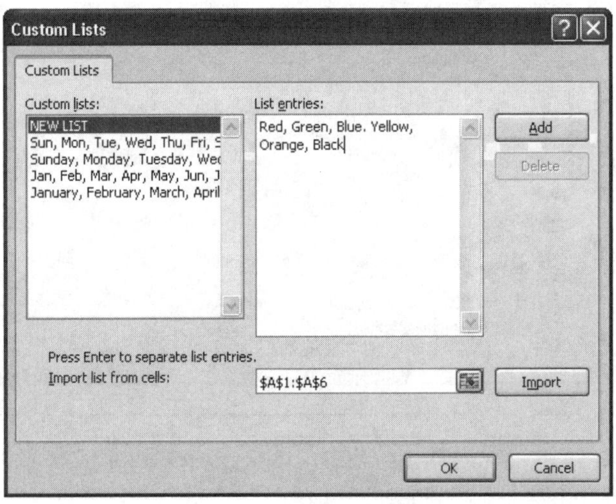

Figure 2-9. Here, a new custom list of colors is being added.

3. **In the "Custom lists" box on the left side of the dialog box, select NEW LIST.**

   This action tells Excel that you're ready to create a new list.

4. **In the "List entries" box on the right side of the dialog box, type in your list.**

   Separate each item with a comma or by pressing Enter. The list in Figure 2-9 shows a series of color names separated by commas.

   If you've already typed your list into your worksheet, you can save some work. Instead of retyping the list, click inside the text box labeled "Import list from cells." Then, click the worksheet and drag to select the cells that contain the list. (Each item in the list must be in a separate cell, and the whole list should be in a series of adjacent cells in a single column or a single row.) When you're finished, click Import, and Excel copies the cell entries into the new list you're creating.

5. **Click Add to store your list.**

   At any later point in time, you can return to this dialog box, select the saved list, and modify it in the window on the right. Just click Add to commit your changes after making a change, or click Delete to remove the list entirely.

6. **Click OK to close the Custom Lists dialog box, and OK again to close the Excel Options window.**

   You can now start using the list with the current worksheet or in a new worksheet. Just type the first item in your list and then follow the AutoFill steps outlined in the previous section.

AutoFit

Page 30 (Figure 1-5) explained how you can drag the edge of a column to resize it. For greater convenience, Excel also provides an AutoFit feature that automatically enlarges columns to fit overflowing contents perfectly (unfortunately, it doesn't include a shrink-to-fit option).

The AutoFit feature springs into action in three situations:

- When you type a number or date that's too wide to fit into a cell, Excel automatically widens the column to accommodate the new content. (Excel doesn't automatically expand columns when you type in text, however.)

GEM IN THE ROUGH

A Few More Ways to Adjust Column Width

Excel gives you the ability to precisely control column widths. To change the width of a column, right-click the column header at the top of the column, and then choose Column Width. The standard unadjusted column size is a compact 8.43 characters, but you can change that to any number of characters. (Because different fonts use different size letters, the number of characters you specify here may not correspond directly to the number of characters in your column.)

You can also adjust multiple column widths at the same time. Just select multiple columns (click the first column header, and then drag to the left or to the right to select more columns). Now, when you apply a new width, Excel uses it for all the selected columns.

Finally, you can customize the standard width for columns, which is the width that Excel assigns to columns in every new worksheet that you create. To set the standard width, choose Home → Cells → Format → Default Width from the menu, and then change the number.

- If you double-click the right edge of a column header, Excel automatically expands the column to fit the widest entry it contains. This trick works for all types of data, including dates, numbers, and text.
- If you select Home → Cells → Format → AutoFit Selection, Excel automatically expands the column to fit the content in the active cell. This feature is helpful if you have a column that's made up of relatively narrow entries, but which also has a long column title. In this situation, you may not want to expand the column to the full width of the title. Instead, you may wish to size the column to fit a typical entry and allow the title to spill over to the next column.

NOTE

When a column is already large enough for its content, AutoFit has no effect.

While AutoFit automatically widens columns when you type in a number or date in a cell, you can still shrink a column after you've entered your information.

Keep in mind, however, that when your columns are too narrow, Excel displays the cell data differently, depending on the type of information. When your cells contain *text*, it's entirely possible for one cell to overlap (and thereby obscure) another, a problem first described in Chapter 1. However, if Excel allowed truncated *numbers*, it could be deceiving. For example, if you squash a cell with the price of espresso makers so that they appear to cost $2 (instead of $200), you might wind up ordering a costly gift for all your coworkers. To prevent this problem, Excel never truncates a number or date. Instead, if you've shrunk a cell's width so that the number can't fit, then you'll see a series of number signs (like #####) filling in the whole cell. This warning is just Excel's way of telling you that you're out of space. Once you enlarge the column by hand (or by using AutoFit), the original number reappears. (Until then, you can still see the number stored in the cell by moving to the cell and looking in the formula bar.)

Undo and Redo

While editing a worksheet, an Excel guru can make as many (or more) mistakes as a novice. These mistakes include copying cells to the wrong place, deleting something important, or just making a mess of the cell formatting. Excel masters can recover much more quickly, however, because they rely on Undo and Redo. Get in the habit of calling on these features, and you'll be well on your way to Excel gurudom.

NOSTALGIA CORNER

Do More with Undo

Long-time Excel fans will realize Excel 2007's Undo feature is vastly improved. Previous versions of Excel were limited to a paltry 16 levels of Undo. Excel 2007 goes far better with 100 levels, which lets you travel farther back into the history of your spreadsheet.

Another welcome improvement that you may not have noticed is the fact that Excel 2007 doesn't clear the Undo history when you save your spreadsheet. In previous versions of Excel, this was an exasperating quirk—as soon as you decided to save your work, you lost out on any chance to undo an action. Now, the Undo history remains until you close your workbook.

How do they work? As you create your worksheet, Excel records every change you make. Because the modern computer has vast resources of extra memory and computing power (that is, when it's not running the latest three-dimensional real-time action game), Excel can keep this log without slowing your computer down one bit.

If you make a change to your worksheet that you don't like (say you inadvertently delete your company's entire payroll plan), you can use Excel's Undo history to reverse the change. In the Quick Access toolbar, simply click the Undo button (Figure 2-10), or press the super-useful keyboard shortcut Ctrl+Z. Excel immediately restores your worksheet to its state just before the last change. If you change your mind again, you can revert to the changed state (known to experts as "undoing your undo") by choosing Edit → Redo, or pressing Ctrl+Y.

Things get interesting when you want to go farther back than just one previous change, because Excel doesn't just store one change in memory. Instead, it tracks the last *100* actions you made. And it tracks just about anything you do to a worksheet, including cell edits, cell formatting, cut and paste operations, and much more. As a result, if you make a series of changes you don't like, or if you discover a mistake a little later down the road, then you can step back through the entire series of changes, one at a time. Every time you press Ctrl+Z, you go back one change in the history. This ability to reverse multiple changes makes Undo one of the most valuable features ever added to any software package.

TIP

The Undo feature means you don't need to be afraid of performing a change that may not be what you want. Excel experts often try out new actions, and then simply reverse them if the actions don't have the desired effect.

The Undo feature raises an interesting dilemma. When you can go back 100 levels into the history of your document, how do you know exactly what changes you're reversing? Most people don't remember the previous 100 changes they made to a worksheet, which makes it all too easy to reverse a change you actually *want* to keep. Excel provides the solution by not only keeping track of old worksheet versions, but also by keeping a simple description of each change. You don't see this description if you use the Ctrl+Z and Ctrl+Y shortcuts. However, when you hover over the button in the Quick Access toolbar, you'll see the action you're undoing listed there.

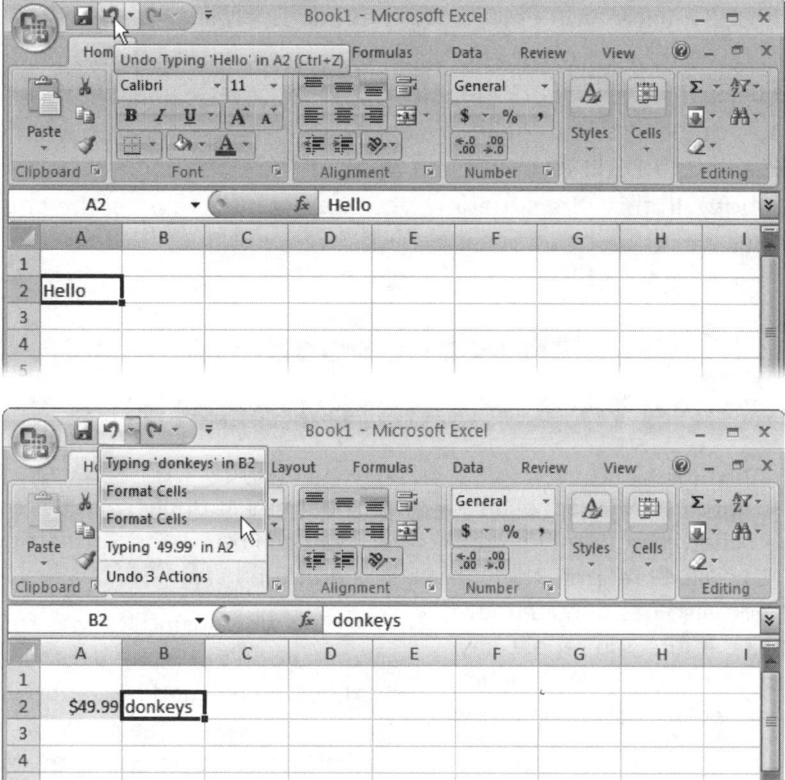

Figure 2-10. Top: When you hover over the Undo button, you see a text description for the most recent action, which is what you'll undo if you click away. Here, the text Hello has just been typed into a cell, as Excel explains.

Bottom: Click the down-pointing arrow on the edge of the Undo button to see a history of all your recent actions, from most recent (top) to oldest (bottom). If you click an item that's down the list, you'll perform a mega-undo operation that undoes all the selected actions. In this example, three actions are about to be rolled back—the text entry in cell B2, and two format operations (which changed the number format and the background fill of cell A2).

For example, if you type *hello* into cell A1, and then delete it, when you hover over the Undo button in the Quick Access toolbar, it says "Undo Clear (Ctrl+Z)". When you choose this option, the word *hello* returns. And if you hover over the Undo button again, it now says, "Undo Typing 'hello' in A2 (Ctrl+Z)", as shown in Figure 2-10, top.

NOTE

Occasionally, when you perform an advanced analysis task with an extremely complex worksheet, Excel may decide it can't afford to keep an old version of your worksheet in memory. When Excel hits this point, it warns you before you make the change, and gives you the chance to either cancel the edit or continue (without the possibility of undoing the change). In this rare situation, you may want to cancel the change, save your worksheet as a backup, and then continue.

GEM IN THE ROUGH

Using Redo to Automate Repetitive Tasks

Redo is commonly used to reverse an Undo. In other words, if you cancel an action and then change your mind, you can use Redo to quickly reapply the change. But Redo also has a much more interesting ability: it lets you repeat any action multiple times. The neat thing is that you can repeat this action *on other cells*.

For example, imagine you hit Ctrl+B to change a cell to bold. When you open the Edit menu, you'll see that the Redo item now says Repeat Font. If you move to another cell and hit Ctrl+Y, Excel applies the bold formatting to the new cell. In this case, you're not saving much effort, because it's just as easy to use Ctrl+B or Ctrl+Y. However, imagine you finish an operation that applies a set of sophisticated formatting changes to a cell. For example, say you increase the font size, bold the text, and apply a border around the cell (Chapter 5 tells you how to do these things).

When you press Ctrl+Y, Excel applies all the changes at once—which is much easier than calling up the Formatting dialog box and then selecting the same options.

The trick when using Redo is to make sure you don't perform another action until you've finished repeating your changes. For example, if you make some formatting changes and then stop to delete an incorrect cell value, then you can no longer use Redo to apply your formatting because Excel applies the last change that you made—in this case, clearing the cell. (Of course, when you mistakenly apply Redo, you can always call on Undo to get out of the mess.)

If you're ever in doubt about what'll happen when you use Redo, just hover over the Redo button in the Quick Access toolbar. You'll see a text description, like Repeat Font or Repeat Column Width.

3 MOVING DATA AROUND A WORKSHEET

- Selecting Cells
- Moving Cells Around
- Adding and Moving Columns or Rows

SIMPLE SPREADSHEETS ARE A GOOD WAY TO GET A HANDLE ON EXCEL. But in the real world, you often need a spreadsheet that's more sophisticated—one that can grow and change as you start to track more information. For example, on the expenses worksheet you created in Chapter 1, perhaps you'd like to add information about which stores you've been shopping in. Or maybe you'd like to swap the order in which your columns appear. To make changes like these, you need to add a few more skills to your Excel repertoire.

This chapter covers the basics of spreadsheet modification, including how to select cells, how to move data from one place to another, and how to change the structure of your worksheet. What you learn here will make you a master of spreadsheet manipulation.

Selecting Cells

First things first: before you can make any changes to an existing worksheet, you need to select the cells you want to modify. Happily, selecting cells in Excel—try saying that five times fast—is easy. You can do it many different ways, and it's worth learning them all. Different selection techniques come in handy in different situations, and if you master all of them in conjunction with the formatting features described in Chapter 5, you'll be able to transform the look of any worksheet in seconds.

Making Continuous Range Selections

Simplest of all is selecting a *continuous range* of cells. A continuous range is a block of cells that has the shape of a rectangle (high school math reminder: a square is a kind of rectangle), as shown in Figure 3-1. The easiest way to select a continuous range is to click the top-left cell you want to select. Then drag to the right (to select more columns) or down (to select more rows). As you go, Excel highlights the selected cells in blue. Once you've highlighted all the cells you want, release the mouse button. Now you can perform an action, like copying the cells' contents, formatting the cells, or pasting new values into the selected cells.

	A	B	C	D
1	Date Purchased	Item	Price	
2	7/7/2007	Cowbell	$43.99	
3	7/7/2007	Fresh Fruit	$3.00	
4	7/10/2007	IBM Laptop	$750.00	
5				

	A	B	C	D
1	Date Purchased	Item	Price	
2	7/7/2007	Cowbell	$43.99	
3	7/7/2007	Fresh Fruit	$3.00	
4	7/10/2007	IBM Laptop	$750.00	
5				

Figure 3-1. Top: The three selected cells (A1, B1, and C1) cover the column titles.

Bottom: This selection covers the nine cells that make up the rest of the worksheet. Notice that Excel doesn't highlight the first cell you select.

In the simple expense worksheet from Chapter 1, for example, you could first select the cells in the top row and then apply bold formatting to make the column titles stand out. (Once you've selected the top three cells, press Ctrl+B, or chose Home → Font → Bold.)

Note

When you select some cells and then press an arrow key or click into another cell *before* you perform any action, Excel clears your selection.

Excel gives you a few useful shortcuts for making continuous range selections (some of these are illustrated in Figure 3-2):

- Instead of clicking and dragging to select a range, you can use a two-step technique. First, click the top-left cell. Then hold down Shift and click the cell at the bottom-right corner of the area you want to select. Excel highlights all the cells in between automatically. This technique works even if both cells aren't visible at the same time; just scroll to the second cell using the scroll bars, and make sure you don't click any other cell on your way there.
- If you want to select an entire column, click the header at the top of the column. For example, if you want to select the second column, then click the gray "B" box above the column. Excel selects all the cells in this column, right down to row 1,048,576.

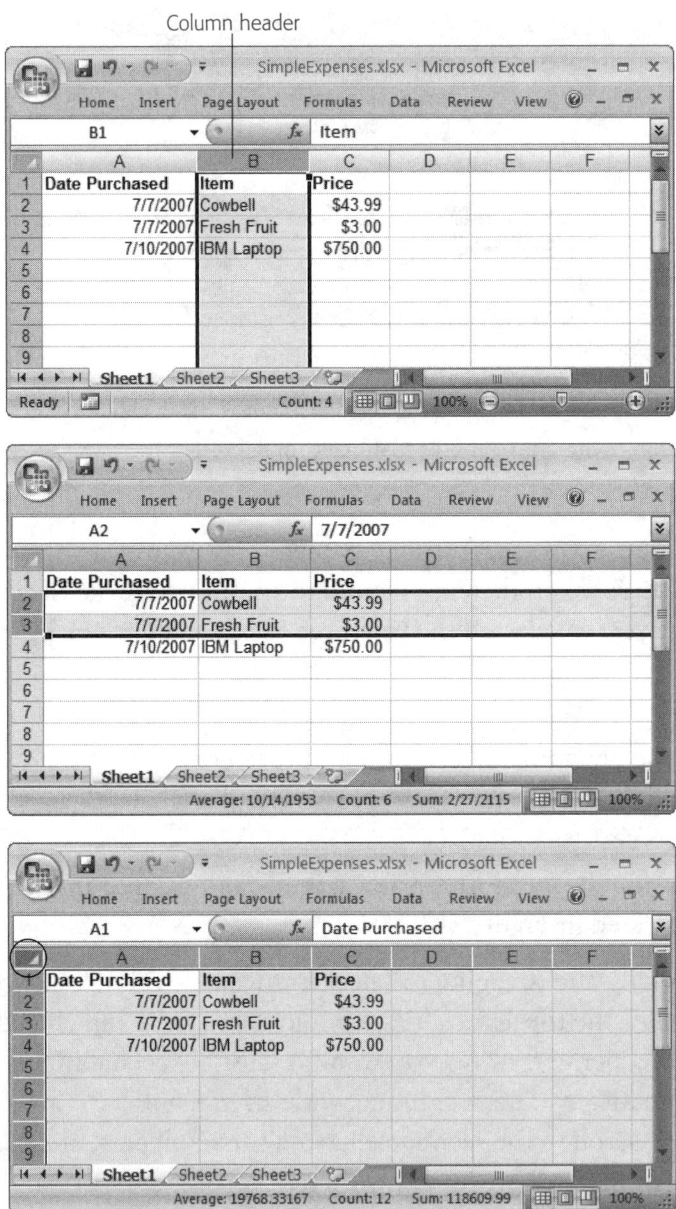

Figure 3-2. Top: Click a column header to select that entire column.

Middle: Click a row number to select that entire row.

Bottom: To select every cell in the worksheet, click the empty gray square just outside the top-left corner of the worksheet (circled).

- If you want to select an entire row, click the numbered row header on the left edge of the row. For example, you can select the second row by clicking the gray "2" box to the left of the row. All the columns in this row will be selected.
- If you want to select multiple adjacent columns, click the leftmost column header, and then drag to the right until all the columns you want are selected. As you drag, a tooltip appears indicating how many columns you've selected. For example, if you've selected three columns, you'll see a tooltip with the text 3C (C stands for "column").
- If you want to select multiple adjacent rows, click the topmost row header and then drag down until all the rows you want are selected. As you drag, a tooltip appears indicating how many rows you've selected. For example, if you've selected two rows, you'll see a tooltip with the text 2R (R stands for "row").
- If you want to select all the cells in the entire worksheet, click the blank gray box that's just outside the top-left corner of the worksheet. This box is immediately to the left of the column headers and just above the row headers.

TIME-SAVING TIP

A Truly Great Calculation Trick

Excel provides a seriously nifty calculation tool in the status bar. Just select two or more cells, and look down to the status bar where you'll see the number of cells you've selected (the count), along with their sum and their average (shown in Figure 3-3).

To choose what calculations appear in the status bar, right-click anywhere on the status bar, and then, in the menu that appears, choose one of the following options:

- **Average.** The average of all the selected numbers or dates.
- **Count.** The number of selected cells (including any cells with text in them).
- **Numerical Count.** The number of selected cells that contain numbers or dates.
- **Minimum.** The selected number or date with the smallest value (for dates this means the earliest date).
- **Maximum.** The selected number or date with the largest value (for dates this means the latest date).
- **Sum.** The sum of all selected numbers. Although you can use Sum with date values, because of the way Excel stores date values, adding dates together generates meaningless results.

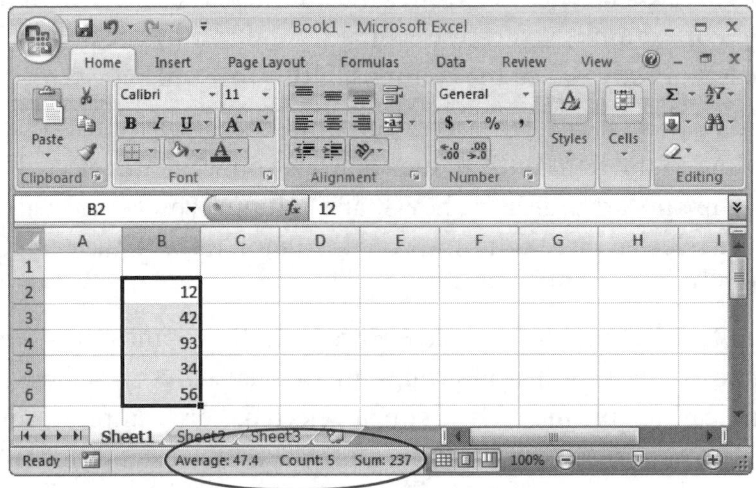

Figure 3-3. The nicest detail about the status bar's quick calculations is that you can mix-and-match several at a time. Here, you see the count, average, and sum of the selected cells.

TIP

When you're selecting multiple rows or columns, make sure you click *between* the column header's left and right edges, not on either edge. When you click the edge of the column header, you end up resizing the column instead of making a selection.

Making Non-Contiguous Selections

In some cases, you may want to select cells that are *non-contiguous* (also known as nonadjacent), which means they don't form a neat rectangle. For example, you might want to select columns A and C, but not column B. Or, you might want to select a handful of cells scattered throughout the worksheet.

The trick to non-contiguous cell selection is using the Ctrl key. All you need to do is select the cells you want while holding down Ctrl. You can select individual cells by Ctrl-clicking them, or you can select multiple blocks of cells on different parts of the sheet by clicking and dragging in several different places while holding down Ctrl.

You can also combine the Ctrl key with any of the shortcuts discussed earlier to select entire columns or rows as a part of your selection. Excel highlights in blue the cells you select (except for the last cell selected, which, as shown in Figure 3-4, isn't highlighted because it becomes the active cell).

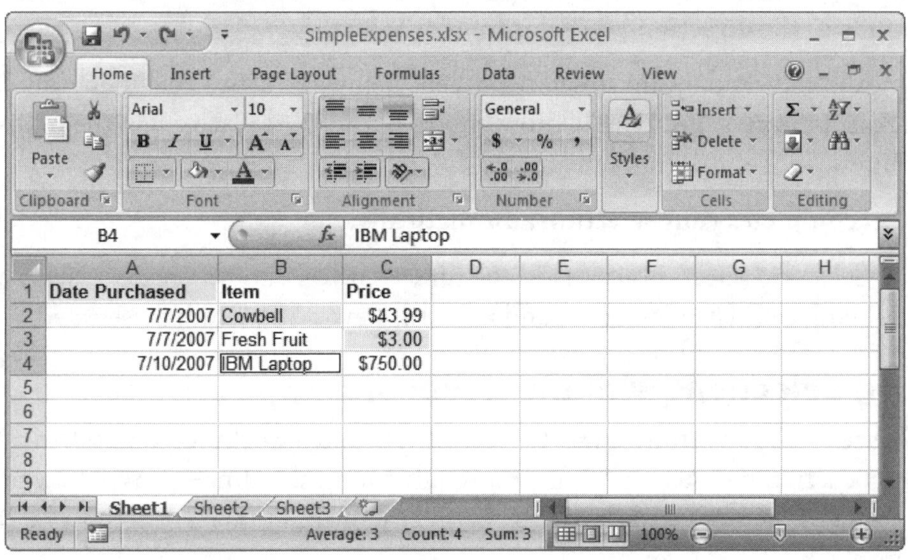

Figure 3-4. This figure shows a non-contiguous selection that includes four cells (A1, B2, C3, and B4). The last selected cell (B4) isn't highlighted because it's the active cell. This behavior is a little bit different from a continuous selection, in which the first selected cell is always the active cell. With a non-contiguous selection, the last selected cell becomes the active cell.

NOTE

Excel restricts what you can do with non-contiguous selections. For example, you can format the cells in a non-contiguous selection, but you can't cut or copy the selection.

Automatically Selecting Your Data

Excel provides a nifty shortcut that can help you select a series of cells without dragging or Shift-clicking anything. It's called AutoSelect, and its special power is to select all the data values in a given row or column until it encounters an empty cell.

To use AutoSelect, follow these steps:

1. **Move to the first cell that you want to select.**

   Before continuing, decide which direction you want to extend the selection.

2. **Hold down Shift. Now, double-click whichever edge of the active cell corresponds to the direction you want to AutoSelect.**

   For example, if you want to select the cells below the active cell, then double-click its bottom edge. (You'll know you're in the right place when the mouse pointer changes to a four-way arrow.)

3. **Excel completes your selection automatically.**

   AutoSelection selects every cell in the direction you choose until it reaches the first blank cell. The blank cell (and any cells beyond it) won't be selected.

Making Selections with the Keyboard

The mouse can be an intuitive way to navigate around a worksheet and select cells. It can also be a tremendous time-suck, especially for nimble-fingered typists who've grown fond of the keyboard shortcuts that let them speed through actions in other programs.

Fortunately, Excel is ready to let you use the keyboard to select cells in a worksheet. Just follow these steps:

1. **Start by moving to the first cell you want to select.**

   Whichever cell you begin on becomes the anchor point from which your selected area grows. Think of this cell as the corner of a rectangle you're about to draw.

2. **Now, hold down Shift, and move to the right or left (to select columns) and down or up (to select more rows), using the arrow keys.**

   As you move, the selection grows. Instead of holding down Shift, you can also just press F8 once, which turns on extend mode. When extend mode is on, you'll see the text Extend Selection in the status bar. As you move, Excel selects cells just as though you were holding down Shift. You can turn off extend mode by pressing F8 once you've finished marking your range.

Making a non-contiguous selection is almost as easy. The trick is you need to switch between extend mode and another mode called add mode. Just follow these steps:

1. **Move to the first cell you want to select.**

   You can add cells to a non-contiguous range one at a time, or by adding multiple continuous ranges. Either way, you start with the first cell you want to select.

2. **Press F8.**

   This key turns on extend mode. You'll see the text Extend Selection appear in the Status bar to let you know extend mode is turned on.

3. **If you want to select more than one cell, use the arrow keys to extend your selection.**

   If you just want to select the currently active cell, do nothing; you're ready to go onto the next step. When you want to add a whole block of cells, you can mark out your selection now. Remember, at this point you're still selecting a continuous range. In the steps that follow you can add several distinct continuous ranges to make a non-contiguous selection.

4. **Press Shift+F8 to add the highlighted cells to your non-contiguous range.**

   When you hit Shift+F8, you switch to add mode, and you see the text "Add to Selection" appear in the status bar.

5. **You now have two choices: You can repeat steps 1 to 4 to add more cells to your selection; or, you can perform an action with the current selection, like applying new formatting.**

   You can repeat steps 1 to 4 as many times as you need to add more groups of cells to your non-contiguous range. These new cells (either individuals or groups) don't need to be near each other or in any way connected to the other cells you've selected. If you change your mind, and decide you don't want to do anything with your selection after all, press F8 twice—once to move back into extend mode, and then again to return to normal mode. Now, the next time you press an arrow key, Excel releases the current selection.

TIP

You can also use the keyboard to activate AutoSelect. Just hold down the Shift key, and use one of the shortcut key combinations that automatically jumps over a range of cells. For example, when you hold down Shift and then press Ctrl+→, you'll automatically jump to the last occupied cell in the current row with all the cells in between selected. For more information about the shortcut keys, see Table 1-1 on page 33.

POWER USERS' CLINIC

Selecting Cells with the Go To Feature

In Chapter 1, you learned how you could use the Go To feature to jump from one position in a cell to another. A little known Excel secret also lets you use the Go To feature to select a range of cells.

It works like this: Start off at the top-left cell of the range you want to select. Then, open the Go To window by selecting Home → Editing → Find & Select → Go To, or by pressing Ctrl+G. Type in the address of the bottom-right cell in the selection you want to highlight. Now, here's the secret: Hold down Shift when you click the OK button. This action tells Excel to select the range of cells as it moves to the new cell.

For example, if you start in cell A1, and use the Go To window to jump to B3, then you'll select a block of six cells: A1, A2, A3, B1, B2, and B3.

Moving Cells Around

One of the most common reasons to select groups of cells on a worksheet is to copy or move them from one place to another. Excel is a champion of the basic cut-and-paste feature, and it also gives you worthwhile enhancements that let you do things like drag-and-drop blocks of cells and copy multiple selections to the clipboard at the same time.

Before you get started shuffling data from one place to another, here are a few points to keep in mind:

- Excel lets you cut or copy a single cell or a continuous range of cells. When you cut or copy a cell, *everything* goes with it, including the data and the current formatting.

- When you paste cells onto your worksheet, you have two basic choices. You can paste the cells into a new, blank area of the worksheet, or, you can paste the cells in a place that already contains data. In this second case, Excel overwrites the existing cells with the new pasted data.
- Cutting and copying cells works almost exactly the same way. The only difference you'll see is that when you perform a cut-and-paste operation (as opposed to a copy-and-paste operation), Excel erases the source data once the operation's complete. However, Excel doesn't remove the source cells from the worksheet. Instead, it just leaves them empty. (The next section shows you what to do if you do want to remove or insert cells, not just the data they contain.)

A Simple Cut-and-Paste or Copy-and-Paste

Here's the basic procedure for any cut-and-paste or copy-and-paste operation.

1. **Select the cells you want to cut or copy.**

   You can use any of the tricks you learned in the previous section to highlight a continuous range of cells. (You can't cut and paste non-contiguous selections.) When you want to cut or copy only a single cell, just move to the cell—you don't actually need to select it.

2. **If you want to cut your selection, choose Home → Clipboard → Cut (or Ctrl+X). When you want to copy your selection, choose Home → Clipboard → Copy (or Ctrl+C).**

   Excel highlights your selection with a *marquee border* (Figure 3-5), so-called because the border blinks like the twinkling lights around an old-style movie theater marquee.

3. **Move to the new location in the spreadsheet where you want to paste the cells.**

   If you selected one cell, move to the new cell where you want to place the data. If you selected multiple cells, then move to the top-left corner of the area where you want to paste your selection. If you have existing data below or to the right of this cell, Excel overwrites it with the new content you're pasting.

   It's valid to paste over part of the data you're copying. For example, you could make a selection that consists of columns A, B, and C, and paste that selection

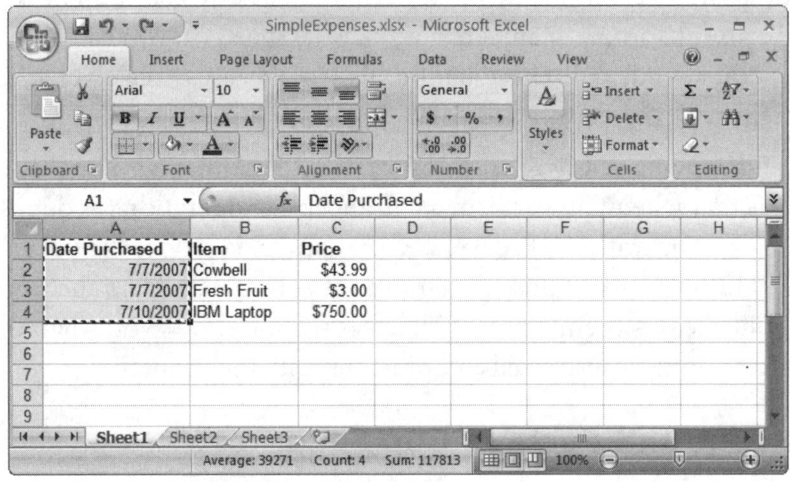

Figure 3-5. In this example, cells A1 to A4 have been copied. The next step is to move to the place where you want to paste the cells, and then press Enter to complete the operation.

starting at column B. In this case, the pasted data appears in columns B, C, and D, and Excel overwrites the original content in these columns (although the original content remains in column A).

4. **Paste the data by selecting Home → Clipboard → Paste (or press Ctrl+V or Enter on the keyboard).**

   This action completes your cut-and-paste or copy-and-paste operation. When you're performing a cut-and-paste, Excel removes the original data from the spreadsheet just before pasting it in the new location.

TIP

Instead of cutting or copying a block of cells, you can also move the entire column or row that contains the cells. Begin by highlighting one or more columns or rows (by selecting the column or row headers). For example, you could select column A by clicking the column header, and then cut it. You could then right-click the column B header, and choose Paste to move the column A values into column B. When you copy entire columns, Excel automatically adjusts the column widths as part of the copy operation, so the destination column winds up the same width as the source column.

FREQUENTLY ASKED QUESTION

The Mysterious Number Signs

What does it mean when I see ####### in a cell?

A series of number (or pound) signs is Excel's way of telling you that a column isn't wide enough to display the number or date that it contains (see Figure 3-6). Sometimes these signs appear when you're copying a big number into a smaller cell.

Excel doesn't use the number signs with text cells—if those cells aren't large enough to hold their data, the words simply spill over to the adjacent cell (if it's blank), or become truncated (if the adjacent cell has some content). This behavior wouldn't be acceptable with numbers because if Excel cut off a portion of a number, it would appear to be a completely different number.

Fortunately, it's easy to solve this problem—just position the mouse pointer at the right edge of the cell header, and then drag it to the right to enlarge the column. Provided you've made the column large enough, the missing number reappears. For a quicker solution, double-click the right edge of the column to automatically make it large enough.

This error doesn't usually occur while you're entering information for the first time because Excel automatically resizes columns to accommodate any numbers you type in. The problem is more likely to crop up if you shrink a column afterward, or if you cut some numeric cells from a wide column and paste them into a much narrower column. To verify the source of your problem, just move to the offending cell, and then check the formula bar to see your complete number or date.

A Fancy Cut-and-Paste or Copy-and-Paste

If you want a really quick way to cut and paste data, you can use Excel's drag-and-drop feature. It works like this:

1. **Select the cells you want to move.**

   Just drag your pointer over the block of cells you want to select.

2. **Click the border of the selection box, and don't release the mouse button.**

   You'll know that you're in the right place when the mouse pointer changes to a four-way arrow. You can click any edge, but *don't* click in the corner.

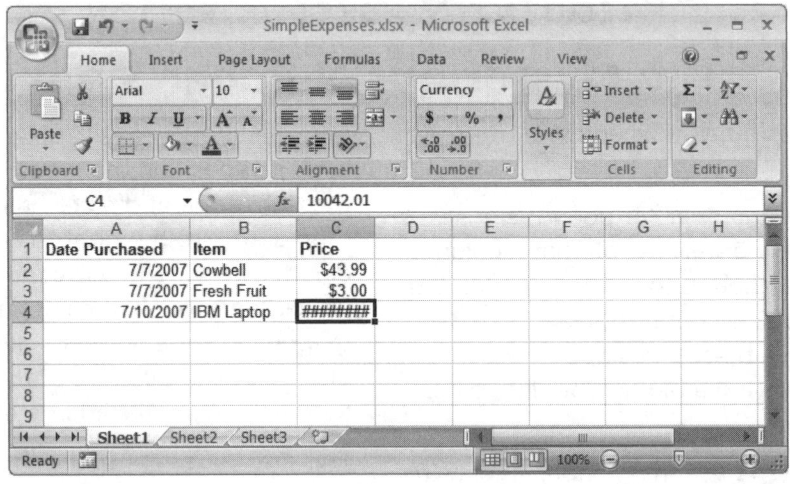

Figure 3-6. Cell C4 has a wide number in an overly narrow column. You can see the mystery number only if you move to the cell and check out the formula bar (it's 10,042.01), or expand the column to a more reasonable width.

3. **Drag the selection box to its new location. If you want to copy (rather than simply move) the text, hold down the Ctrl key while you drag.**

   As you drag, a light gray box shows you where Excel will paste the cells.

4. **Release the mouse button to move the cells.**

   If you drop the cells into a region that overlaps with other data, Excel prompts you to make sure that you want to overwrite the existing cells. This convenience isn't provided with ordinary cut-and-paste operations. (Excel uses it for drag-and-drop operations because it's all too easy to inadvertently drop your cells in the wrong place, especially while you're still getting used to this feature.)

The Clipboard

In Windows' early days, you could copy only a single piece of information at a time. If you copied two pieces of data, only the most recent item you copied would remain in the clipboard, a necessary way of life in the memory-starved computing days of yore. But nowadays, Excel boasts the ability to hold 24 separate cell selections in the Office clipboard. This information remains available as long as you have at least one Office application open.

NOTE

Even though the Office clipboard holds 24 pieces of information, you won't be able to access all this information in Windows applications that aren't part of the Office suite. If you want to paste Excel data into a non-Office application, you'll be able to paste only the data that was added to the clipboard most recently.

When you use the Home → Clipboard → Paste command (or Ctrl+V), you're using the ordinary Windows clipboard. That means you always paste the item most recently added to the clipboard. But if you fire up the Office clipboard, you can hold a lot more. Go to the Home → Clipboard section of the ribbon, and then click the dialog box launcher (the small arrow-in-a-square icon in the bottom-right corner) to open the Clipboard panel. Now Excel adds all the information you copy to *both* the Windows clipboard and the more capacious Office clipboard. Each item that you copy appears in the Clipboard panel (Figure 3-7).

Using the Clipboard panel, you can perform the following actions:

- Click Paste All to paste all the selections into your worksheet. Excel pastes the first selection into the current cell, and then begins pasting the next selection starting in the first row underneath that, and so on. As with all paste operations, the pasted cells overwrite any existing content in your worksheet.
- Click Delete All to remove all the selections from the clipboard. This is a useful approach if you want to add more data to the Clipboard, and you don't want to confuse this information with whatever selection you previously copied.
- Click a selection in the list to paste it into the current location in the worksheet.
- Click the drop-down arrow at the right of a selection item to show a menu that allows you to paste that item or remove it from the clipboard.

Depending on your settings, the Clipboard panel may automatically spring into action. To configure this behavior, click the Options button at the bottom of the Clipboard panel to display a menu of options. These include:

- **Show Office Clipboard Automatically.** If you turn on this option, the Clipboard panel automatically appears if you copy more than one piece of information to the clipboard. (Remember, without the Clipboard panel, you can access only the last piece of information you've copied.)

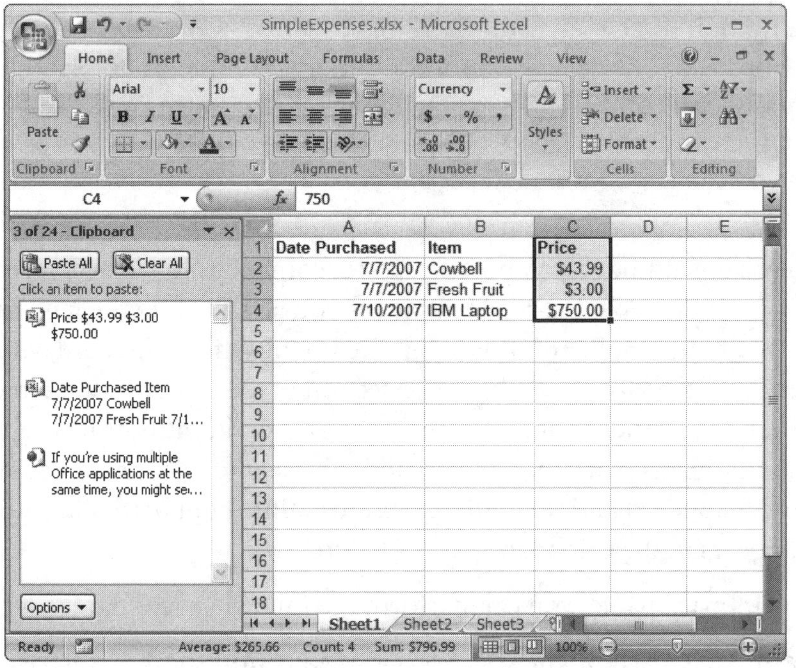

Figure 3-7. The Clipboard panel shows a list of all the items you've copied to it since you opened it (up to a limit of 24 items). Each item shows the combined content for all the cells in the selection. For example, the first item in this list includes four cells: the Price column title followed by the three prices. If you're using multiple Office applications at the same time, you may see scraps of Word documents, PowerPoint presentations, or pictures in the clipboard along with your Excel data. The icon next to the item always tells you which program the information came from.

- **Show Office Clipboard When Ctrl+C Pressed Twice.** If you turn on this option, the Clipboard panel appears if you press the Ctrl+C shortcut twice in a row, without doing anything else in between.
- **Collect Without Showing Office Clipboard.** If you turn on this option, it overrides the previous two settings, ensuring that the Clipboard panel never appears automatically. You can still call up the Clipboard panel manually, of course.
- **Show Office Clipboard Icon on Taskbar.** If you turn on this option, a clipboard icon appears in the system tray at the right of the taskbar. You can double-click this icon to show the Clipboard panel while working in any Office application. You can also right-click this icon to change clipboard settings or to tell the Office clipboard to stop collecting data.

- **Show Status Near Taskbar When Copying.** If you turn on this option, you'll see a tooltip near the Windows system tray whenever you copy data. (The *system tray* is the set of notification icons at the bottom-right corner of your screen, in the Windows taskbar.) The icon for the Office clipboard shows a clipboard icon, and it displays a message like "4 of 24 - Item Collected" (which indicates you have just copied a fourth item to the clipboard).

UP TO SPEED

Cutting or Copying Part of a Cell

Excel's cut-and-paste and copy-and-paste features let you move data in one or more cells. But what if you simply want to take a snippet of text from a cell, and transfer it to another cell or even another application? Excel makes this operation possible, but you need to work a little differently.

First, move to the cell that contains the content you want to cut or copy, and then place it in edit mode by double-clicking it with the mouse or pressing F2. You can now scroll through the cell content using the arrow keys. Move to the position where you want to start chopping or copying, hold down Shift, and then arrow over to the right. Keep moving until you've selected all the text you want to cut or copy. Then, hit Ctrl+C to copy the text, or Ctrl+X to cut it. (When you cut text, it disappears immediately, just like in other Windows applications.) Hit F2 or Enter to exit edit mode once you're finished.

The final step is to paste your text somewhere else. You can move to another cell that has data in it already, press F2 to enter edit mode again, move to the correct position in that cell, and then press Ctrl+V. However, you can also paste the text directly into a cell by just moving to the cell and pressing Ctrl+V without placing it into edit mode. In this case, the data you paste overwrites the current content in the cell.

Special Pasting

When you copy cells, *everything* comes along for the ride, including text, numbers, and formatting. For example, if you copy a column that has one cell filled with bold text and several other cells filled with dollar amounts (including the dollar sign), when you paste this column into its new location, the numbers will still have the dollar sign and the text will still have bold formatting. If you want to change this behavior, you can use the Paste Special command.

It works like this. First, copy your cells in the normal way. (Don't cut them, or the Paste Special feature won't work.) Then, move to where you want to paste the information, and choose Home → Clipboard → Paste → Paste Special (instead of Home → Clipboard → Paste). A new dialog box appears with a slew of options (Figure 3-8).

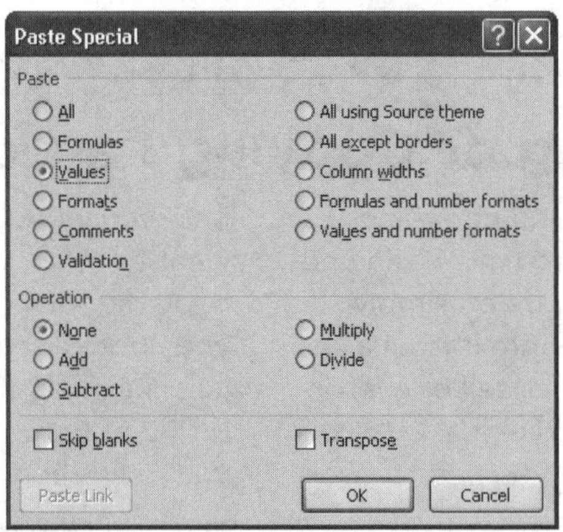

Figure 3-8. The Paste Special window allows you to choose exactly what Excel will paste, and it also lets you apply a few other settings. Here, Excel will paste the cell values but not the formatting.

These options are divided into two main groups: Paste and Operation. The Paste settings determine what content Excel pastes. This is the most useful part of the window. These settings include:

- **All.** This option is the same as a normal paste operation, and it pastes both formatting and numbers.
- **Formulas.** This option pastes only cell content—numbers, dates, and text—without any formatting. If your source range includes any formulas, Excel also copies the formulas.
- **Values.** This option pastes only cell content—numbers, dates, and text—without any formatting. If your source range includes any formulas, Excel pastes the *result* of that formula (the calculated number) but not the actual formula.

- **Formats.** This option applies the formatting from the source selection, but it doesn't actually copy any data.
- **Comments.** This option copies only the comments that you've added to cells.
- **Validation.** This option copies only cells that use validation (an advanced tool for checking data before it's entered into a cell).
- **All Except Borders.** This option is the same as All, except it ignores any borders that you've applied to the cell. Border formatting is described on page 160.
- **Column Widths.** This option is the same as All, and it also adjusts the columns in the paste region so that they have the same widths as the source columns.
- **Formulas and Number Formats.** This option doesn't paste any data. Here, Excel pastes only formulas and any settings used for formatting how numbers appear. (In other words, you'll lose format settings that control the font, cell fill color, and borders.)
- **Values and Number Formats.** This option pastes everything without any formatting, except for the formatting used to configure how numbers appear. (In other words, you'll lose format settings that control the font, cell fill color, and borders.)

The Operation settings are a little wacky—they allow you to combine the cells you're pasting with the contents of the cells you're pasting into, either by adding, subtracting, multiplying, or dividing the two sets of numbers. It's an intriguing idea, but few people use these settings because they're not intuitive.

Further down the Paste Special dialog box, the "Skip blanks" checkbox tells Excel not to overwrite a cell if the cell you're pasting from is empty. The Transpose checkbox inverts your information before it pastes it, so that all the columns become rows and the rows become columns. Figure 3-9 shows an example.

Finally, you can use the Paste Link button to paste a link that refers to the original data instead of a duplicate copy of the content. That means that if you modify the source cells, Excel automatically modifies the copies. In fact, if you take a closer look at the copied cells in the formula bar, you'll find that they don't contain the actual data. Instead, they contain a formula that points to the source cell. For example, if you paste cell A2 as a link into cell B4, the cell B4 contains the reference =A2. You'll learn more about cell references and formulas in Chapter 7.

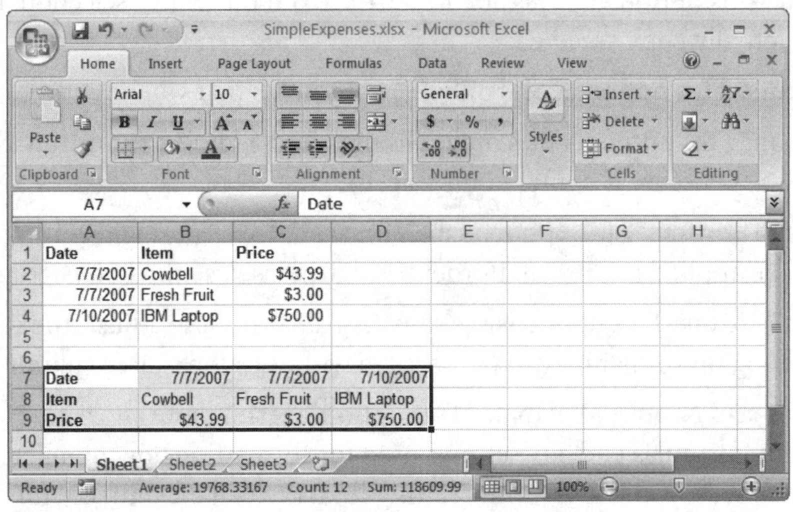

Figure 3-9. With the Transpose option (from the Paste Special dialog box), Excel's pasted the table at the top and transposed it on the bottom.

TIP

Once you know your way around the different pasting options, you can often find a quicker way to get the same result. Instead of choosing Home → Clipboard → Paste → Paste Special, you can choose one of the options in the Home → Clipboard → Paste menu. You won't find all the options that are in the Paste Special dialog box, but you do find commonly used options like Paste Values and Transpose.

Even if you don't use the Paste Special command, you can still control some basic paste settings. After you paste any data in Excel, a paste icon appears near the bottom-right corner of the pasted region. (Excel nerds know this icon as a *smart tag.*) If you click this icon, you'll see a drop-down menu that includes the most important options from the Paste Special dialog box, as shown in Figure 3-10.

NOTE

The paste icon appears only after a copy-and-paste operation, not a cut-and-paste operation. If you paste cells from the Clipboard panel, the paste icon still appears, but it provides just two options: keeping the source formatting or pasting the data only.

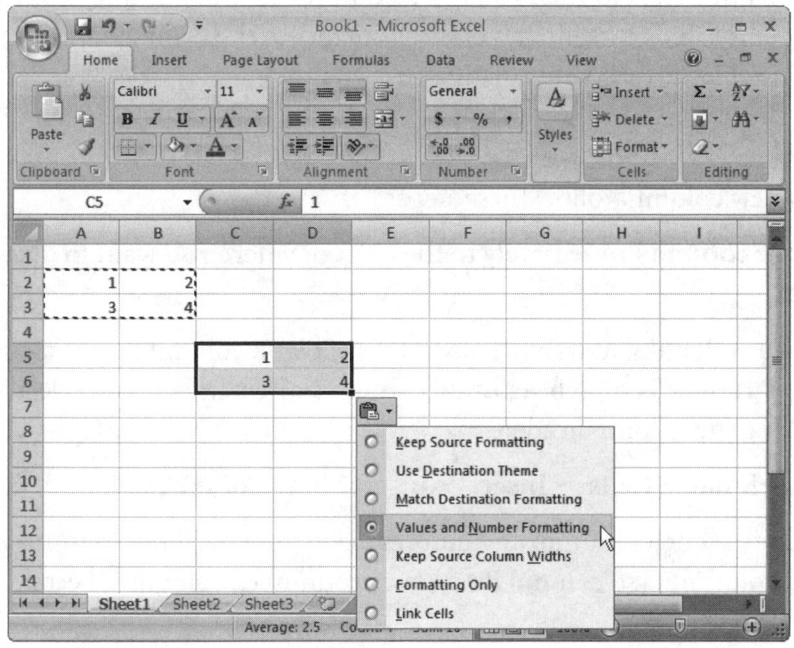

Figure 3-10. The paste icon appears following the completion of every paste operation, letting you control a number of options, including whether the formatting matches the source or destination cells. If you choose Values and Number Formatting, Excel copies the cell content and the number formats, but ignores other formatting information like font and cell color. The number format determines how the number is displayed (for example, how many decimal places and whether a dollar sign is used). Chapter 4 covers formatting.

Adding and Moving Columns or Rows

The cut-and-paste and copy-and-paste operations let you move data from one cell (or group of cells) to another. But what happens if you want to make some *major* changes to your worksheet itself? For example, imagine you have a spreadsheet with 10 filled columns (A to J) and you decide you want to add a new column between columns C and D. You could cut all the columns from D to J, and then paste them starting at E. That would solve the problem, and leave the C column free for your new data. But the actual task of selecting these columns can be a little awkward, and it only becomes more difficult as your spreadsheet grows in size.

A much easier option is to use two dedicated Excel commands designed for inserting new columns and rows into an existing spreadsheet. If you use these features, you won't need to disturb your existing cells at all.

Inserting Columns

To insert a new column, follow these steps:

1. **Select the column immediately to the *right* of where you want to place the new column.**

   That means that if you want to insert a new, blank column between columns A and B, start by selecting the existing column B. Remember, you select a column by clicking the column header.

2. **Choose Home → Cells → Insert → Insert Sheet Columns.**

   Excel inserts a new column, and automatically moves all the columns to the right of column A (so column B becomes column C, column C becomes column D, and so on).

Inserting Rows

Inserting rows is just as easy as inserting new columns. Just follow these steps:

1. **Select the row that's immediately *below* where you want to place the new row.**

   That means that if you want to insert a new, blank row between rows 6 and 7, start by selecting the existing row 7. Remember, you select a row by clicking the row number header.

2. **Choose Home → Cells → Insert → Insert Sheet Rows.**

   Excel inserts a new row, and all the rows beneath it are automatically moved down one row.

NOTE

In the unlikely event that you have data at the extreme right edge of the spreadsheet, in column XFD, Excel doesn't let you insert a new column anywhere in the spreadsheet because the data would be pushed off into the region Beyond The Spreadsheet's Edges. Similarly, if you have data in the very last row (row 1,048,576), Excel doesn't let you insert more rows. If you do have data in either of these spots and try to insert a new column or row, Excel displays a warning message.

Inserting Copied or Cut Cells

Usually, inserting entirely new rows and columns is the most straightforward way to change the structure of your spreadsheet. You can then cut and paste new information into the blank rows or columns. However, in some cases, you may simply want to insert cells into an *existing* row or column.

To do so, begin by copying or cutting a cell or group of cells, and then select the spot you want to paste into. Next, choose Home → Cells → Insert → Insert Copied Cells from the menu (or Home → Cells → Insert → Insert Cut Cells if you're performing a cut instead of a copy operation). Unlike the cut-and-paste feature, when you insert cells, you won't overwrite the existing data. Instead, Excel asks you whether the existing cells should be shifted down or to the right to make way for the new cells (as shown in Figure 3-11).

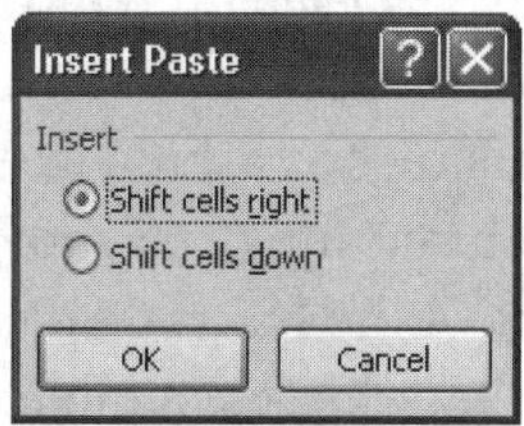

Figure 3-11. When you insert copied cells, Excel asks whether it should move the existing cells down or to the right.

You need to be careful when you use the Insert Copied Cells feature. Because you're shifting only certain parts of your worksheet, it's possible to mangle your data, splitting the information that should be in one row or one column into multiple rows or columns! Fortunately, you can always back out of a tight spot using Undo.

Deleting Columns and Rows

In Chapter 1, you learned that you can quickly remove cell values by moving to the cell and hitting the Delete key. You can also delete an entire range of values by selecting multiple cells, and then hitting the Delete key. Using this technique, you can quickly wipe out an entire row or column.

However, using delete simply clears the cell content. It doesn't remove the cells or change the structure of your worksheet. If you want to simultaneously clear cell values and adjust the rest of your spreadsheet to fill in the gap, you need to use the Home → Cell → Delete command.

For example, if you select a column by clicking the column header, you can either clear all the cells (by pressing the Delete key), or remove the column by choosing Home → Cells → Delete. Deleting a column in this way is the reverse of inserting a column. All the columns to the right are automatically moved one column to the left to fill in the gap left by the column you removed. Thus, if you delete column B, column C becomes the new column B, column D becomes column C, and so on. If you take out row 3, row 4 moves up to fill the void, row 5 becomes row 4, and so on.

Usually, you'll use Home → Cells → Delete to remove entire rows or columns. However, you can also use it just to remove specific cells in a column or row. In this case, Excel prompts you with a dialog box asking whether you want to fill in the gap by moving cells in the current column up, or by moving cells in the current row to the left. This feature is the reverse of the Insert Copied Cells feature, and you'll need to take special care to make sure you don't scramble the structure of your spreadsheet when you use this approach.

4

MANAGING WORKSHEETS AND WORKBOOKS

- Worksheets and Workbooks
- Find and Replace
- Spell Check

So far, you've learned how to create a basic worksheet with a table of data. That's great for getting started, but as power users, professional accountants, and other Excel jockeys quickly learn, some of the most compelling reasons to use Excel involve *multiple* tables that share information and interact with each other.

For example, say you want to track the performance of your company: you create one table summarizing your firm's yearly sales, another listing expenses, and a third analyzing profitability and making predictions for the coming year. If you create these tables in different spreadsheet files, you have to copy shared information from one location to another, all without misplacing a number or making a mistake. And what's worse, with data scattered in multiple places, you're missing the chance to use some of Excel's niftiest charting and analytical tools. Similarly, if you try cramming a bunch of tables onto the same worksheet page, you can quickly create formatting and cell management problems.

Fortunately, a better solution exists. Excel lets you create spreadsheets with multiple pages of data, each of which can conveniently exchange information with other pages. Each page is called a *worksheet*, and a collection of one or more worksheets is called a *workbook* (which is also sometimes called a *spreadsheet file*). In this chapter, you'll learn how to manage the worksheets in a workbook. You'll also take a look at two more all-purpose Excel features: Find and Replace (a tool for digging through worksheets in search of specific data) and the spell checker.

Worksheets and Workbooks

Many workbooks contain more than one table of information. For example, you might have a list of the items you've purchased over two consecutive years. You might find it a bit challenging to arrange these different tables. You could stack them (Figure 4-1) or place them side by side (Figure 4-2), but neither solution is perfect.

Most Excel masters agree that the best way to arrange separate tables of information is to use separate worksheets for each table. When you create a new workbook, Excel automatically fills it with three blank worksheets named Sheet1, Sheet2, and Sheet3. Often, you'll work exclusively with the first worksheet (Sheet1), and not even realize that you have two more blank worksheets to play with—not to mention the ability to add plenty more.

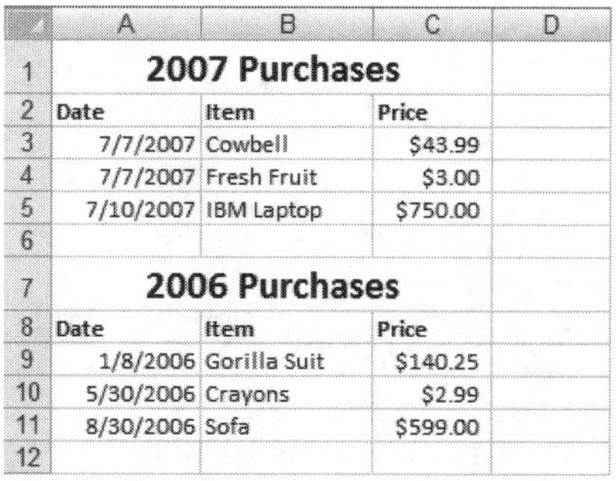

	A	B	C	D
1	2007 Purchases			
2	Date	Item	Price	
3	7/7/2007	Cowbell	$43.99	
4	7/7/2007	Fresh Fruit	$3.00	
5	7/10/2007	IBM Laptop	$750.00	
6				
7	2006 Purchases			
8	Date	Item	Price	
9	1/8/2006	Gorilla Suit	$140.25	
10	5/30/2006	Crayons	$2.99	
11	8/30/2006	Sofa	$599.00	
12				

Figure 4-1. Stacking tables on top of each other is usually a bad idea. If you need to add more data to the first table, then you have to move the second table. You'll also have trouble properly resizing or formatting columns because each column contains data from two different tables.

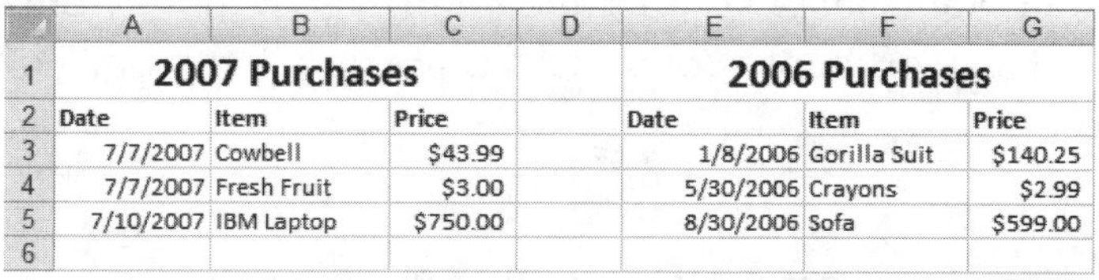

	A	B	C	D	E	F	G
1	2007 Purchases				2006 Purchases		
2	Date	Item	Price		Date	Item	Price
3	7/7/2007	Cowbell	$43.99		1/8/2006	Gorilla Suit	$140.25
4	7/7/2007	Fresh Fruit	$3.00		5/30/2006	Crayons	$2.99
5	7/10/2007	IBM Laptop	$750.00		8/30/2006	Sofa	$599.00
6							

Figure 4-2. You're somewhat better off putting tables side by side, separated by a blank column, than you are stacking them, but this method can create problems if you need to add more columns to the first table. It also makes for a lot of side-to-side scrolling.

To move from one worksheet to another, you have a few choices:

- Click the worksheet tabs at the bottom of Excel's grid window (just above the status bar), as shown in Figure 4-3.
- Press Ctrl+Page Down to move to the next worksheet. For example, if you're currently in Sheet1, this key sequence jumps you to Sheet2.
- Press Ctrl+Page Up to move to the previous worksheet. For example, if you're currently in Sheet2, this key sequence takes you back to Sheet1.

Excel keeps track of the active cell in each worksheet. That means if you're in cell B9 in Sheet1, and then move to Sheet2, when you jump back to Sheet1 you'll automatically return to cell B9.

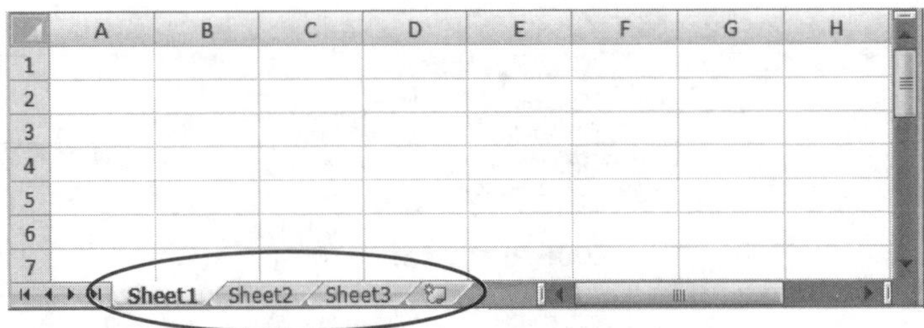

Figure 4-3. Worksheets provide a good way to organize multiple tables of data. To move from one worksheet to another, click the appropriate Worksheet tab at the bottom of the grid. Each worksheet contains a fresh grid of cells.

TIP

Excel includes some interesting viewing features that let you look at two different worksheets at the same time, even if these worksheets are in the same workbook. You'll learn more about custom views in Chapter 6.

Adding, Removing, and Hiding Worksheets

When you open a fresh workbook in Excel, you automatically get three blank worksheets in it. You can easily add more worksheets. Just click the Insert Worksheet button, which appears immediately to the right of your last worksheet tab (Figure 4-4). You can also use the Home → Cells → Insert → Insert Sheet command, which works the same way but inserts a new worksheet immediately to the *left* of the current worksheet. (Don't panic; page 113 shows how you can rearrange worksheets after the fact.)

If you continue adding worksheets, you'll eventually find that all the worksheet tabs won't fit at the bottom of your workbook window. If you run out of space, you need to use the scroll buttons (which are immediately to the left of the worksheet tabs) to scroll through the list of worksheets. Figure 4-5 shows the scroll buttons.

Insert Worksheet

Figure 4-4. Every time you click the Insert Worksheet button, Excel inserts a new worksheet after your existing worksheets and assigns it a new name. For example, if you start with the standard Sheet1, Sheet2, and Sheet3 and click the Insert Worksheet button, then Excel adds a new worksheet named—you guessed it—Sheet4.

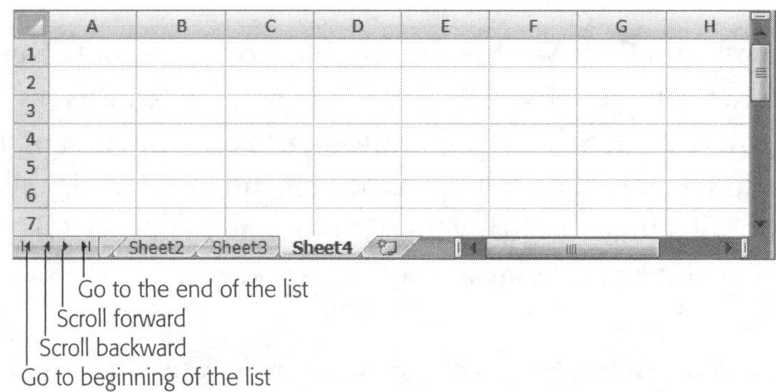

Figure 4-5. Using the scroll buttons, you can move between worksheets one at a time or jump straight to the first or last tab. These scroll buttons control only which tabs you see—you still need to click the appropriate tab to move to the worksheet you want to work on.

TIP

If you have a huge number of worksheets and they don't all fit in the strip of worksheet tabs, there's an easier way to jump around. Right-click the scroll buttons to pop up a list with all your worksheets. You can then move to the worksheet you want by clicking it in the list.

Removing a worksheet is just as easy as adding one. Simply move to the worksheet you want to get rid of, and then choose Home → Cells → Delete → Delete Sheet (you can also right-click a worksheet tab and choose Delete). Excel won't complain if you ask it to remove a blank worksheet, but if you try to remove a sheet that contains any data, it presents a warning message asking for your confirmation. Also, if you're down to one last worksheet, Excel won't let you remove it. Doing so would create a tough existential dilemma for Excel—a workbook that holds no worksheets—so the program prevents you from taking this step.

WARNING

Be careful when deleting worksheets, as you can't use Undo (Ctrl+Z) to reverse this change! Undo also doesn't work to reverse a newly inserted sheet.

Excel starts you off with three worksheets for each workbook, but changing this setting's easy. You can configure Excel to start with fewer worksheets (as few as one), or many more (up to 255). Select Office button → Excel Options, and then choose the Popular section. Under the heading "When creating new workbooks" change the number in the "Include this many sheets" box, and then click OK. This setting takes effect the next time you create a new workbook.

NOTE

Although you're limited to 255 sheets in a new workbook, Excel doesn't limit how many worksheets you can add *after* you've created a workbook. The only factor that ultimately limits the number of worksheets your workbook can hold is your computer's memory. However, modern day PCs can easily handle even the most ridiculously large, worksheet-stuffed workbook.

Deleting worksheets isn't the only way to tidy up a workbook or get rid of information you don't want. You can also choose to *hide* a worksheet temporarily. When you hide a worksheet, its tab disappears but the worksheet itself remains part of your spreadsheet file, available whenever you choose to unhide it. Hidden worksheets also don't appear on printouts. To hide a worksheet, right-click the worksheet tab and choose Hide. (Or, for a more long-winded approach, choose Home → Cells → Format → Hide & Unhide → Hide Sheet.)

To redisplay a hidden worksheet, right-click any worksheet tab and choose Unhide. The Unhide dialog box appears along with a list of all hidden sheets, as shown in Figure 4-6. You can then select a sheet from the list and click OK to unhide it. (Once again, the ribbon can get you the same window—just point yourself to Home → Cells → Format → Hide & Unhide → Unhide Sheet.)

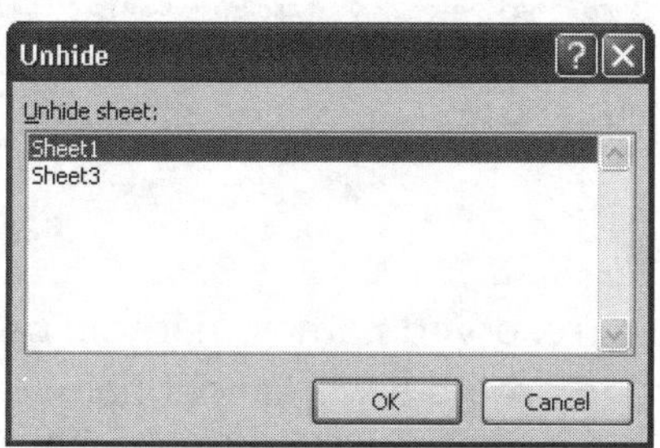

Figure 4-6. This workbook contains two hidden worksheets. To restore one, just select it from the list, and then click OK. Unfortunately, if you want to show multiple hidden sheets, you have to use the Unhide Sheet command multiple times. Excel has no shortcut for unhiding multiple sheets at once.

Naming and Rearranging Worksheets

The standard names Excel assigns to new worksheets—Sheet1, Sheet2, Sheet3, and so on—aren't very helpful for identifying what they contain. And they become even less helpful if you start adding new worksheets, since the new sheet numbers don't necessarily indicate the position of the sheets, just the order in which you created them.

For example, if you're on Sheet 3 and you add a new worksheet (by choosing Home → Cells → Insert → Insert Sheet), then the worksheet tabs read: Sheet1, Sheet2, Sheet4, Sheet3. (That's because the Insert Sheet command inserts the new sheet just before your current sheet.) Excel doesn't expect you to stick with these auto-generated names. Instead, you can rename them by right-clicking the worksheet tab and selecting Rename, or just double-click the sheet name. Either way, Excel highlights the worksheet tab, and you can type a new name directly onto the tab. Figure 4-7 shows worksheet tabs with better names.

Figure 4-7. Worksheet names can be up to 31 characters long and can include letters, numbers, some symbols, and spaces.

NOTE

Excel has a small set of reserved names that you can never use. To witness this problem, try to create a worksheet named History. Excel doesn't let you because it uses the History worksheet as part of its change tracking features. Use this Excel oddity to impress your friends.

Sometimes Excel refuses to insert new worksheets exactly where you'd like them. Fortunately, you can easily rearrange any of your worksheets just by dragging their tabs from one place to another, as shown in Figure 4-8.

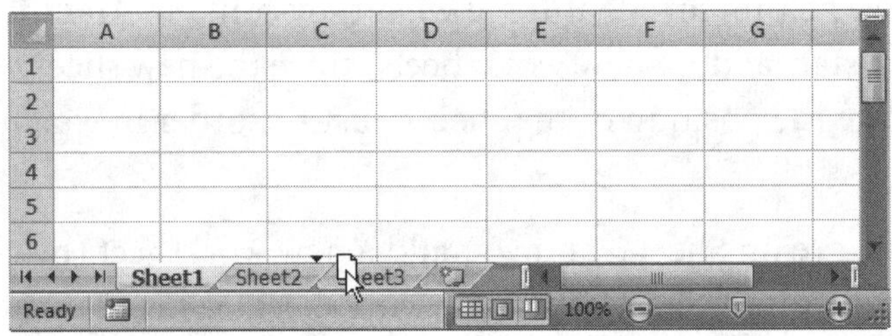

Figure 4-8. When you drag a worksheet tab, a tiny page appears beneath the arrow cursor. As you move the cursor around, you'll see a black triangle appear, indicating where the worksheet will land when you release the mouse button.

Tip

You can use a similar technique to create *copies* of a worksheet. Click the worksheet tab and begin dragging, just as you would to move the worksheet. However, before releasing the mouse button, press the Ctrl key (you'll see a plus sign [+] appear). When you let go, Excel creates a copy of the worksheet in the new location. The original worksheet remains in its original location. Excel gives the new worksheet a name with a number in parentheses. For example, a copy of Sheet1 is named Sheet1 (2). As with any other worksheet tab, you can change this name.

GEM IN THE ROUGH

Colorful Worksheet Tabs

Names aren't the only thing you can change when it comes to newly added worksheets. Excel also lets you modify a worksheet tab's background color. This minor convenience has no effect on your data or your printout, but it can help you quickly find an important worksheet if it has lots of neighbors.

To change the background color of a worksheet tab, right-click the tab, and then select Tab Color (or move to the appropriate worksheet and Home → Cells → Format → Tab Color). A list of color choices appears; make your selection by clicking the color you want.

Find and Replace

When you're dealing with great mounds of information, you may have a tough time ferreting out the nuggets of data you need. Fortunately, Excel's find feature is great for helping you locate numbers or text, even when they're buried within massive workbooks holding dozens of worksheets. And if you need to make changes to a bunch of identical items, the find-and-replace option can be a real timesaver.

The "Find and Replace" feature includes both simple and advanced options. In its basic version, you're only a quick keystroke combo away from a word or number you *know* is lurking somewhere in your data pile. With the advanced options turned on, you can do things like search for cells that have certain formatting characteristics and apply changes automatically. The next few sections dissect these features.

The Basic Find

Excel's find feature is a little like the Go To tool described in Chapter 1, which lets you move across a large expanse of cells in a single bound. The difference is that Go To moves to a *known* location, using the cell address you specify. The find feature, on the other hand, searches every cell until it finds the content you've asked Excel to look for. Excel's search works similarly to the search feature in Microsoft Word, but it's worth keeping in mind a few additional details:

- Excel searches by comparing the content you enter with the content in each cell. For example, if you searched for the word *Date*, Excel identifies as a match a cell containing the phrase *Date Purchased.*
- When searching cells that contain numeric or date information, Excel always searches the *display text*. For example, say a cell displays dates using the day-month-year format, like *2-Dec-05*. You can find this particular cell by searching for any part of the displayed date (using search strings like *Dec* or *2-Dec-05*). But if you use the search string *12/2/2005,* you won't find a match because the search string and the display text are different. A similar behavior occurs with numbers. For example, the search strings *$3* and *3.00* match the currency value *$3.00*. However, the search string *3.000* won't turn up anything because Excel won't be able to make a full text match.
- Excel searches one cell at a time, from left to right. When it reaches the end of a row, it moves to the first column of the next row.

To perform a find operation, follow these steps:

1. **Move to the cell where you want the search to begin.**

   If you start off halfway down the worksheet, for example, the search covers the cells from there to the end of the worksheet, and then "loops over" and starts at cell A1. If you select a group of cells, Excel restricts the search to just those cells. You can search across a set of columns, rows, or even a non-contiguous group of cells.

2. **Choose Home → Editing → Find & Select → Find, or press Ctrl+F.**

   The "Find and Replace" window appears, with the Find tab selected.

NOTE

To assist frequent searches, Excel lets you keep the "Find and Replace" window hanging around (rather than forcing you to use it or close it, as is the case with many other dialog boxes). You can continue to move from cell to cell and edit your worksheet data even while the "Find and Replace" window remains visible.

3. **In the "Find what" combo box, enter the word, phrase, or number you're looking for.**

   If you've performed other searches recently, you can reuse these search terms. Just choose the appropriate search text from the "Find what" drop-down list.

4. **Click Find Next.**

   Excel jumps to the next matching cell, which becomes the active cell. However, Excel doesn't highlight the matched text or in any way indicate *why* it decided the cell was a match. (That's a bummer if you've got, say, 200 words crammed into a cell.) If it doesn't find a matching cell, Excel displays a message box telling you it couldn't find the requested content.

   If the first match isn't what you're looking for, you can keep looking by clicking Find Next again to move to the next match. Keep clicking Find Next to move through the worksheet. When you reach the end, Excel resumes the search at the beginning of your worksheet, potentially bringing you back to a match you've already seen. When you're finished with the search, click Close to get rid of the "Find and Replace" window.

Find All

One of the problems with searching in Excel is that you're never quite sure how many matches there are in a worksheet. Sure, clicking Find Next gets you from one cell to the next, but wouldn't it be easier for Excel to let you know right away how many matches it found?

Enter the Find All feature. With Find All, Excel searches the entire worksheet in one go, and compiles a list of matches, as shown in Figure 4-9.

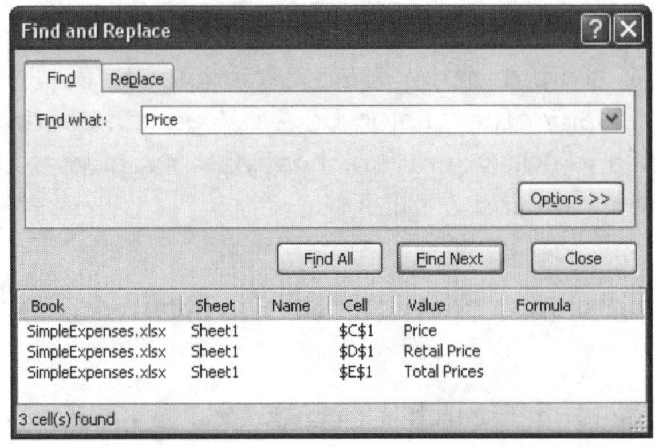

Figure 4-9. In the example shown here, the search for Price matched three cells in the worksheet. The list shows you the complete text in the matching cell and the cell reference (for example, $C$1, which is a reference to cell C1).

The Find All button doesn't lead you through the worksheet like the find feature. It's up to you to select one of the results in the list, at which point Excel automatically moves you to the matching cell.

The Find All list won't automatically refresh itself: After you've run a Find All search, if you *add* new data to your worksheet, you need to run a new search to find any newly added terms. However, Excel does keep the text and numbers in your found-items list synchronized with any changes you make in the worksheet. For example, if you change cell D5 to Total Price, the change appears in the Value column in the found-items list *automatically*. This tool is great for editing a worksheet because you can keep track of multiple changes at a single glance.

Finally, the Find All feature is the heart of another great Excel guru trick: it gives you another way to change multiple cells at once. After you've performed the Find All search, select all the entries you want to change from the list by clicking them while you hold down Ctrl (this trick allows you to select several at once). Click in the formula bar, and then start typing the new value. When you're finished, hit Ctrl+Enter to apply your changes to every selected cell. Voilà—it's like "Find and Replace", but you're in control!

More Advanced Searches

Basic searches are fine if all you need to find is a glaringly unique phrase or number (*Pet Snail Names* or *10,987,654,321*). But Excel's advanced search feature gives you lots of ways to fine-tune your searches or even search more than one worksheet. To conduct an advanced search, begin by clicking the "Find and Replace" window's Options button, as shown in Figure 4-10.

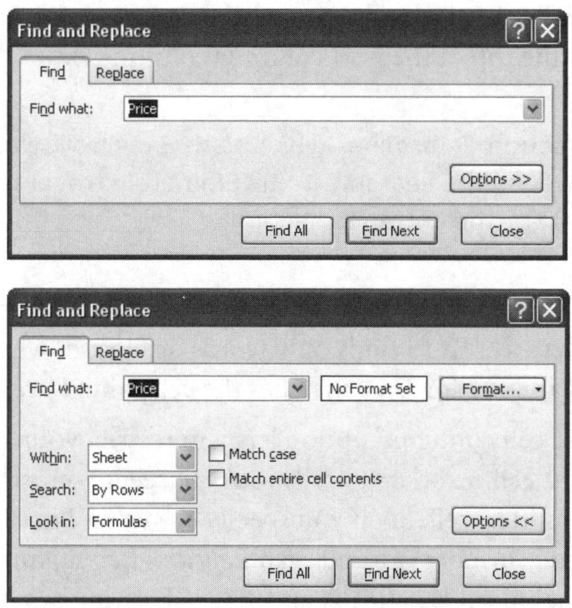

Figure 4-10. In the standard "Find and Replace" window (top), when you click Options, Excel gives you a slew of additional settings (bottom) so you can configure things like search direction, case sensitivity, and format matching.

You can set any or all of the following options:

- If you want your search to span multiple worksheets, go to the Within box, and then choose Workbook. The standard option, Sheet, searches all the cells in the currently active worksheet. If you want to continue the search in the other worksheets in your workbook, choose Workbook. Excel examines the worksheets from left to right. When it finishes searching the last worksheet, it loops back and starts examining the first worksheet.

- The Search pop-up menu lets you choose the direction you want to search. The standard option, By Rows, completely searches each row before moving on to the next one. That means that if you start in cell B2, Excel searches C2, D2, E2, and so on. Once it's moved through every column in the second row, it moves onto the third row and searches from left to right.

  On the other hand, if you choose By Columns, Excel searches all the rows in the current column before moving to the next column. That means that if you start in cell B2, Excel searches B3, B4, and so on until it reaches the bottom of the column and then starts at the top of the next column (column C).

NOTE

The search direction determines which path Excel follows when it's searching. However, the search will still ultimately traverse every cell in your worksheet (or the current selection).

- The "Match case" option lets you specify whether capitalization is important. If you select "Match case", Excel finds only words or phrases whose capitalization matches. Thus, searching for *Date* matches the cell value *Date,* but not *date.*
- The "Match entire cell contents" option lets you restrict your searches to the entire contents of a cell. Excel ordinarily looks to see if your search term is contained *anywhere* inside a cell. So, if you specify the word *Price*, Excel finds cells containing text like *Current Price* and even *Repriced Items*. Similarly, numbers like *32* match cell values like *3253, 10032,* and *1.321*. Turning on the "Match entire cell contents" option forces Excel to be precise.

NOTE

Remember, Excel searches for numbers as they're *displayed* (as opposed to looking at the underlying values that Excel uses to store numbers internally). That means that if you're searching for a number formatted using the dollar Currency format ($32.00, for example), and you've turned on the "Match entire cell contents" checkbox, you'll need to enter the number exactly as it appears on the worksheet. Thus, *$32.00* would work, but *32* alone won't help you.

POWER USERS' CLINIC

Using Wildcards

Sometimes you sorta, kinda know what you're looking for—for example, a cell with some version of the word "date" in it (as in "date" or "dated" or "dating"). What you really need is a search tool that's flexible enough to keep its eyes open for results that are *similar* but not exactly alike. Power searchers will be happy to know that Excel lets you use *wildcards* in your searches. Wildcards are search symbols that let you search for variations on a word.

The asterisk (*) wildcard represents a group of one or more characters. A search for *s*nd* finds any word that begins with the letter *s* and ends with the letters *nd*; for example, it would find words like *sand*, *sound*, *send*, or even the bizarre series of characters *sgrthdnd*.

The question mark ? wildcard represents any single character. For example, a search for *f?nd* turns up *find* or *fund*, but not *friend*.

Wildcards are particularly useful when you're using the "Match entire cell contents" option. For example, if you turn on the "Match entire cell contents" option and enter the search term *date** you'll find any cell that *starts* with the word *date*. In contrast, if you performed the same search without turning the "Match entire cell contents" option on, you'd find any cell *containing* the word *date*.

If you happen to want to search for special characters like the asterisk or the question mark, you'll need to use the tilde (~) before the wildcard. For example, the search string ~* searches for cells that contain the asterisk symbol.

Finding Formatted Cells

Excel's "Find and Replace" is an equal opportunity search tool: It doesn't care what the contents of a cell look like. But what if you know, for example, that the data you're looking for is formatted in bold, or that it's a number that uses the Currency format? You can use these formatting details to help Excel find the data you want and ignore cells that aren't relevant.

To use formatting details as part of your search criteria, follow these steps:

1. **Launch the Find tool.**

   Choose Home → Editing → Find & Select → Find, or press Ctrl+F. Make sure that the "Find and Replace" window is showing the advanced options (by clicking the Options button).

2. **Click the Format button next to the "Find what" search box.**

   The Find Format dialog box appears (Figure 4-11). It contains the same options as the Format Cell dialog box discussed on page 136.

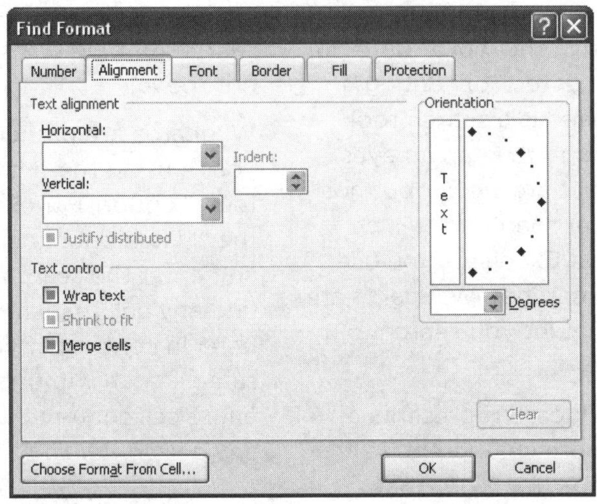

Figure 4-11. In the Find Format dialog box, Excel won't use any formatting option that's blank or grayed out as part of it's search criteria. For example, here, Excel won't search based on alignment. Checkboxes are a little trickier. In some versions of Windows, it looks like the checkbox is filled with a solid square (as with the "Merge cells" setting in this example). In other versions of Windows, it looks like the checkbox is dimmed and checked at the same time. Either way, this visual cue indicates that Excel won't use the setting as part of its search.

3. **Specify the format settings you want to look for.**

   Using the Find Format dialog box, you can specify any combination of number format, alignment, font, fill pattern, borders, and formatting. Chapter 5 explains all these formatting settings in detail.

4. **When you're finished, click OK to return to the "Find and Replace" window.**

   Next to the "Find what" search box, a preview appears indicating the formatting of the cell that you'll be searching for, as shown in Figure 4-12.

   To remove these formatting restrictions, click the pop-up menu to the right of the Format button and then choose Clear Find.

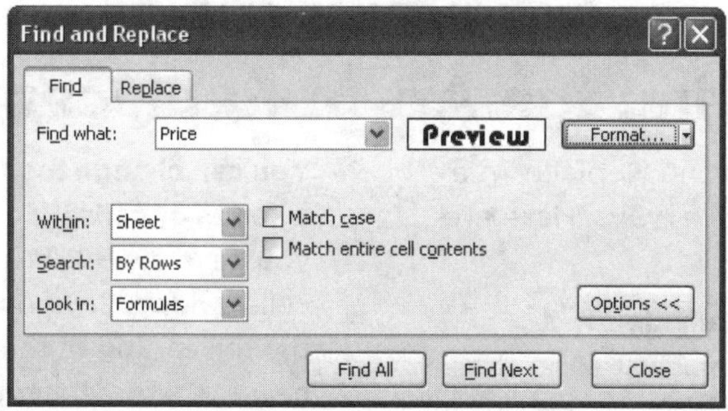

Figure 4-12. The Find Format dialog box shows a basic preview of your formatting choices. In this example, the search will find cells containing the word Price that also use white lettering, a black background, and the Bauhaus font.

TIP

Rather than specifying all the format settings manually, you can copy them from another cell. Just click the Choose Format From Cell button at the bottom of the Find Format dialog box. The pointer changes to a plus symbol with an eyedropper next to it. Next, click any cell that has the formatting you want to match. Keep in mind that when you use this approach, you copy *all* the format settings.

Finding and Replacing Values

You can use Excel's search muscles to find not only the information you're interested in, but also to modify cells quickly and easily. Excel lets you make two types of changes using its *replace* tool:

- **You can automatically change cell content.** For example, you can replace the word *Colour* with *Color* or the number *$400* with *$40*.
- **You can automatically change cell formatting.** For example, you can search for every cell that contains the word *Price* or the number *$400* and change the fill color. Or, you can search for every cell that uses a specific font, and modify these cells so they use a new font.

POWER USERS' CLINIC

Mastering the Art of Replacement

You can use the "Find and Replace" feature in many imaginative ways. Here are just a few examples:

* **You can automatically delete a specific piece of text.** Just enter the appropriate "Find what" text, and leave the "Replace with" box blank.
* **You can change the formatting used in specific cells.** Just type the same text in both the "Find what" and "Replace with" text, and then click the Format button next to the "Replace with" combo box to set some formatting attributes. (You don't need to specify any formatting settings for your "Find what" search criteria.)
* **You can change the formatting used in a series of cells.** For example, imagine you have a worksheet that has several cells bolded. Say you want to adjust the formatting of these cells to use a new font. To perform this operation, leave both the "Find what" and "Replace with" boxes blank. Then, set the formatting search criteria to look for the bold font attribute, and set the replacement formatting to use the new font. Click Replace All, and all the cells that currently have bold formatting acquire the new font. You might find mastering this technique tricky, but it's one of the most powerful formatting tricks around.

Here's how to perform a replace operation. The box below gives some super-handy tricks you can do with this process.

1. **Move to the cell where the search should begin.**

   Remember, if you don't want to search the entire spreadsheet, just select the range of cells you want to search.

2. **Choose Home → Editing → Find & Select → Replace, or press Ctrl+H.**

   The "Find and Replace" window appears, with the Replace tab selected, as shown in Figure 4-13.

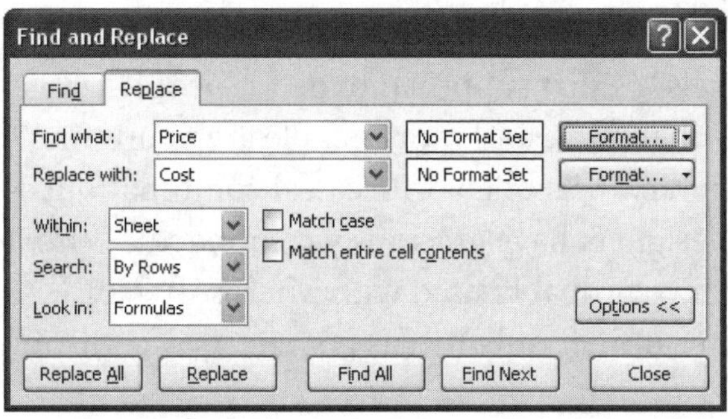

Figure 4-13. The Replace tab looks pretty similar to the Find tab. Even the advanced options are the same. The only difference is that you also need to specify the text you want to use as a replacement for the search terms you find.

3. **In the "Find what" box, enter your search term. In the "Replace with" box, enter the replacement text.**

   Type the replacement text exactly as you want it to appear. If you want to set any advanced options, click the Options button (see the earlier sections "More Advanced Searches" and "Finding Formatted Cells" for more on your choices).

4. **Perform the search.**

   You've got four different options here. *Replace All* immediately changes all the matches your search identifies. *Replace* changes only the first matched item (you can then click Replace again to move on to subsequent matches or to select any of the other three options). *Find All* works just like the same feature described in the box on page 124. *Find Next* moves to the next match, where you can click Replace to apply your specified change, or click any of the other three buttons. The replace options are good if you're confident you want to make a change; the find options work well if you first want to see what changes you're about to make (although you can reverse either option using Ctrl+Z to fire off the Undo command).

NOTE

It's possible for a single to contain more than one match. In this case, clicking Replace replaces every occurrence of that text in the entire cell.

Spell Check

A spell checker in Excel? Is that supposed to be for people who can't spell 138 correctly? The fact is that more and more people are cramming text—column headers, boxes of commentary, lists of favorite cereal combinations—into their spreadsheets. And Excel's designers have graciously responded by providing the very same spell checker that you've probably used with Microsoft Word. As you might expect, Excel's spell checker examines only text as it sniffs its way through a spreadsheet.

NOTE

The same spell checker works in almost every Office application, including Word, PowerPoint, and Outlook.

To start the spell checker, follow these simple steps:

1. **Move to where you want to start the spell check.**

   If you want to check the entire worksheet from start to finish, move to the first cell. Otherwise, move to the location where you want to start checking. Or, if you want to check a portion of the worksheet, select the cells you want to check.

   Unlike the "Find and Replace" feature, Excel's spell check can check only one worksheet at a time.

2. **Choose Review → Proofing → Spelling, or press F7.**

   The Excel spell checker starts working immediately, starting with the current cell and moving to the right, going from column to column. After it finishes the last column of the current row, checking continues with the first column of the next row.

   If you don't start at the first cell (A1) in your worksheet, Excel asks you when it reaches the end of the worksheet whether it should continue checking from the beginning of the sheet. If you say yes, it checks the remaining cells and stops when it reaches your starting point (having made a complete pass through all of your cells).

When the spell check finishes, a dialog box informs you that all cells have been checked. If your cells pass the spell check, this dialog box is the only feedback you receive. On the other hand, if Excel discovers any potential spelling errors during its check, it displays a Spelling window, as shown in Figure 4-14, showing the offending word and a list of suggestions.

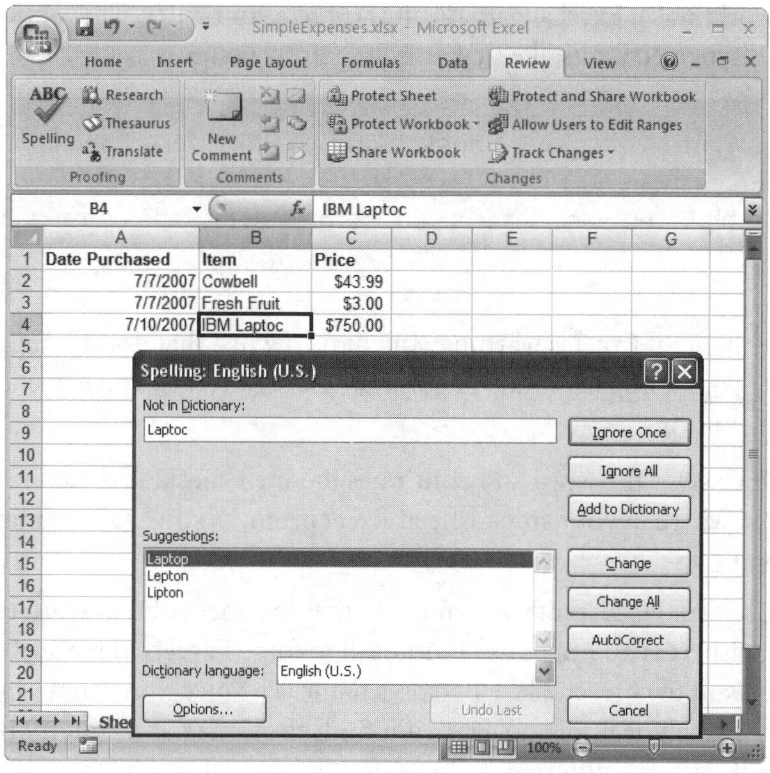

Figure 4-14. When Excel encounters a word it thinks is misspelled, it displays the Spelling window. The cell containing the word—but not the actual word itself—gets highlighted with a black border. Excel doesn't let you edit your file while the Spelling window is active. You either have to click one of the options on the Spelling window or cancel the spell check.

The Spelling window offers a wide range of choices. If you want to use the list of suggestions to perform a correction, you have three options:

- Click one of the words in the list of suggestions, and then click Change to replace your text with the proper spelling. Double-clicking the word has the same effect.
- Click one of the words in the list of suggestions, and click Change All to replace your text with the proper spelling. If Excel finds the same mistake elsewhere in your worksheet, it repeats the change automatically.

- Click one of the words in the list of suggestions, and click AutoCorrect. Excel makes the change for this cell, and for any other similarly misspelled words. In addition, Excel adds the correction to its AutoCorrect list (described on page 71). That means if you type the same unrecognized word into another cell (or even another workbook), Excel automatically corrects your entry. This option is useful if you've discovered a mistake that you frequently make.

TIP

If Excel spots an error but it doesn't give you the correct spelling in its list of suggestions, just type the correction into the "Not in Dictionary" box and hit Enter. Excel inserts your correction into the corresponding cell.

On the other hand, if Excel is warning you about a word that doesn't represent a mistake (like your company name or some specialized term), you can click one of the following buttons:

- **Ignore Once** skips the word and continues the spell check. If the same word appears elsewhere in your spreadsheet, Excel prompts you again to make a correction.
- **Ignore All** skips the current word and all other instances of that word throughout your spreadsheet. You might use Ignore All to force Excel to disregard something you don't want to correct, like a person's name. The nice thing about Ignore All is that Excel doesn't prompt you again if it finds the same name, but it does prompt you again if it finds a different spelling (for example, if you misspelled the name).
- **Add to Dictionary** adds the word to Excel's custom dictionary. Adding a word is great if you plan to keep using a word that's not in Excel's dictionary. (For example, a company name makes a good addition to the custom dictionary.) Not only does Excel ignore any occurrences of this word, but if it finds a similar but slightly different variation of that word, it provides the custom word in its list of suggestions. Even better, Excel uses the custom dictionary in every workbook you spell check.
- **Cancel** stops the operation altogether. You can then correct the cell manually (or do nothing) and resume the spell check later.

GEM IN THE ROUGH

Other Proofing Tools

Spreadsheet spell checking is a useful proofing tool. But Excel doesn't stop there. It piles in a few more questionable extras to help you enhance your workbooks. You'll find them all in the Review → Proofing section of the ribbon.

Along with the spellchecker, Excel offers these goodies:

* **Research.** Click this button to open a Research window, which appears on the right side of the Excel window, and lets you retrieve all kinds of information from the Web. The Research window provides a small set of Internet-driven services, including the ability to search a dictionary for a detailed definition, look in the Encarta encyclopedia, or get a delayed stock market quote from MSN Money.
* **Thesaurus.** Itching to promulgate your prodigious prolixity? (Translation: wanna use big words?) The thesaurus can help you take ordinary language and transform it into clear-as-mud jargon. Or, it can help you track down a synonym that's on the edge of your tongue. Either way, use this tool with care.
* **Translate.** Click this button to translate words or short phrases from one language to another. This feature isn't included in the standard Office installation, so you may need to have the Office DVD handy the first time you click this button.

Spell Checking Options

Excel lets you tweak how the spell checker works by letting you change a few basic options that control things like the language used and which, if any, custom dictionaries Excel examines. To set these options (or just to take a look at them), choose Office button → Excel Options, and then select the Proofing section (Figure 4-15). You can also reach these options by clicking the Spelling window's Options button while a spell check is underway.

The most important spell check setting is the language (at the bottom of the window), which determines what dictionary Excel uses. Depending on the version of Excel that you're using and the choices you made while installing the software, you might be using one or more languages during a spell check operation.

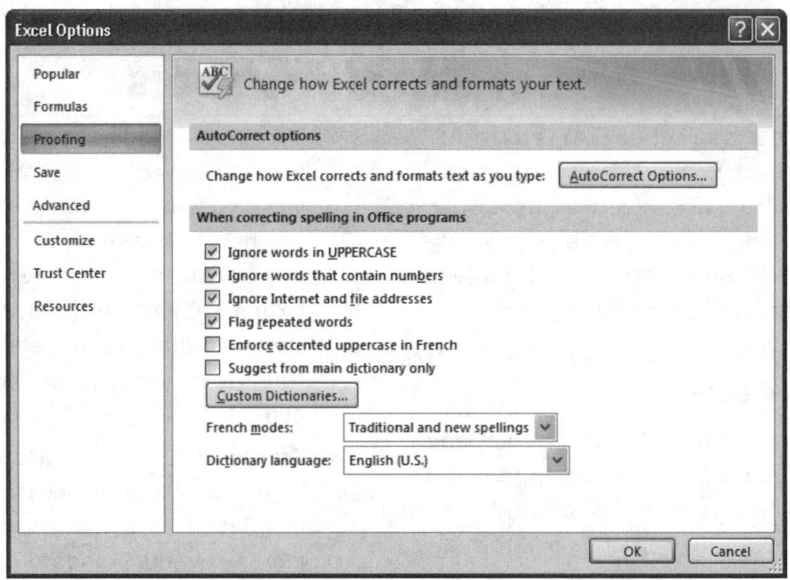

Figure 4-15. The spell checker options allow you to specify the language and a few other miscellaneous settings. This figure shows the standard settings that Excel uses when you first install it.

Some of the other spelling options you can set include:

- **Ignore words in UPPERCASE.** If you choose this option, Excel won't bother checking any word written in all capitals (which is helpful when your text contains lots of acronyms).
- **Ignore words that contain numbers.** If you choose this option, Excel won't check words that contain numeric characters, like *Sales43* or *H3ll0*. If you don't choose this option, Excel flags these entries as errors unless you've specifically added them to the custom dictionary.
- **Ignore Internet and file addresses.** If you choose this option, Excel ignores words that appear to be file paths (like *C:\Documents and Settings*) or Web site addresses (like *http://FreeSweatSocks.com*).

- **Flag repeated words.** If you choose this option, Excel treats words that appear consecutively ("the the") as an error.
- **Suggest from main dictionary only.** If you choose this option, the spell checker doesn't suggest words from the custom dictionary. However, it still *accepts* a word that matches one of the custom dictionary entries.

You can also choose the file Excel uses to store custom words—the unrecognized words that you add to the dictionary while a spell check is underway. Excel automatically creates a file named custom.dic for you to use, but you might want to use another file if you're sharing someone else's custom dictionary. (You can use more than one custom dictionary at a time. If you do, Excel combines them all to get one list of custom words.) Or, you might want to edit the list of words if you've mistakenly added something that shouldn't be there.

To perform any of these tasks, click the Custom Dictionaries button, which opens the Custom Dictionaries dialog box (Figure 4-16). From this dialog box, you can remove your custom dictionary, change it, or add a new one.

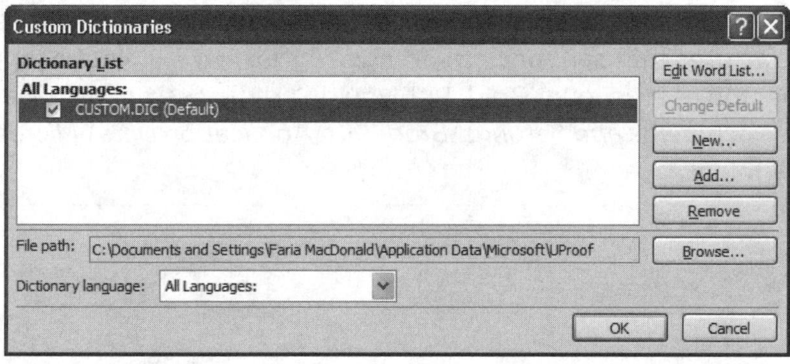

Figure 4-16. Excel starts you off with a custom dictionary named custom.dic (shown here). To add an existing custom dictionary, click Add and browse to the file. Or, click New to create a new, blank custom dictionary. You can also edit the list of words a dictionary contains (select it and click Edit Word List). Figure 4-17 shows an example of dictionary editing.

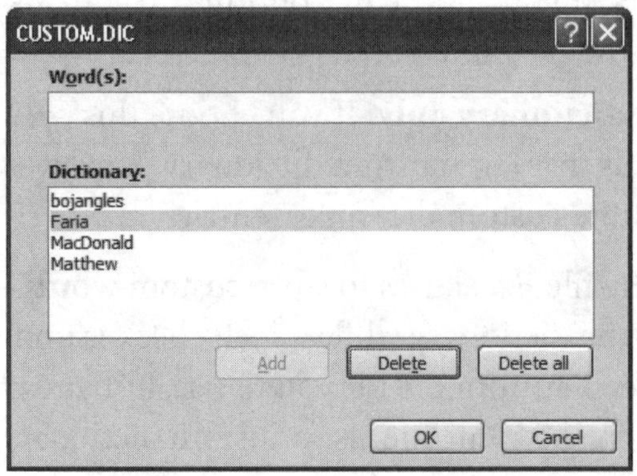

Figure 4-17. This custom dictionary is fairly modest. It contains three names and an unusual word. Excel lists the words in alphabetical order. You can add a new word directly from this window (type in the text and click Add), remove one (select it and click Delete), or go nuclear and remove them all (click Delete All).

NOTE

All custom dictionaries are ordinary text files with the extension .dic. Unless you tell it otherwise, Excel assumes that custom dictionaries are located in the *Application Data\Microsoft\UProof* folder in the folder Windows uses for user-specific settings. For example, if you're logged in under the user account Brad_Pitt, you'd find the custom dictionary in the *C:\Documents and Settings\Brad_Pitt\Application Data\ Microsoft\ UProof* folder.

5 FORMATTING CELLS

- Formatting Cell Values
- Formatting Cell Appearance
- Smart Ways to Apply Formatting

WHEN YOU CREATE A BASIC WORKBOOK, you've taken only the first step toward mastering Excel. If you plan to print your data, email it to colleagues, or show it off to friends, you need to think about whether you've formatted your worksheets in a viewer-friendly way. The careful use of color, shading, borders, and fonts can make the difference between a messy glob of data and a worksheet that's easy to work with and understand.

But formatting isn't just about deciding, say, where and how to make your text bold. Excel also lets you control the way numerical values are formatted. In fact, there are really two fundamental aspects of formatting in any worksheet:

- **Cell appearance.** Cell appearance includes cosmetic details like color, typeface, alignment, and borders. When most people think of formatting, they think of cell appearance first.
- **Cell values.** Cell value formatting controls the way Excel displays numbers, dates, and times. For numbers, this includes details like whether to use scientific notation, the number of decimal places displayed, and the use of currency symbols, percent signs, and commas. With dates, cell value formatting determines what parts of the date are shown in the cell, and in what order.

In many ways, cell value formatting is more significant than cell appearance because it can change the meaning of your data. For example, even though 45%, $0.45, and .450 are all the same number, your spreadsheet readers will see a failing test score, a cheap price for chewing gum, and a world-class batting average.

NOTE

Keep in mind that regardless of how you *format* your cell values, Excel maintains an unalterable *value* for every number entered. For more on how Excel internally stores numbers, see the box on page 141.

In this chapter, you'll learn about cell value formatting, and then unleash your inner artist with cell appearance formatting. You'll also learn the most helpful ways to use formatting to improve a worksheet's readability, and how to save time with nifty features like the Format Painter, styles, and themes.

Formatting Cell Values

Cell value formatting is one aspect of worksheet design you don't want to ignore, because the values Excel stores can differ from the numbers that it displays in the worksheet, as shown in Figure 5-1. In many cases, it makes sense to have the numbers that appear in your worksheet differ from Excel's *underlying* values, since a worksheet that's displaying numbers to, say, 13 decimal places, can look pretty cluttered.

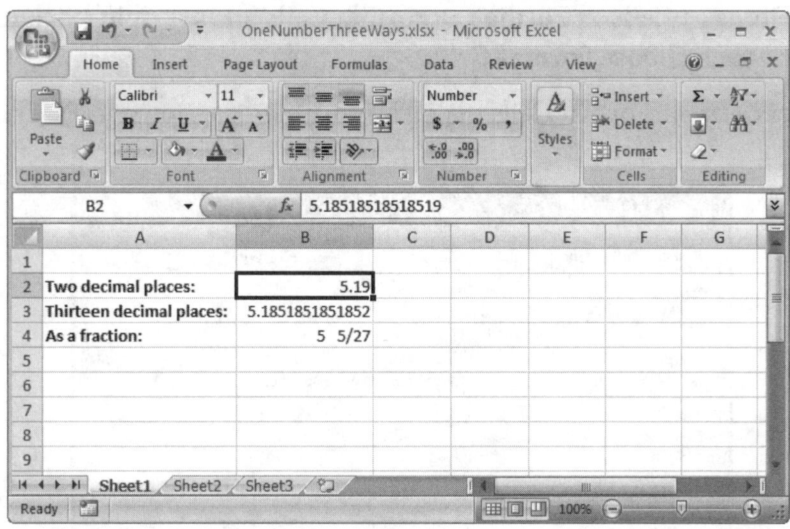

Figure 5-1. This worksheet shows how different formatting can affect the appearance of the same data. Each of the cells B2, B3, and B4 contains the exact same number: 5.18518518518519. In the formula bar, Excel always displays the exact number it's storing, as you see here with cell B2. However, in the worksheet itself, each cell's appearance differs depending on how you've formatted the cell.

To format a cell's value, follow these steps:

1. **Select the cells you want to format.**

   You can apply formatting to individual cells or a collection of cells. Usually, you'll want to format an entire column at once because all the values in a column typically contain the same type of data. Remember, to select a column, you simply need to click the column header (the gray box at the top with the column letter).

NOTE

Technically, a column contains *two* types of data: the values you're storing within the actual cells and the column title in the topmost cell (where the text is). However, you don't need to worry about unintentionally formatting the column title because Excel applies number formats only to numeric cells (cells that contain dates, times, or numbers). Excel doesn't use the number format for the column title cell because it contains text.

2. **Select Home → Cells → Format → Format Cells, or just right-click the selection, and then choose Format Cells.**

   In either case, the Format Cells dialog box appears, as shown in Figure 5-2.

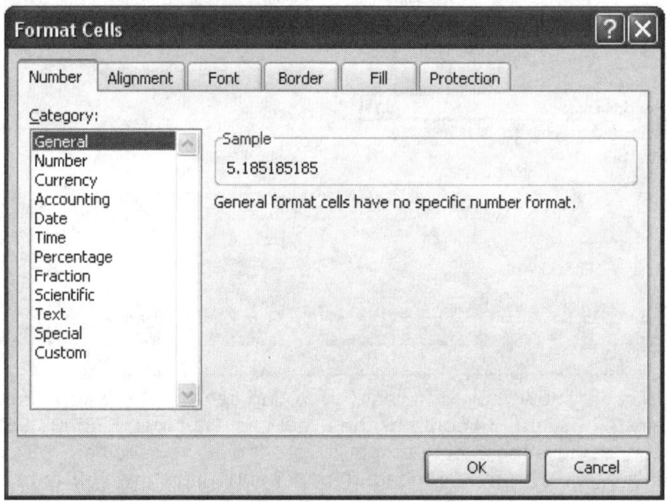

Figure 5-2. The Format Cells dialog box provides one-stop shopping for cell value and cell appearance formatting. The first tab, Number, lets you configure how numeric values are formatted. You can use the Alignment, Font, Border, and Fill tabs to control the cell's appearance.

3. **Set the format options.**

   The Number tab's options let you choose how Excel translates the cell value into a display value. For example, you can change the number of decimal places that Excel uses to show the number. (Number formatting choices are covered in much more detail in the next section, "Formatting Numbers.")

Most of the Format Cells dialog box's other tabs are for cell appearance formatting, which is covered later in this chapter.

NOTE

Once you apply formatting to a cell, it retains that formatting even if you clear the cell's contents (by selecting it and pressing Delete). In addition, formatting comes along for the ride if you copy a cell, so if you copy the content from cell A1 to cell A2, the formatting comes with it. Formatting includes both cell value formatting *and* cell appearance.

The only way to remove formatting is to highlight the cell and select Home → Editing → Clear → Clear Formats. This command removes the formatting, restoring the cell to its original, General number format (which you'll learn more about next), but it doesn't remove any of the cell's content.

4. **Click OK.**

   Excel applies your formatting changes and changes the appearance of the selected cells accordingly.

You'll spend a lot of time in this chapter at the Format Cells dialog box. As you've already seen, the most obvious way to get there is to choose Home → Format → Cells → Format Cells. However, your mouse finger's sure to tire out with that method. Fortunately, there's a quicker route—you can use one of three *dialog box launchers*. Figure 5-3 shows the way.

Formatting Numbers

In the Format Cells dialog box, the Number tab lets you control how Excel displays numeric data in a cell. Excel gives you a lengthy list of predefined formats (as shown in Figure 5-4). Remember, Excel uses number formats when the cell contains only numeric information. Otherwise, Excel simply ignores the number format. For example, if you enter *Half past 12* in a column full of times, Excel considers it plain ol' text—although, under the hood, the cell's numerical formatting stays put, and Excel uses it if you change the cell content to a time.

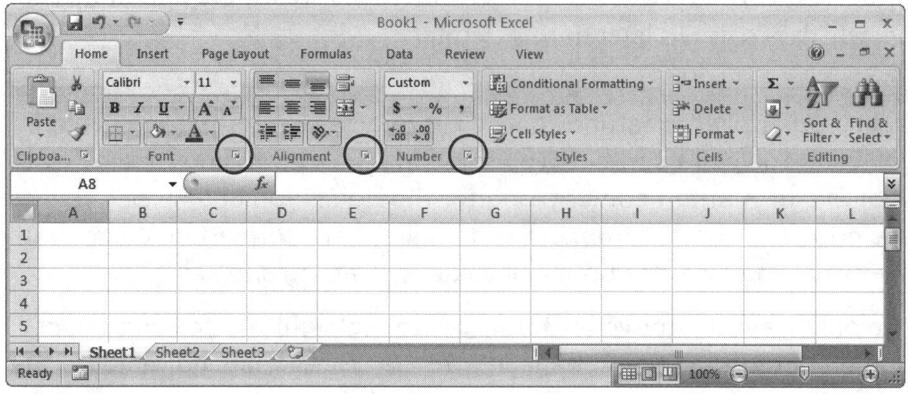

Figure 5-3. The ribbon's Home tab gives you a quick way to open the Format Cells dialog box from three different spots: the Font, the Alignment, or the Number tab.

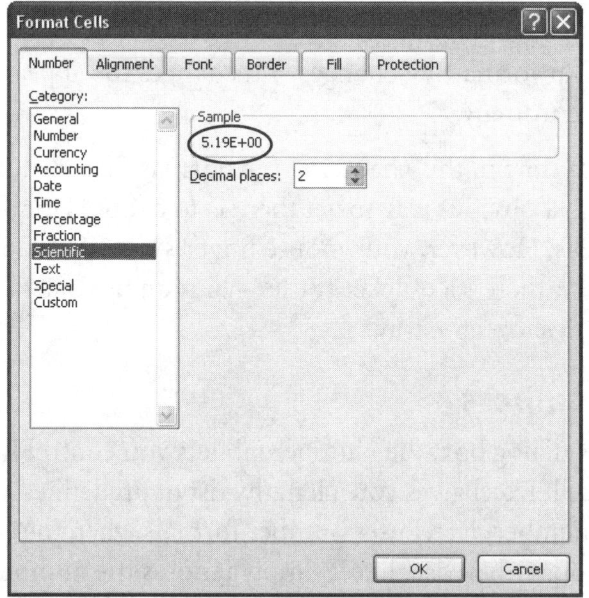

Figure 5-4. You can learn about the different number formats by selecting a cell that already has a number in it, and then choosing a new number format from the Category list (Home → Cells → Format → Format Cells). When you do so, Excel uses the Format Cells dialog box to show how it'll display the number if you apply that format. In this example, you see that the cell value, 5.18518518518519, will appear as 5.19E+00, which is scientific notation with two decimal places.

When you create a new spreadsheet, every cell starts out with the same number format: General. This format comes with a couple of basic rules:

- If a number has any decimal places, Excel displays them, provided they fit in the column. If the number's got more decimal places than Excel can display, then it leaves out the ones that don't fit. (It rounds up the last displayed digit, when appropriate). If you change a column width, then Excel automatically adjusts the amount of digits it displays.
- Excel removes leading and trailing zeros. Thus, 004.00 becomes 4. The only exception to this rule occurs with numbers between –1 and 1, which retain the 0 before the decimal point. For example, Excel displays the number .42 as 0.42.

As you saw in Chapter 2, the way you type in a number can change a cell's formatting. For example, if you enter a number with a currency symbol, the number format of the cell changes automatically to Currency. Similarly, if you enter three numbers separated by dashes (-) or backward slashes (/), Excel assumes you're entering a date, and adjusts the number format to Date.

However, rather than rely on this automatic process, it's far better just to enter ordinary numbers and set the formatting explicitly for the whole column. This approach prevents you from having different formatting in different cells (which can confuse even the sharpest spreadsheet reader), and it makes sure you get exactly the formatting and precision you want. You can apply formatting to the column before or after you enter the numbers. And it doesn't matter if a cell is currently empty; Excel still keeps track of the number format you've applied.

Different number formats provide different options. For example, if you choose the Currency format, then you can choose from dozens of currency symbols. When you use the Number format, you can choose to add commas (to separate groups of three digits) or parentheses (to indicate negative numbers). Most number formats let you set the number of decimal places.

The following sections give a quick tour of the predefined number formats available in the Format Cells dialog box's Number tab. Figure 5-5 gives you an overview of how different number formats affect similar numbers.

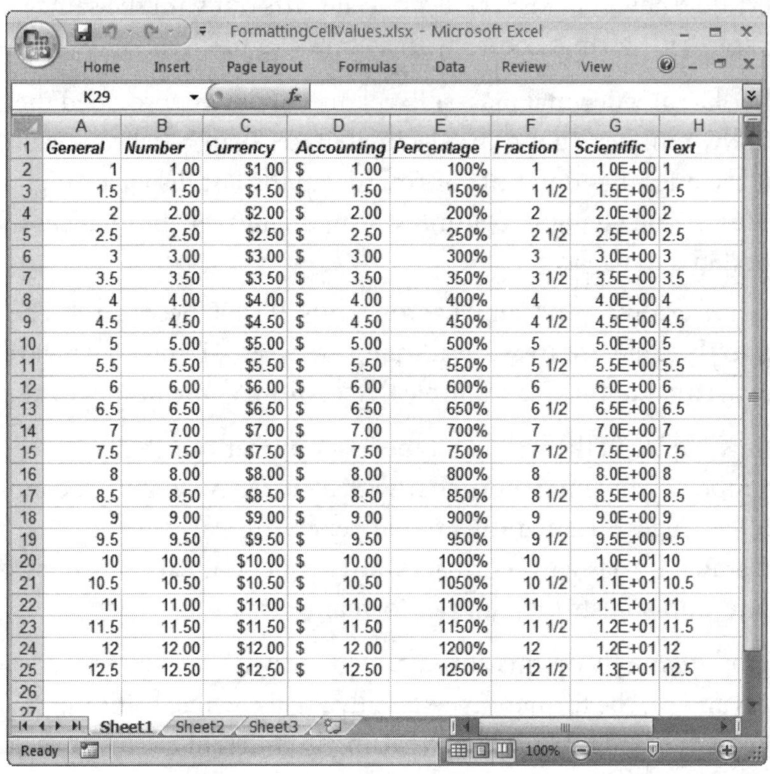

	A	B	C	D	E	F	G	H
1	General	Number	Currency	Accounting	Percentage	Fraction	Scientific	Text
2	1	1.00	$1.00	$ 1.00	100%	1	1.0E+00	1
3	1.5	1.50	$1.50	$ 1.50	150%	1 1/2	1.5E+00	1.5
4	2	2.00	$2.00	$ 2.00	200%	2	2.0E+00	2
5	2.5	2.50	$2.50	$ 2.50	250%	2 1/2	2.5E+00	2.5
6	3	3.00	$3.00	$ 3.00	300%	3	3.0E+00	3
7	3.5	3.50	$3.50	$ 3.50	350%	3 1/2	3.5E+00	3.5
8	4	4.00	$4.00	$ 4.00	400%	4	4.0E+00	4
9	4.5	4.50	$4.50	$ 4.50	450%	4 1/2	4.5E+00	4.5
10	5	5.00	$5.00	$ 5.00	500%	5	5.0E+00	5
11	5.5	5.50	$5.50	$ 5.50	550%	5 1/2	5.5E+00	5.5
12	6	6.00	$6.00	$ 6.00	600%	6	6.0E+00	6
13	6.5	6.50	$6.50	$ 6.50	650%	6 1/2	6.5E+00	6.5
14	7	7.00	$7.00	$ 7.00	700%	7	7.0E+00	7
15	7.5	7.50	$7.50	$ 7.50	750%	7 1/2	7.5E+00	7.5
16	8	8.00	$8.00	$ 8.00	800%	8	8.0E+00	8
17	8.5	8.50	$8.50	$ 8.50	850%	8 1/2	8.5E+00	8.5
18	9	9.00	$9.00	$ 9.00	900%	9	9.0E+00	9
19	9.5	9.50	$9.50	$ 9.50	950%	9 1/2	9.5E+00	9.5
20	10	10.00	$10.00	$ 10.00	1000%	10	1.0E+01	10
21	10.5	10.50	$10.50	$ 10.50	1050%	10 1/2	1.1E+01	10.5
22	11	11.00	$11.00	$ 11.00	1100%	11	1.1E+01	11
23	11.5	11.50	$11.50	$ 11.50	1150%	11 1/2	1.2E+01	11.5
24	12	12.00	$12.00	$ 12.00	1200%	12	1.2E+01	12
25	12.5	12.50	$12.50	$ 12.50	1250%	12 1/2	1.3E+01	12.5
26								

Figure 5-5. Each column contains the same list of numbers. Although this worksheet shows an example for each number format (except dates and times), it doesn't show all your options. Each number format has its own settings (like the number of decimal places) that affect how Excel displays data.

General

The General format is Excel's standard number format; it applies no special formatting other than the basic rules described on page 141. General is the only number format (other than Text) that doesn't limit your data to a fixed number of decimal places. That means if you want to display numbers that differ wildly in precision (like 0.5, 12.334, and 0.120986398), it makes sense to use General format. On the other hand, if your numbers have a similar degree of precision (for example, if you're logging the number of miles you run each day), the Number format makes more sense.

UP TO SPEED

The Relationship Between Formatting and Values

The format that you choose for a number doesn't affect Excel's internal storage of that number. For example, if a cell contains the fraction 1/3, then Excel stores this value as 0.333333333333333. (The exact number of decimal places varies, depending on the number you've entered, due to the slight approximations computers need to make when converting fractional numbers into 0s and 1s.) When deciding how to format a cell, you may choose to show only two decimal places, in which case the number appears in your worksheet as 0.33. Or, maybe you choose just one decimal place, in which case the number is simply 0.3. In both cases, Excel still keeps the full 15 or so decimal places on hand. To tell the difference between the displayed number and the real number that Excel stores behind the scenes, just move to the cell. Then look at the formula bar, which always shows you the real deal.

Because of this difference between the stored value and the displayed number, there may be some situations in which it looks like Excel's making a mistake. For example, imagine you have three cells, and each stores 0.333333333333333 but displays only 0.3. When you add these three cell values together, you won't end up with 0.3 + 0.3 + 0.3 = 0.9. Instead, you'll add the more precise stored values and end up with a number that's infinitesimally close to, but not quite, 1. Excel rounds this number up to 1.

This is almost always the way you want Excel to work because you know full well that if you add up 1/3 three times you end up with 1. But, if you need to, you can change this behavior.

To change what Excel does, select Office button → Excel Options, chose the Advanced section, and then scroll down to the "When calculating this workbook" group of settings. A "Set precision as displayed" checkbox appears. When you turn on this checkbox, Excel adjusts all the values in your current spreadsheet so that the stored value matches the displayed value. Unfortunately, with this choice, you'll get less precise data. For example, if you use this option with the 1/3 example, Excel stores the display value 0.3 instead of 0.333333333333333. Because you can't reverse this change, Excel warns you and asks for a final confirmation when you try to apply the "Precision as displayed" setting.

Number

The Number format is like the General format but with three refinements. First, it uses a fixed number of decimal places (which you set). That means that the decimal point always lines up (assuming you've formatted an entire column). The Number format also allows you to use commas as a separator between groups of three digits, which is handy if you're working with really long numbers. Finally, you can choose to have negative numbers displayed with the negative sign, in parentheses, or in red lettering.

Currency

The Currency format closely matches the Number format, with two differences. First, you can choose a currency symbol (like the dollar sign, pound symbol, Euro symbol, and so on) from an extensive list; Excel displays the currency symbol before the number. Second, the Currency format always includes commas. The Currency format also supports a fixed number of decimal places (chosen by you), and it allows you to customize how negative numbers are displayed.

Accounting

The Accounting format is modeled on the Currency format. It also allows you to choose a currency symbol, uses commas, and has a fixed number of decimal places. The difference is that the Accounting format uses a slightly different alignment. The currency symbol is always at the far left of the cell (away from the number), and there's always an extra space that pads the right side of the cell. Also, the Accounting format always shows negative numbers in parentheses, which is an accounting standard. Finally, the number 0 is never shown when using the Accounting format. Instead, a dash (-) is displayed in its place. There's really no reason to prefer the Currency or the Accounting format. Think of it as a personal decision, and choose whichever looks nicest on your worksheet. The only exception is if you happen to *be* an accountant, in which case you really have no choice in the matter—stick with your namesake.

Percentage

The Percentage format displays fractional numbers as percentages. For example, if you enter 0.5, that translates to 50%. You can choose the number of decimal places to display.

There's one trick to watch out for with the Percentage format. If you forget to start your number with a decimal, then Excel quietly "corrects" your numbers. For example, if you type 4 into a cell that uses the Percentage format, Excel interprets this as 4%. As a result, it actually stores the value 0.04. A side effect of this quirkiness is that if you want to enter percentages larger than 100%, you can't enter them as decimals. For example, to enter 200%, you need to type in 200 (not 2.00).

Fraction

The Fraction format displays your number as a fraction instead of a number with decimal places. The Fraction format doesn't mean you have to enter the number as a fraction (although you can if you want by using the forward slash, like 3/4). Instead it means that Excel converts any number you enter and display it as a fraction. Thus, to have 1/4 appear you can either enter .25 or 1/4.

NOTE

If you try to enter 1/4 and you *haven't* formatted the cell to use the Fraction number format, then you won't get the result you want. Excel assumes you're trying to enter a date (in this case, January 4th of the current year). To avoid this misunderstanding, change the number format *before* you type in your fraction. Or, enter it as *0 1/4* (zero and one quarter).

People often use the Fraction format for stock market quotes, but it's also handy for certain types of measurements (like weights and temperatures). When using the Fraction format, Excel does its best to calculate the closest fraction, which depends on a few factors including whether an exact match exists (entering .5 always gets you 1/2, for example) and what type of precision level you've picked when selecting the Fraction formatting.

You can choose to have fractions with three digits (for example, 100/200), two digits (10/20), or just one digit (1/2), using the top three choices in the Type list. For example, if you enter the number 0.51, Excel shows it as 1/2 in one-digit mode, and the more precise 51/100 in three-digit mode. In some cases, you may want all numbers to use the same denominator (the bottom number in the fraction) so that it's easy to compare different numbers. (Don't you wish Excel had been around when you were in grammar school?) In this case, you can choose to show all fractions as halves (with a denominator of 2), quarters (a denominator of 4), eighths (8), sixteenths (16), tenths (10), and hundredths (100). For example, the number 0.51 would be shown as 2/4 if you chose quarters.

TIP

Entering a fraction in Excel can be awkward because Excel may attempt to convert it to a date. To prevent this confusion, always start by entering 0 and then a space. For example, instead of typing 2/3 enter 0 2/3 (which means zero and two-thirds). If you have a whole number and a fraction, like 1 2/3, you'll also be able to duck the date confusion.

Scientific

The Scientific format displays numbers using scientific notation, which is ideal when you need to handle numbers that range widely in size (like 0.0003 and 300) *in the same column*. Scientific notation displays the first non-zero digit of a number, followed by a fixed number of digits, and then indicates what power of 10 that number needs to be multiplied by to generate the original number. For example, 0.0003 becomes 3.00×10^{-4} (displayed in Excel as 3.00E-04). The number 300, on the other hand, becomes 3.00×10^{2} (displayed in Excel as 3.00E02). Scientists—surprise, surprise—like the Scientific format for doing things like recording experimental data or creating mathematical models to predict when an incoming meteor will graze the Earth.

Text

Few people use the Text format for numbers, but it's certainly possible to do so. The Text format simply displays a number as though it were text, although you can still perform calculations with it. Excel shows the number exactly as it's stored internally, positioning it against the left edge of the column. You can get the same effect by placing an apostrophe before the number (although that approach won't allow you to use the number in calculations).

TIMESAVING TIP

Shortcuts in the Ribbon

You don't need to waste hours jumping between your worksheet and the Format Cells dialog box. The ribbon gets you to some of the most commonly used number formats in the Home → Number section.

The Home → Number section's most prominent part is the drop-down list of number formats (Figure 5-6). Just underneath are buttons that let you apply one of the three most common formats: Accounting, Percent, or Number. Just to the right are two buttons that let you increase or decrease the number of decimal places that you see at once.

One of the neatest features is the list of currency options for the Accounting button. If you click the drop-down arrow on the Accounting button (which looks like a dollar sign), then you see a list with different currency symbols you can choose (like Pounds, Euros, Chinese Yuan, and so on). But if you click the other portion of the Accounting button (not the arrow), then you get the currency symbol that's appropriate based on your computer's regional settings.

Formatting Dates and Times

Excel gives you lots of options here. You can use everything from compact styles like 3/13/07 to longer formats that include the day of the week, like Sunday, March 13, 2007. Time formats give you a similar range of options, including the ability to use a 12-hour or 24-hour clock, show seconds, show fractional seconds, and include the date information.

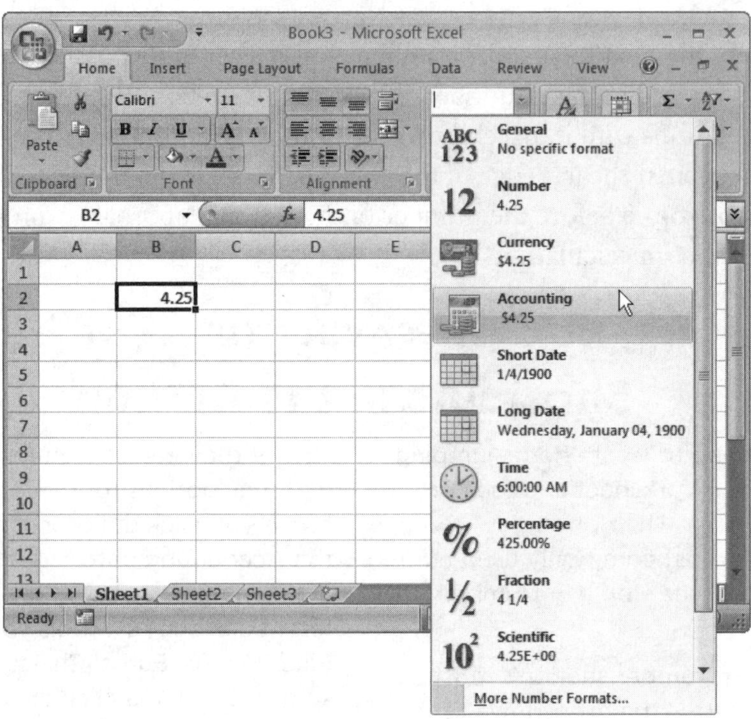

Figure 5-6. The all-around quickest way to apply a number format is to select some cells, and then, from the number format list, choose an option. Best of all, you see a small preview of what the value in the first selected cell will look like if you apply the format.

To format dates and times, first open the Format Cells dialog box shown in Figure 5-7 (Home → Cells → Format → Format Cells). Choose Date or Time from the column on the left and then choose the format from the list on the right. Date and Time both provide a slew of options.

Excel has essentially two types of date and time formats:

- **Formats that take the regional settings of the spreadsheet viewer's computer into account.** With these formats, dates display differently depending on the computer that's running Excel. This choice is a good one because it lets everyone see dates in just the way they want to, which means no time-consuming arguments about month-day-year or day-month-year ordering.

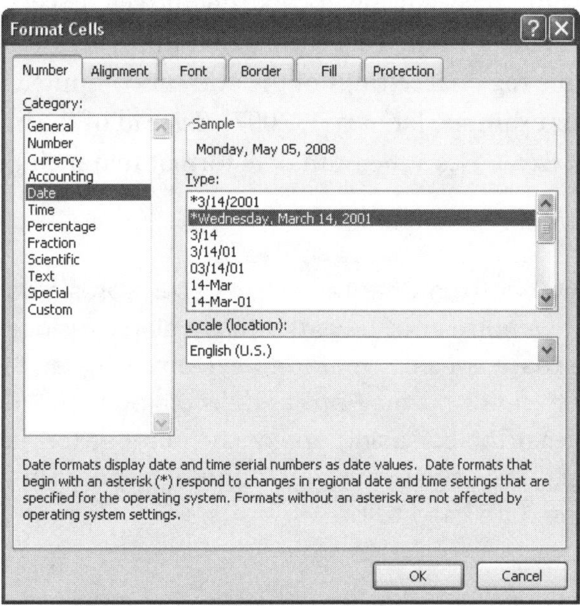

Figure 5-7. Excel gives you dozens of different ways to format dates and times. You can choose between formats that modify the date's appearance depending on the regional settings of the computer viewing the Excel file, or you can choose a fixed date format. When using a fixed date format, you don't have to stick to the U.S. standard. Instead, choose the appropriate region from the Locale list box. Each locale provides its own set of customized date formats.

- **Formats that *ignore* the regional settings of individual computers.** These formats define a fixed pattern for month, day, year, and time components, and display date-related information in exactly the same way on all computers. If you need to absolutely make sure a date is in a certain format, use this choice.

The first group (the formats that rely on a computer's regional settings) is the smallest. It includes two date formats (a compact, number-only format and a long, more descriptive format) and one time format. In the Type list, these formats are at the top and have an asterisk next to them.

The second group (the formats that are independent of a computer's regional settings) is much more extensive. In order to choose one of these formats, you first select a region from the Locale list, and then you select the appropriate date or time format. Some examples of locales include "English (United States)" and "English (United Kingdom)."

If you enter a date without specifically formatting the cell, Excel usually uses the short region-specific date format. That means that the order of the month and year vary depending on the regional settings of the current computer. If you incorporate the month name (for example, January 1, 2007), instead of the month number (for example, 1/1/2007), Excel uses a medium date format that includes a month abbreviation, like 1-Jan-2007.

NOTE

You may remember from Chapter 2 that Excel stores a date internally as the cumulative number of days that have elapsed since a certain long-ago date that varies by operating system. You can take a peek at this internal number using the Format Cells dialog box. First, enter your date. Then, format the cell using one of the number formats (like General or Number). The underlying date number appears in your worksheet where the date used to be.

Special Formats for Special Numbers

You wouldn't ever want to perform mathematical operations with some types of numeric information. For example, it's hard to image a situation where you'd want to add or multiply phone numbers or Social Security numbers.

When entering these types of numbers, therefore, you may choose to format them as plain old text. For example, you could enter the text (555) 123-4567 to represent a phone number. Because of the parentheses and the dash (-), Excel won't interpret this information as a number. Alternatively, you could just precede your value with an apostrophe (') to explicitly tell Excel that it should be treated as text (you might do this if you don't use parentheses or dashes in a phone number).

But whichever solution you choose, you're potentially creating more work for yourself because you have to enter the parentheses and the dash for each phone number you enter (or the apostrophe). You also increase the likelihood of creating inconsistently formatted numbers, especially if you're entering a long list of them. For example, some phone numbers may end up entered in slightly similar but somewhat different formats, like 555-123-4567 and (555)1234567.

To avoid these problems, apply Excel's Special number format (shown in Figure 5-8), which converts numbers into common patterns. And lucky you: In the Special number format, one of the Type options is Phone Number (other formats are for Zip codes and Social Security numbers).

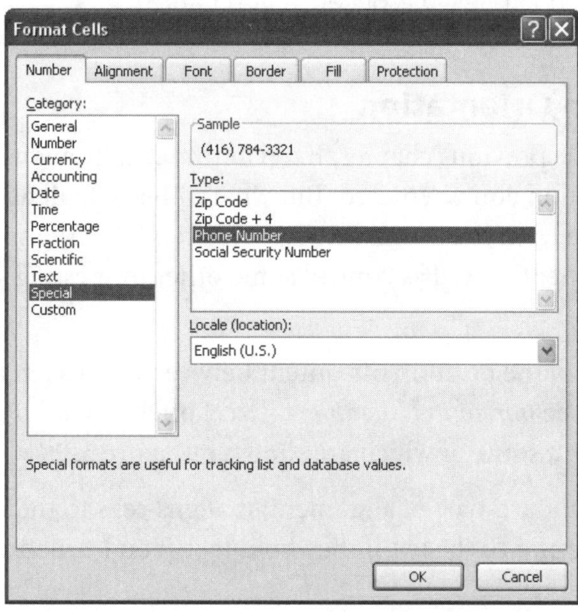

Figure 5-8. Special number formats are ideal for formatting sequences of digits into a common pattern. For example, in the Type list, if you choose Phone Number, then Excel converts the sequence of digits 5551234567 into the proper phone number style—(555) 123-4567—with no extra work required on your part.

Formatting Cell Appearance

Formatting cell values is important because it helps maintain consistency among your numbers. But to really make your spreadsheet readable, you're probably going to want to enlist some of Excel's tools for controlling things like alignment, color, and borders and shading.

To format a cell's appearance, first select the single cell or group of cells that you want to work with, and then choose Home → Cells → Format → Format Cells, or just right-click the selection, and then choose Format Cells. The Format Cells dialog box that appears is the place where you adjust your settings.

TIP

Even a small amount of formatting can make a worksheet easier to interpret by drawing the viewer's eye to important information. Of course, as with formatting a Word document or designing a Web page, a little goes a long way. Don't feel the need to bury your worksheet in exotic colors and styles just because you can.

Alignment and Orientation

As you learned in the previous chapter, Excel automatically aligns cells according to the type of information you've entered. But what if this default alignment isn't what you want? Fortunately, in the Format Cells dialog box, the Alignment tab lets you easily change alignment as well as control some other interesting settings, like the ability to rotate text.

Excel lets you control the position of content between a cell's left and right borders, which is known as the *horizontal alignment*. Excel offers the following choices for horizontal alignment, some of which are shown in Figure 5-9:

- **General** is the standard type of alignment; it aligns cells to the right if they hold numbers or dates and to the left if they hold text. You learned about this type of alignment in Chapter 2.
- **Left (Indent)** tells Excel to always line up content with the left edge of the cell. You can also choose an indent value to add some extra space between the content and the left border.
- **Center** tells Excel to always center content between the left and right edges of the cell.
- **Right (Indent)** tells Excel to always line up content with the right edge of the cell. You can also choose an indent value to add some extra space between the content and the right border.
- **Fill** copies content multiple times across the width of the cell, which is almost never what you want.

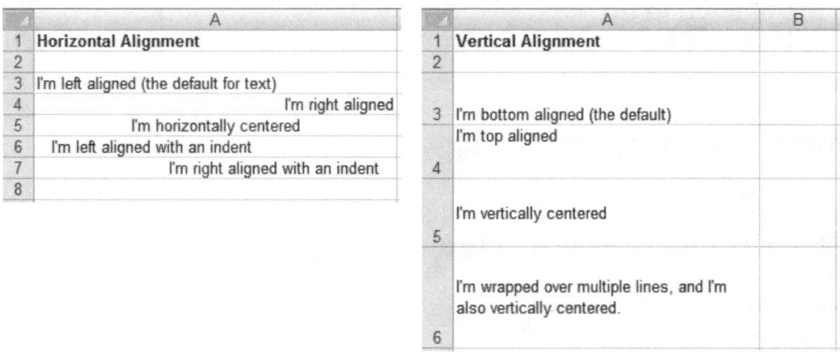

Figure 5-9. Left: Horizontal alignment options in action.
Right: This sheet shows how vertical alignment and cell wrapping work with cell content.

- **Justify** is the same as Left if the cell content fits on a single line. When you insert text that spans more than one line, Excel *justifies* every line except the last one, which means Excel adjusts the space between words to try and ensure that both the right and left edges line up.
- **Center Across Selection** is a bit of an oddity. When you apply this option to a single cell, it has the same effect as Center. If you select more than one adjacent cell in a row (for example, cell A1, A2, A3), this option centers the value in the first cell so that it appears to be centered over the full width of all cells. However, this happens only as long as the other cells are blank. This setting may confuse you a bit at first because it can lead to cell values being displayed over cells in which they aren't stored. Another approach to centering large text titles and headings is to use cell merging (as described on page 154).
- **Distributed (Indent)** is the same as Center—if the cell contains a numeric value or a single word. If you add more than one word, then Excel enlarges the spaces between words so that the text content fills the cell perfectly (from the left edge to the right edge).

Vertical alignment controls the position of content between a cell's top and bottom border. Vertical alignment becomes important only if you enlarge a row's height so that it becomes taller than the contents it contains. To change the height of a row, click the bottom edge of the row header (the numbered cell on the left side of the worksheet), and drag it up or down. As you resize the row, the content stays fixed at the bottom. The vertical alignment setting lets you adjust the cell content's positioning.

Excel gives you the following vertical alignment choices, some of which are shown in Figure 5-9:

- **Top** tells Excel that the first line of text should start at the top of the cell.
- **Center** tells Excel that the block of text should be centered between the top and bottom border of the cell.
- **Bottom** tells Excel that the last line of text should end at the bottom of the cell. If the text doesn't fill the cell exactly, then Excel adds some padding to the top.
- **Justify** is the same as Top for a single line of text. When you have more than one line of text, Excel increases the spaces between each line so that the text fills the cell completely from the top edge to the bottom edge.
- **Distributed** is the same as Justify for multiple lines of text. If you have a single line of text, this is the same as Center.

If you have a cell containing a large amount of text, you may want to increase the row's height so you can display multiple lines. Unfortunately, you'll notice that enlarging a cell doesn't automatically cause the text to flow into multiple lines and fill the newly available space. But there's a simple solution: just turn on the "Wrap text" checkbox (on the Alignment tab of the Format Cells dialog box). Now, long passages of text flow across multiple lines. You can use this option in conjunction with the vertical alignment setting to control whether Excel centers a block of text, or lines it up at the bottom or top of the cell. Another option is to explicitly split your text into lines. Whenever you want to insert a line break, just press Alt+Enter, and start typing the new line.

TIP

After you've expanded a row, you can shrink it back by double-clicking the bottom edge of the row header. When you haven't turned on text wrapping, this action shrinks the row back to its standard single-line height.

Finally, the Alignment tab allows you to rotate content in a cell up to 180 degrees, as shown in Figure 5-10. You can set the number of degrees in the Orientation box on the right of the Alignment tab. Rotating cell content automatically changes the size of the cell. Usually, you'll see it become narrower and taller to accommodate the rotated content.

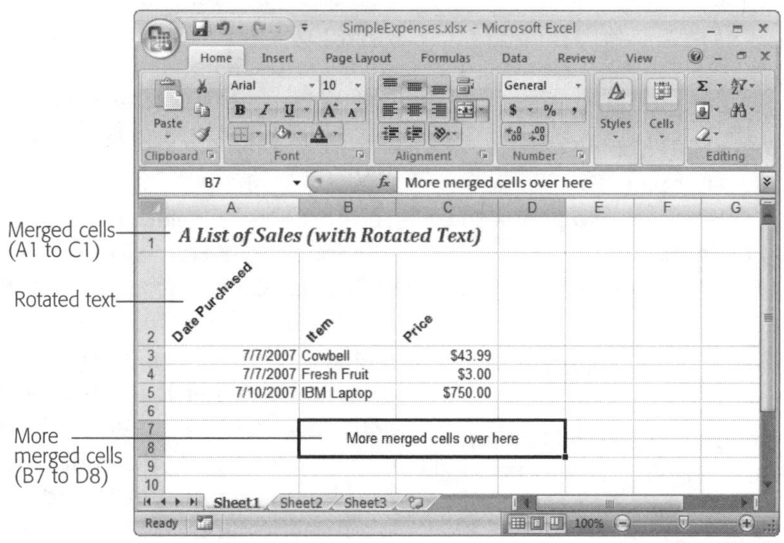

Figure 5-10. Here's a worksheet that demonstrates one of Excel's most commonly used formatting tricks (merged cells), along with one of its most exotic (rotated text).

TIP

You can use the Home → Alignment section of the ribbon to quickly change alignment, indenting, rotation, and wrapping, without opening the Format Cells dialog box.

Fonts and Color

As in almost any Windows program, you can customize the text in Excel, applying a dazzling assortment of colors and fancy typefaces. You can do everything from enlarging headings to colorizing big numbers. Here are the individual font details you can change:

FREQUENTLY ASKED QUESTION

Shrinking Text and Merging Cells So You Can Fit More Text into a Cell

I'm frequently writing out big chunks of text that I'd love to scrunch into a single cell. Do I have any options other than text wrapping?

You betcha. When you need to store a large amount of text in one cell, text wrapping is a good choice. But it's not your only option. You can also shrink the size of the text or merge multiple cells, both from the Format Cells dialog box's Alignment tab.

To shrink a cell's contents, select the "Shrink to fit" checkbox. Be warned, however, that if you have a small column that doesn't use wrapping, this option can quickly reduce your text to vanishingly small proportions.

Joining multiple cells together removes the cells' shared borders and creates one mega-sized cell. Usually, you'll do this to accommodate a large amount of content that can't fit in a single cell (like a long title that you want to display over every column). For example, if you merge cells A1, B1, and C1, you end up with a single cell named A1 that stretches over the full width of the A, B, and C columns, as shown in Figure 5-10.

To merge cells, select the cells you want to join, choose Home → Cells → Format → Format Cells, and then, on the Alignment tab, turn on the "Merge cells" checkbox. There's no limit to how many cells you can merge. (In fact, you can actually convert your entire worksheet into a single cell if you want to go crazy.) And if you change your mind, don't worry—you simply need to select the single merged cell, choose Home → Cells → Format → Format Cells again, and then turn off the "Merge cells" checkbox to redraw the original cells.

- **The font style.** (For example, Arial, Times New Roman, or something a little more shocking, like Futura Extra Bold.) Arial is the standard font for new worksheets.
- **The font size, in points.** The default point size is 10, but you can choose anything from a minuscule 1-point to a monstrous 409-point. Excel automatically enlarges the row height to accommodate the font.

- **Various font attributes, like italics, underlining, and bold.** Some fonts have complimentary italic and bold typefaces, while others don't (in which case Windows uses its own algorithm to make the font bold or italicize it).
- **The font color.** This option controls the color of the text. (Page 162 covers how to change the color of the entire cell.)

To change font settings, first highlight the cells you want to format, choose Home → Cells → Format → Format Cells, and then click the Font tab (Figure 5-11).

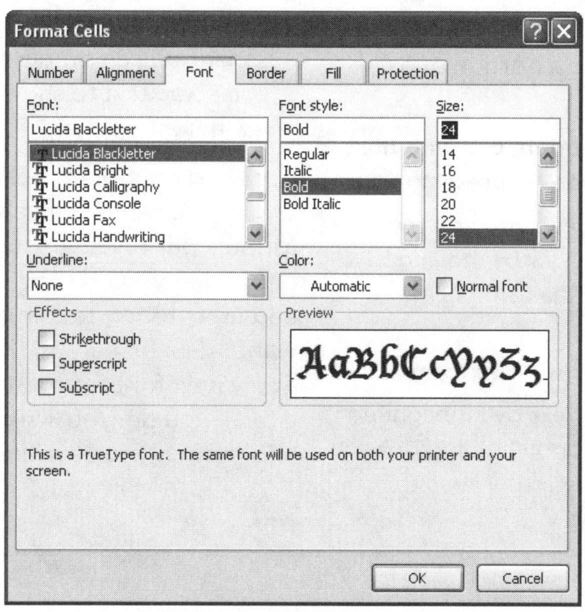

Figure 5-11. Here's an example of how to apply an exotic font through the Format Cells dialog box. Keep in mind that when displaying data, and especially numbers, sans-serif fonts are usually clearer and look more professional than serif fonts. (Serif fonts have little embellishments, like tiny curls, on the ends of the letters; sans-serif fonts don't.) Arial, the default spreadsheet font, is a sans-serif font.

TIP

Thanks to Excel's handy Redo feature, you can repeatedly apply a series of formatting changes to different cells. After you make your changes in the Format Cells dialog box, simply select the new cell you want to format in the same way, and then hit Ctrl+Y to repeat the last action.

POWER USERS' CLINIC

Formatting Individual Characters

The ribbon lets you perform one task that you can't with the Format Cells dialog box: applying formatting to just a part of a cell. For example, if a cell contains the text "New low price", you could apply a new color or bold format to the word "low."

To apply formatting to a portion of a cell, follow these steps:

1. **Move to the appropriate cell, and then put it into edit mode by pressing F2.**

   You can also put a cell into edit mode by double-clicking it, or by moving to it and clicking inside the formula bar's text.

2. **Select the text you want to format.**

   You can select the text by highlighting it with the mouse, or by holding down Shift while using the arrow keys to mark your selection.

3. **Choose a font option from the ribbon's Home → Font section.**

   You can also change the size, the color, or the bold, italic, or underline settings. And if you don't want to waste time choosing the Home tab if you're currently somewhere else in the ribbon, then you can simply right-click the selected text to show a pop-up toolbar with font options.

Applying multiple types of text formatting to the same cell can get tricky. The formula bar doesn't show the difference, and, when you edit the cell, you may not end up entering text in the font you want. Also, be careful that you don't apply new font formatting to the cell later; if you do, you'll wipe out all the font information you've added to the cell.

Rather than heading to the Format Cells dialog box every time you want to tweak a font, you can use the ribbon's handy shortcuts. The Home → Font section displays buttons for changing the font and font size. You also get a load of tiny buttons for applying basics like bold, italic, and underline, applying borders, and changing the text and background colors. (Truth be told, the formatting toolbar is way more convenient for setting fonts because its drop-down menu shows a long list of font names, whereas the font list in the Format Cells dialog box is limited to showing an impossibly restrictive six fonts at a time. Scrolling through that cramped space is like reading the phone book on index cards.)

Without a doubt, the most useful ribbon formatting feature is *live preview*, a frill that shows you the result of a change *before* you've even applied it. Figure 5-12 shows live preview in action.

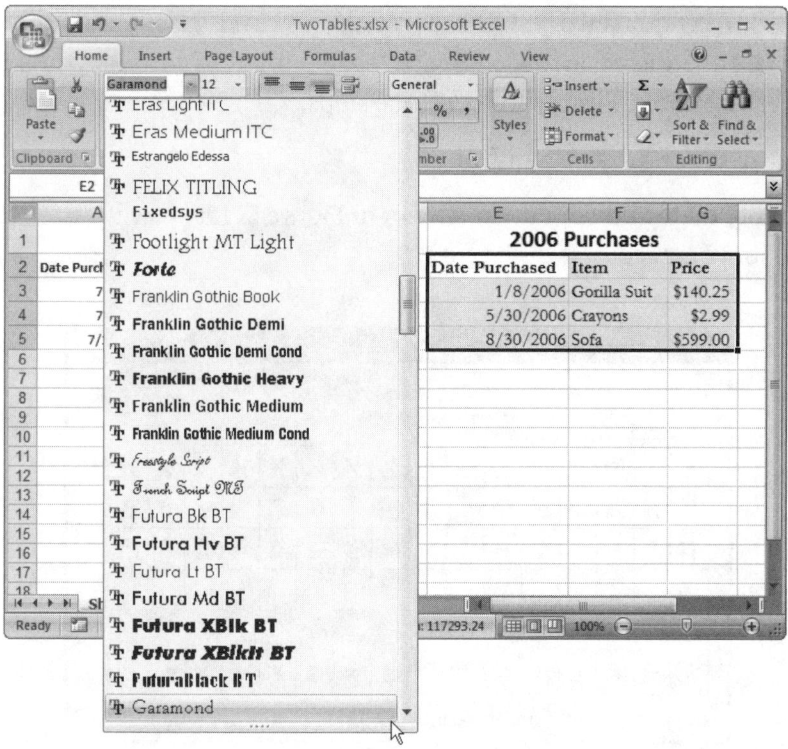

Figure 5-12. Right now, this spreadsheet's creator is just thinking about using the stylish Garamond font for this table. However, the moment she hovers over Benguiat (higher up in the font list), Excel switches the currently selected cells on the worksheet to that font, providing a preview of the change. The best part: When she moves the mouse pointer away, the formatting disappears instantaneously. To make the changes stick, all she needs to do is click the font. This live preview feature works with font names, font sizes, and colors.

NOTE

No matter what font you apply, Excel, thankfully, always displays the cell contents in the formula bar in easy-to-read Calibri font. That makes things easier if you're working with cells that've been formatted using difficult-to-decipher script fonts, or really large or small text sizes.

Special characters

Most fonts contain not only digits and the common letters of the alphabet, but also some special symbols that you can type directly on your keyboard. One example is the copyright symbol ©, which you can insert into a cell by entering the text *(C)*, and letting AutoCorrect do its work. Other symbols, however, aren't as readily available. One example is the special arrow character →. To use this symbol, you'll need the help of Excel's symbols. Simply follow these steps:

1. **Choose Insert → Text → Symbol.**

   The Symbol dialog box opens, as shown in Figure 5-13. Now it's time to hunt for the symbol you need.

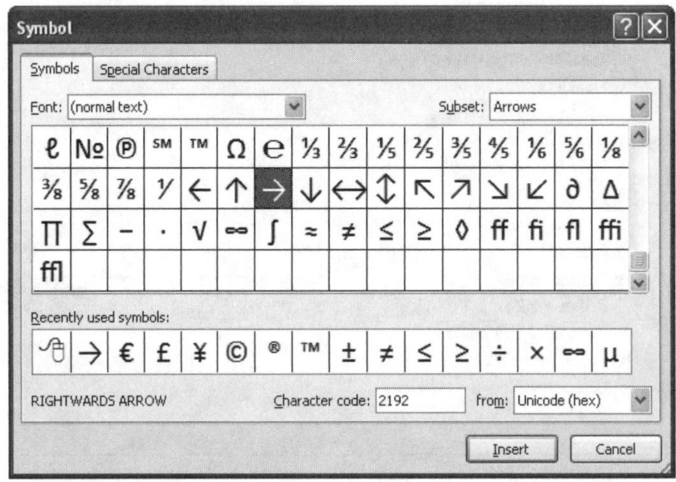

Figure 5-13. The Symbol dialog box lets you insert one or more special characters. You can choose extended characters that are supported by most fonts (like currency symbols, non-English letters, arrows, and so on). Alternatively, you can use a font that's all about fancy characters, like the Wingdings font that's chock full of tiny graphical icons.

2. **Choose the font and subset (the group of symbols you want to explore).**

   If you're looking for a fairly common symbol (like a mathematical sign, an arrow, an accented letter, or a fraction), you probably don't need to change the font. In the Font box, keep the default selection of "(normal text)", and then, from the Subset box at the right, choose the type of symbol. For example, choose the Arrows subset to see arrow symbols that point in different directions.

If you want funkier alternatives, choose a fancy font from the Font box on the left. You should be able to find at least one version of the Wingdings font in the list. Wingdings has the most interesting symbols to use. It's also the most likely to be on other people's computers, which makes a difference if you're planning to email your worksheet to other people. If you get your symbols from a really bizarre font that other people don't have, they won't be able to see your symbols.

NOTE

Wingdings is a special font included with Windows that's made up entirely of symbols like happy faces and stars, none of which you find in standard fonts. You can try and apply the Wingdings font on your own (by picking it from the font list), but you won't know which character to press on your keyboard to get the symbol you want. You're better off using Excel's Symbol dialog box.

3. **Select the character, and then click Insert.**

   Alternatively, if you need to insert multiple special characters, just double-click each one; doing so inserts each symbol right next to each other in the same cell without having to close the window.

TIP

If you're looking for an extremely common special character (like the copyright symbol), you can shorten this whole process. Instead of using the Symbols tab, just click over to the Special Characters tab. Then, look through the small list of commonly used symbols. If you find what you want, just select it, and then click Insert.

There's one idiosyncrasy that you should be aware of if you choose to insert symbols from another font. For example, if you insert a symbol from the Wingdings font into a cell that already has text, then you actually end up with a cell that has two fonts—one for the symbol character and one that's used for the rest of your text. This system works perfectly well, but it can cause some confusion. For example, if you apply a new font to the cell after inserting a special character, Excel adjusts the entire contents of the cell to use the new font, and your symbol changes into the corresponding character in the new font (which usually isn't what you want). These problems can crop up any time you deal with a cell that has more than one font.

On the other hand, if you kept the font selection on "(normal text)" when you picked your symbol, you won't see this behavior. That's because you picked a more commonplace symbol that's included in the font you're already using for the cell. In this case, Excel doesn't need to use two fonts at once.

NOTE

When you look at the cell contents in the formula bar, you always see the cell data in the standard Calibri font. This consistency means, for example, that a Wingdings symbol doesn't appear as the icon that shows up in your worksheet. Instead, you see an ordinary letter or some type of extended non-English character, like æ.

Borders and Fills

The best way to call attention to important information isn't to change fonts or alignment. Instead, place borders around key cells or groups of cells and use shading to highlight important columns and rows. Excel provides dozens of different ways to outline and highlight any selection of cells.

Once again, the trusty Format Cells dialog box is your control center. Just follow these steps:

1. **Select the cells you want to fill or outline.**

   Your selected cells appear highlighted.

2. **Select Home → Cells → Format → Format Cells, or just right-click the selection, and then choose Format Cells.**

   The Format Cells dialog box appears.

3. **Head directly to the Border tab. (If you don't want to apply any borders, skip straight to step 4.)**

   Applying a border is a multistep process (see Figure 5-14). Begin by choosing the line style you want (dotted, dashed, thick, double, and so on), followed by the color. (Automatic picks black.) Both these options are on the left side of the tab. Next, choose where your border lines are going to appear. The Border box (where the word "Text" appears four times) functions as a nifty interactive test canvas that shows you where your lines will appear. Make your selection either by clicking one of the eight Border buttons (which contain a single bold horizontal, vertical, or diagonal line), or click directly inside the Border box. If you change your mind, clicking a border line makes it disappear.

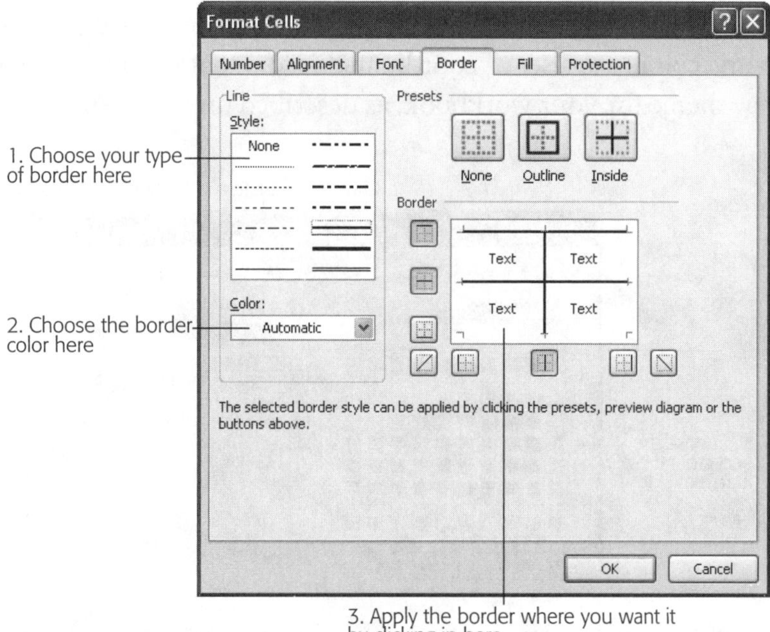

Figure 5-14. Follow the numbered steps in this figure to choose the line style and color, and then apply the border. In this picture, Excel will apply a solid border between the columns and at the top edge of the selection.

For example, if you want to apply a border to the top of your selection, click the top of the Border box. If you want to apply a line between columns inside the selection, click between the cell columns in the Border box. The line appears indicating your choice.

TIP

The Border tab also provides two shortcuts in the tab's Presets section. If you want to apply a border style around your entire selection, select Outline after choosing your border style and color. Choose Inside to apply the border between the rows and columns of your selection. Choosing None removes all border lines.

4. **Click the Fill tab.**

   Here you can select the background color, pattern color, and pattern style to apply shading to the cells in the selection (see Figure 5-15). Click the No Color box to clear any current color or pattern in the selected cells. When picking a pattern color, you may notice that certain colors are described as *theme colors*. These theme colors are a set of coordinated colors that change whenever you pick a new theme for your workbook, as described on page 170.

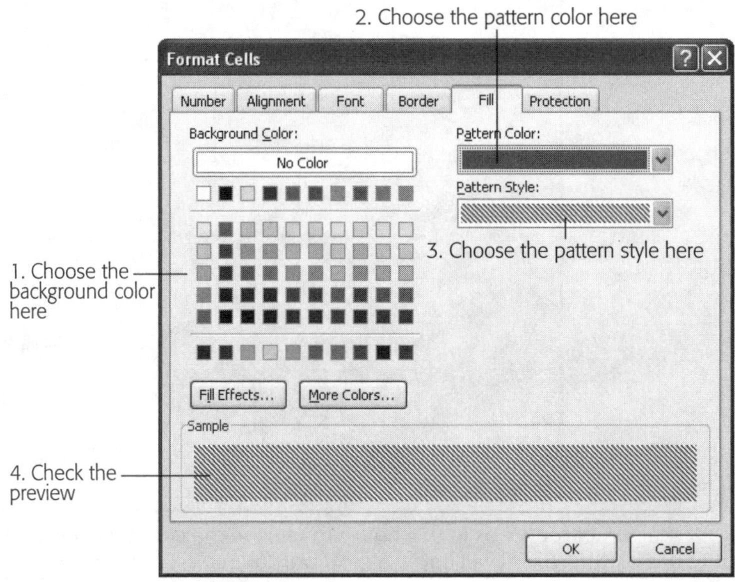

Figure 5-15. Adding a pattern to selected cells is simpler than choosing borders. All you need to do is select the colors you want and, optionally, choose a pattern. The pattern can include a grid, dots, or the diagonal lines shown in this figure.

   To get a really fancy fill, you can use a *gradient*, which is a blend of two colors. For example, with gradients you can create a fill that starts out white on one side of a cell and gradually darkens to blue on the other. To use a gradient fill, click the Fill Effects button, and then follow the instructions in Figure 5-16.

5. **Click OK to apply your changes.**

   If you don't like the modifications you've just applied, you can roll back time by pressing Ctrl+Z to trigger the indispensable Undo command.

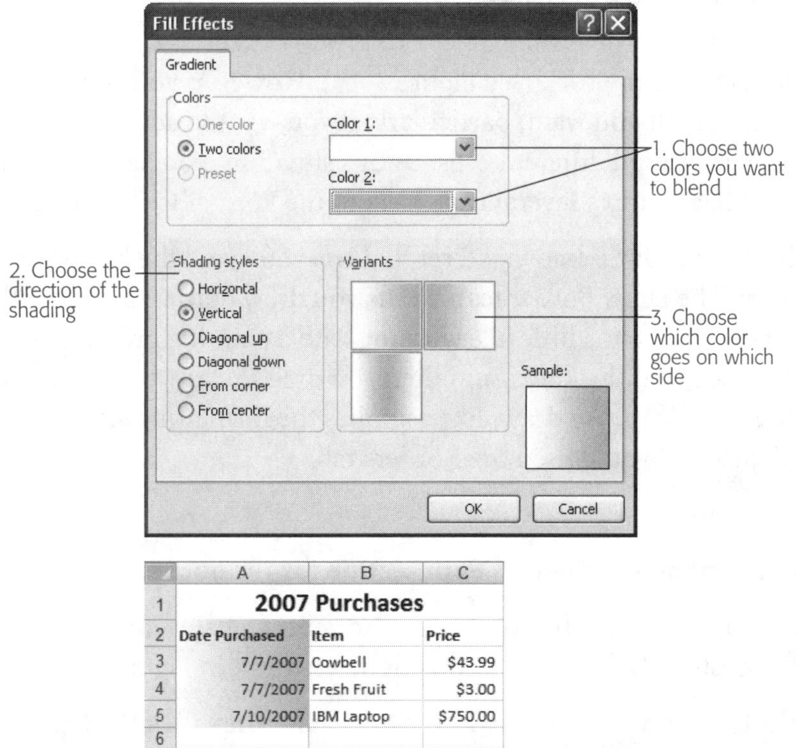

	A	B	C
1	2007 Purchases		
2	Date Purchased	Item	Price
3	7/7/2007	Cowbell	$43.99
4	7/7/2007	Fresh Fruit	$3.00
5	7/10/2007	IBM Laptop	$750.00
6			

Figure 5-16. Top: To create a gradient, you need to pick the two colors that are used to create the blend, and you need to choose the way Excel does the blending (from one side to another, from the top to the bottom, and so on). When applying a gradient fill to a stack of cells, a vertical fill makes the most sense, because that way the gradients in each cell line up and they look like one seamless shaded region. When applying a gradient fill to a row of cells, a horizontal fill looks better for the same reason.

Bottom: A gradient fill on cells A2 to A5.

TIP

You can remove a worksheet's gridlines, which is handy when you want to more easily see any custom borders you've added. To remove gridlines, select View → Show/Hide → Gridlines. (This action affects only the current file, and won't apply to new spreadsheets.)

Drawing Borders by Hand

If you need to add a border around a cell or group of cells, the Format Cells dialog box's Border tab does the trick (see Figure 5-14). However, you could have a hard time getting the result you want, particularly if you want to add a combination of different borders around different cells. In this situation, you have a major project on your hand that requires several trips back to the Format Cells dialog box.

Fortunately, there's a little-known secret that lets you avoid the hassle: Excel's Draw Border feature. The Draw Border feature lets you draw border lines directly on your worksheet. This process is a little like working with a painting program. You pick the border style, color, and thickness, and then you drag to draw the line between the appropriate cells. When you draw, Excel applies the formatting settings to each affected cell, just as if you'd used the Borders tab.

Here's how it works:

1. **Look in the ribbon's Home → Font section for the border button.**

   The name of the border button changes to reflect whatever you used it for last. You can most easily find it by its position, as shown in Figure 5-17.

2. **Click the border button, choose Line Style, and then pick the type of line you want.**

   You can use dashed and solid lines of different thicknesses, just as you can in the Format Cells dialog box's Borders tab.

3. **Click the border button, choose Line Color, and then pick the color you want.**

   Now you're ready to start drawing.

4. **Click the border button, and then choose Draw Border.**

   When you choose Draw Border, your mouse pointer changes into a pencil icon.

5. **Using the border pencil, click a gridline where you want to place your border (Figure 5-18).**

   You can also drag side to side or up and down to draw a longer horizontal or vertical line. And if you drag your pointer down *and* to the side, you create an outside border around a whole block of cells.

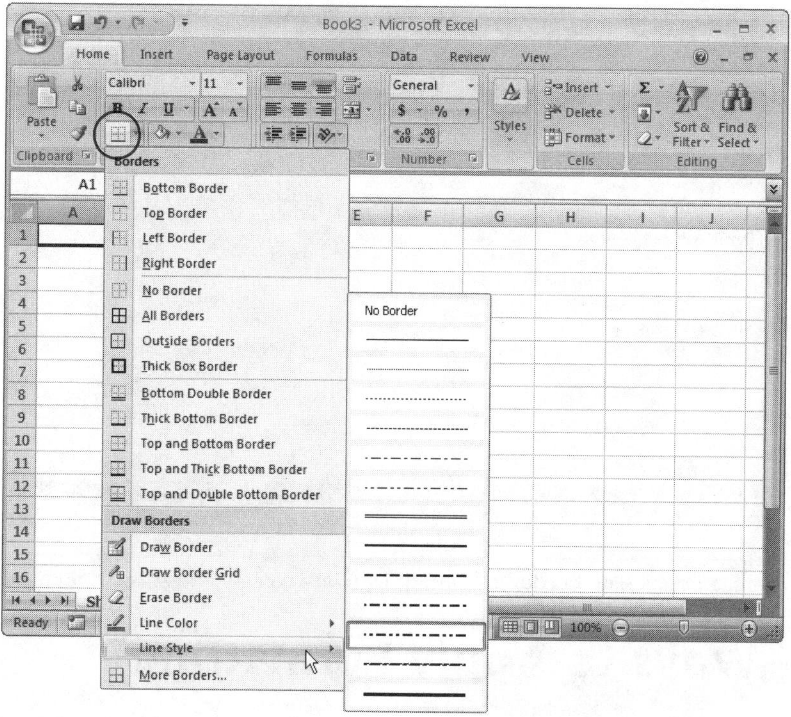

Figure 5-17. When you click the border button (circled), you see a list of border-customizing commands. Before you draw any borders, it makes sense to customize the border style. For example, you could choose Line Style, as shown here, and for color, you'd choose Line Color.

6. **To stop drawing, head back to the border menu, and then choose Draw Border again.**

   If you make a mistake, you can even use an eraser to tidy it all up. Just click the border button, and then choose Erase Border. The mouse pointer changes to an eraser. Now you can click the border you want to remove.

TIP

If you don't want to use the Draw Border feature, you can still make good use of the border button. Just pick a line style and line color, select some cells, and then choose an option from the border menu. For example, if you pick Bottom Border, Excel applies a border with the color and style you chose to the bottom of the current cell selection.

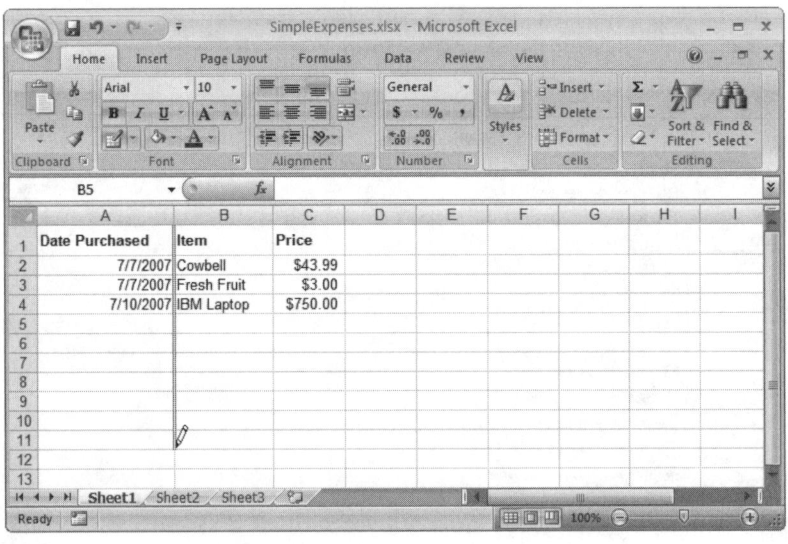

Figure 5-18. Here, a double-line border is being drawn between column A and column B.

Smart Ways to Apply Formatting

Earlier in this chapter, you took a comprehensive tour of Excel's formatting fundamentals. But of course, just because the features exist doesn't mean they're easy to use. Digging through the different options and applying a full range of formatting settings can be a tedious task. Fortunately, Excel also includes a few timesavers that let you speed up many formatting jobs.

In the following sections, you'll try out the essential formatting techniques that every Excel guru loves. They include:

- **The Format Painter,** which provides a quick and dirty way to transfer formatting from one cell to another.
- **Styles,** which let you standardize your favorite formatting choices so you can use them again.
- **Themes,** which give you a toolkit with a collection of ready-to-use styles that can jazz up the dullest worksheet.

None of these tools are new to Excel 2007, but Microsoft has vastly improved the styles and themes so they look better, do more, and are easier to use. Once you master these three timesavers, you'll have the secret to making great-looking worksheets.

The Format Painter

The Format Painter is a simple yet elegant tool that lets you copy all of a cell's format settings—including fonts, colors, fill, borders, and even the number format—from one cell to another. (Apparently, the Excel team decided that the more accurate label "Format Copier" wasn't nearly as exciting as the name Format Painter.)

To use the Format Painter, follow these steps:

1. **Move to a cell that has the formatting you want to copy.**

   You can use the Format Painter to copy formatting from either one cell or a whole group of cells. For example, you could copy the format from two cells that use two different fill colors, and paste that format to a whole range of new cells. These cells would alternate between the two fill colors. Although this is a powerful trick, in most cases, it's easiest to copy the format from a single cell.

2. **Choose Home → Clipboard → Format Painter to switch into "format painting" mode.**

   The pointer changes so that it now includes a paintbrush icon, indicating Excel is ready to copy the format.

3. **Click the cell where you want to apply the format.**

   The moment you release your mouse button, Excel applies the formatting and your pointer changes back to its normal appearance. If you want to copy the selected format to several cells at once, just drag to select a group of cells, rows, or columns, instead of clicking a single cell.

Excel doesn't let you get too carried away with format painting—as soon as you copy the format to a new cell or selection, you exit format painting mode. If you want to copy the desired format to another cell, you have to backtrack to the cell that has your format, and start over again. However, there's a neat trick you can use if you know you're going to repeatedly apply the same format to a bunch of different cells. Instead of single-clicking the Format Painter button, double-click it. You'll remain in format painting mode until you click the Format Painter button again to switch it off.

TIP

The Format Painter is a good tool for quickly copying formatting, but it's no match for another Excel feature called *styles*. With styles, you can define a group of formatting settings, and then apply them wherever you need them. Best of all, if you change the style after you've created it, Excel automatically updates all cells that you've formatted using that style. Styles are described in the next section.

Styles and Themes

Styles let you create a customized collection of format settings, give that collection a name, and store it in a spreadsheet file. You can then apply these settings anywhere you need them. For example, you could create a style called Great Big Header that uses the Cambria font, pumps up the font size to 46 points, and colors the text bright red.

Every Excel spreadsheet starts off with a collection of prebuilt styles. Microsoft designed these styles with two goals in mind: to give you quick access to most common and practical formatting choices, and to make great looking documents. To take a look at the styles waiting for you, choose Home → Styles → Cell Styles. Figure 5-19 shows the gallery of options that you'll see.

You can apply more than one style to the same cell to get a combination of formatting options. For example, you could use the Currency style to get the right number format, and then pick the Bad style to flag a huge debt with a light red background fill. (Bad is simply the name of a prebuilt style that applies a light red background fill and a dark red font color.) If you apply more than one style and they conflict (for example, both styles use a different background color), the style you applied last takes over.

Styles use Excel's live preview feature, which gives you try-before-you-buy formatting. When you select a group of cells and then hover over one of the styles in the ribbon, your selected cells change instantaneously to reflect that style. Run your

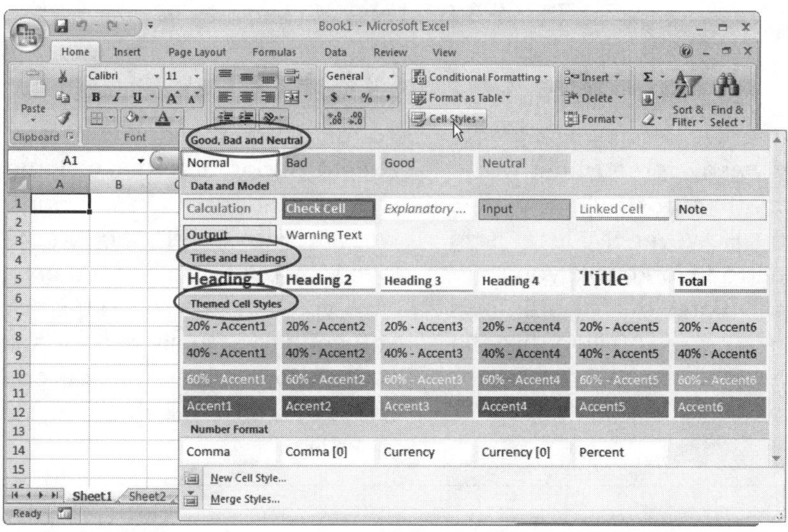

Figure 5-19. Excel's built-in styles are divided into separate categories according to how you might use them. The "Good, Bad, and Neutral" category lets you separate the good news from the bad using the carefully shaded versions of the universal colors red, yellow, and green. The "Titles and Headings" category adds border formatting (page 160) to make great titles. And the Themed Cell Styles category gives you a range of differently colored, differently shaded cells that are chosen to match harmoniously with one another based on the current workbook theme (page 170).

mouse over the different style options, and you see a quickly changing series of different formatting choices. To actually apply a style, click it.

TIP

Longtime Excel users will recognize the Number Format group of styles shown at the bottom of Figure 5-19. These styles are the only ones that Excel included in previous versions. The Number Format styles simply apply a different number format (page 137), like Currency, Percentage, and so on. They don't change other appearance details. However, they're still useful. For example, you could use Currency style for all the dollar figures in your worksheet. Then, at some later point, you could modify that style to set a different currency symbol, alignment, or number of decimal places. This one change updates every cell that uses the Currency style—in this case, all the prices across your entire worksheet.

TIMESAVING TIP

Turning Off Live Preview

Most of the time, live preview is a great way for wishy-washy spreadsheet writers to see formatting possibilities without committing. However, if you're using a heavily formatted workbook, you might find the live preview feature slows you down when you're scrolling through a lot of options. In this case, it might make sense to turn off live preview.

To turn it off, choose Office button → Excel Options, and then pick the Popular section. Under the "Top options for working with Excel", turn off the Enable Live Preview setting, and then click OK. Now you can zip around the ribbon, but you need to actually *apply* a formatting change (by clicking the appropriate button in the ribbon) before you see what it looks like.

Themes: A package of styles

As nice as the prebuilt styles are, they don't suit everyone. For example, the standard style colors favor subdued shades of red, gray, brown, and green, which make sense for the company accountant but aren't the most exciting choice for an urban hipster. To jazz things up, you can choose a different *theme* that features livelier colors. When you do, your entire worksheet gets an immediate facelift—you don't need to track down each individual cell and reformat it.

Technically, a theme is a combination of three ingredients:

- **Fonts.** Every theme has one font that's used for headings and another one that's used for everything else. These two fonts might be different sizes of the same typeface, or two complementary typefaces.
- **Colors.** Every theme has a palette of 12 complementary colors. The cell styles that appear under the Themed Cell Styles heading (see Figure 5-19) draw upon these colors for text and background fills. Best of all, these colors don't reflect the preferences of Cheeto-munching programmers. Instead, bona fide artsy types chose them—in this case, professional designers on the Microsoft payroll.
- **Effects.** Effects are fine alterations that pretty up shapes and other hand-drawn graphics that you can create with Excel's drawing tools. If you don't have any shapes on your worksheet, the effect settings don't do anything.

To choose a theme, choose Page Layout → Themes → Themes to see a gallery of choices (Figure 5-20).

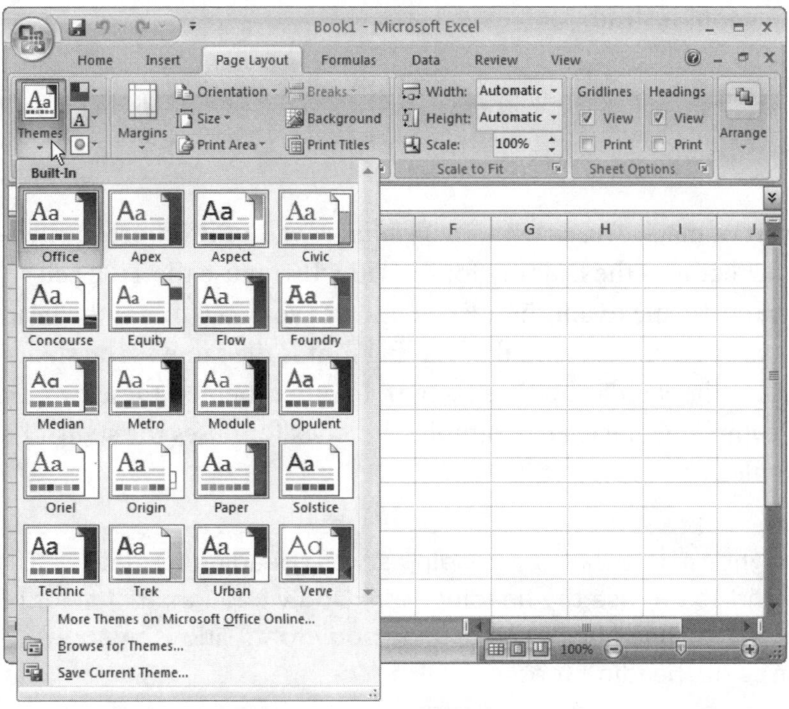

Figure 5-20. Every workbook begins using the crowd-pleasing Office theme, but you have a long list of other options. You can even search Microsoft's Office Online Web site for hot new themes. As you hover over a new theme, your workbook adjusts itself automatically, thanks to the magic of Excel's live preview feature.

The secret to understanding themes is realizing how changing the theme affects your worksheet. In other words, how does Excel apply the theme's fonts, colors, and effects to your worksheet? The following sections break it down.

Fonts. Every workbook has a standard *body font* that it uses in every cell. Excel uses this standard font unless you explicitly choose a different font using the ribbon's Home → Font section or the Format Cells dialog box.

In a brand new Excel spreadsheet, everything you type starts out in easy-on-the-eyes 11-point Calibri font. If you apply a new theme, you get a new standard font. For example, switch to the traditionally styled Apex theme, and you'll get the elegant Book Antiqua font instead.

NOTE

All the fonts used in Excel themes are installed as part of Microsoft Office.

The same sort of magic works with the *heading font*, but it's more limited—in fact, the only style that uses the heading font is Title. If you use the Title cell style and switch from one theme to another, Excel updates your cell to use the heading font from that style. In some themes, the heading font is the same as the standard body font (as it is for the standard Office theme). In other themes, these two fonts are different, but complementary. For example, the Apex font uses the stylish Lucida Sans font for all titles.

NOTE

You might assume that the heading styles (Heading 1, Heading 2, Heading 3, and so on) use the heading font. Oddly enough, that's not how it works. All the heading styles use the body font. Title is the only style that uses the heading font.

If you're feeling a bit reckless, you can override the default font that Excel uses for all new workbooks. To override it, select Office button → Excel Options, and then choose the Popular section. Under the "When creating new workbooks" heading is a "Use this font" and a "Font size" setting where you can set the standard font and font size. Ordinarily, the default font isn't set to a specific font at all—instead, it's set to the special value "Body Font." This tells Excel to apply the standard font from the current theme. Usually, this is the choice you want because it lets you quickly adapt your entire spreadsheet to a theme of your choosing.

Colors. Every theme relies on 12 key colors. When you move from one theme to another, Excel swaps in the new set of colors. Excel alters any place where you've used the 12 theme colors. However, *other* colors aren't affected.

NOTE

Although there are only 12 base colors in a theme, Excel varies the saturation of the color to make it bolder or lighter, based on the style you use. For example, the Office theme includes a steel blue color that you can use at full strength (with the style named Accent 1), or lighten to a faint gray-blue mist (with the style named 20% - Accent 1).

To make this system a bit clearer, imagine a designer runs amok, formatting cells with different background fills. Some of these cells are filled with theme colors, while others are filled with custom colors. (Figure 5-21 shows the difference.) When you switch themes, the cells that have the theme colors are changed, while the other cells aren't.

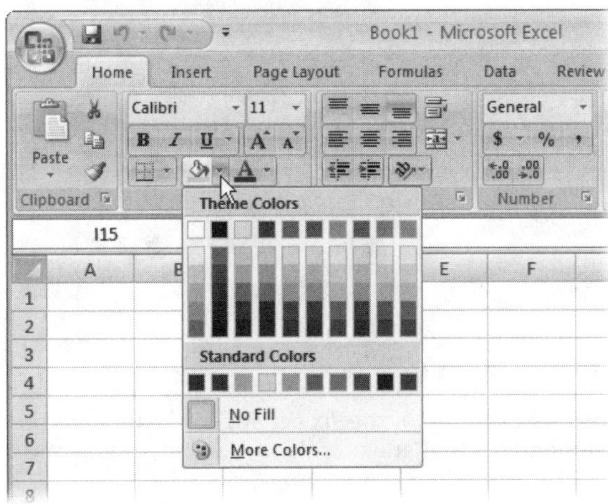

Figure 5-21. When you set the background fill in a cell, you can pick one of the theme colors (at different saturations), you can use a standard color (which gives you the standard red-green-blue lineup), or you can click More Colors to pick a custom color of your own design. You have the same choices when picking the foreground color for your text.

TIP

You're always better off using the theme colors rather than picking a new custom color. That way you can give your workbook a facelift by switching from one theme to another, and the colors still match. On the other hand, if you choose custom colors that look nice with a specific theme, they're likely to clash horribly when you change to another theme.

Experienced Excel workers rarely waste time picking background and foreground colors out of the ribbon. Instead, they use styles. Any time you use one of the styles from the Themed Cell Styles category (Home → Styles → Cell Styles; see Figure 5-19), you're applying a theme-specific color. As a result, if you pick another theme, all the themed cell styles change to use the new color.

The theme system works well because each color in a theme plays a specific role. In other words, some colors are intended for text, while others are designed to play the role of a complementary background; a few more add eye-catching accents. To see the intended purpose of each color, hover over it in the ribbon (Figure 5-22).

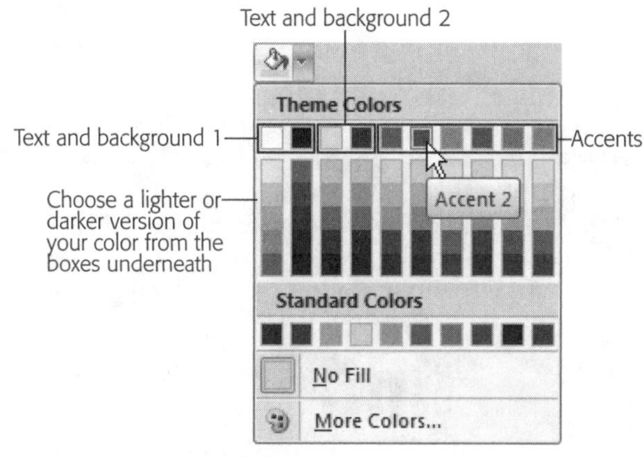

Figure 5-22. Here, the mouse is over one of the six accent colors that are present in every theme. You can also choose from four colors that are intended for standard text and background fills (on the left).

Effects. Effects are the simplest part of any theme because Excel applies them with no work on your part (all you need to do is switch themes, and then the Effects kick in). Excel automatically applies effects to any graphics you've created.

VIEWING AND PRINTING WORKSHEETS

6

- Controlling Your View
- Printing
- Controlling Pagination

THE PREVIOUS CHAPTERS HAVE GIVEN YOU ALL THE TOOLS you need to create nicely formatted worksheets. While this is all well and good, these features can quickly bury you in an avalanche of data. If you want to see more than one part of your workbook at once, or if you want an overview of the entire worksheet, then you have to seize control of Excel's viewing features.

These features include zooming (which lets you magnify cells or just fit more information into your Excel window), panes (which let you see more than one part of a worksheet at once), and freezing (which lets you keep certain cells visible at all times). This chapter teaches you how to use all these tools, and how to store a custom view so your spreadsheet looks just the way you want it.

No matter what your worksheets look like on a screen, sometimes the best way to review them is in print. The second half of this chapter tackles printing your worksheets. You'll learn Excel's basic printing options and a few tricks that can help you preview page breaks and make sure large amounts of data get divided the way you want.

Controlling Your View

So far, most of the worksheets in this book have included only a small amount of data. But as you cram your worksheets with dozens of columns, and hundreds or even thousands of rows, editing becomes much trickier. The most challenging problems are keeping track of where you are in an ocean of information and making sure the data you want stays visible. Double that if you have multiple large worksheets in one workbook.

The following sections introduce the basic tools you can use to view your data, along with a few tips for managing large worksheets.

Zooming

Excel's zoom feature lets you control how much data you'll see in the window. When you *reduce* the zoom percentage—say from 100 percent to 10 percent—Excel shrinks your individual cells, letting you see more of them at once, which also makes it harder to read the data. Very small zoom percentages are ideal for looking at the overall layout of a worksheet. When you *increase* the zoom percentage—say from

100 percent to 200 percent—Excel magnifies your cells, letting you see more detail but fewer cells. Larger zoom percentages are good for editing.

NOTE

Excel lets you zoom in to 400 percent and out all the way to 10 percent.

You can most easily adjust the zoom percent by using the zoom slider in the bottom-right part of the status bar. The zoom slide also displays the current zoom percentage. But if you want to specify the exact zoom percentage by hand (say, 142 percent), then you can choose View → Zoom → Zoom. A Zoom dialog box appears (Figure 6-1).

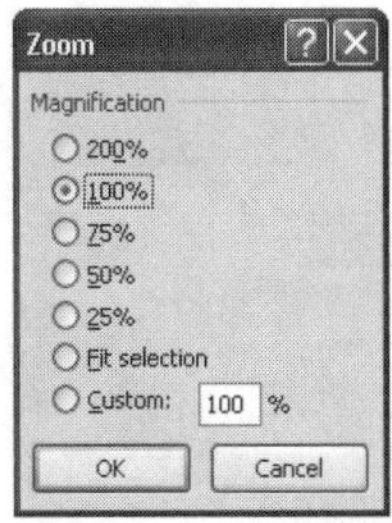

Figure 6-1. Left: Using the Zoom dialog box, you can select a preset zoom percentage or, in the Custom box, type in your own percentage.

Right: But using the Zoom slider is almost always faster than making frequent trips to the Zoom dialog box.

The standard zoom setting is 100 percent, although other factors like the size of the font you're using and the size and resolution of your computer screen help determine how many cells fit into Excel's window. As a rule of thumb, every time you double the zoom, Excel cuts in half the number of rows you can see. Thus, if you can see 20 rows at 100 percent, then you'll see 10 rows at 200 percent.

NOTE

Changing the zoom affects how your data appears in the Excel window, but it won't have any effect on how your data is printed or calculated.

You can also zoom in on a range of cells. When your data extends beyond the edges of your monitor, this handy option lets you shrink a portion to fit your screen. Conversely, if you've zoomed out to get a bird's eye view of all your data, and you want to swoop in on a particular section, Excel lets you expand a portion to fit your screen. To zoom in on a group of cells, first select some cells (Figure 6-2), and then choose View → Zoom → Zoom to Selection (Figure 6-3). (You can perform this same trick by highlighting some cells, opening the Zoom dialog box, and then choosing "Fit selection.") Make sure you select a large section of the worksheet—if you select a small group, you'll end up with a truly jumbo-sized zoom.

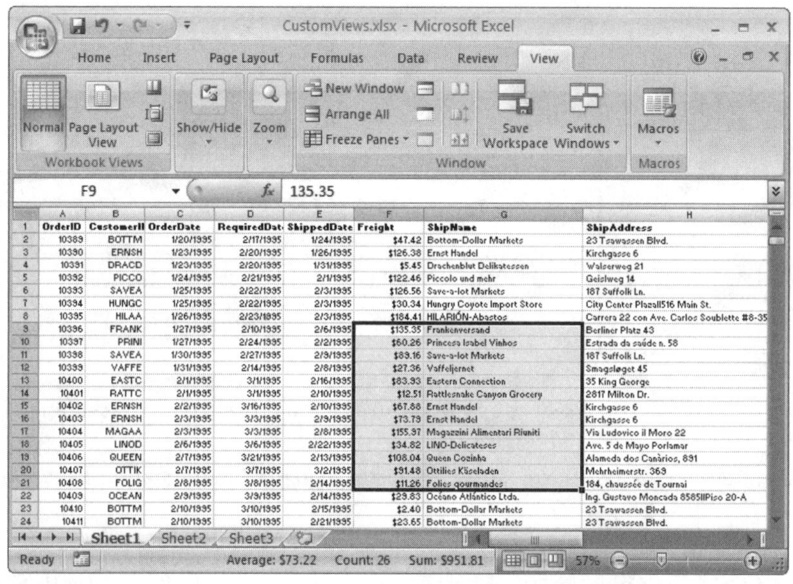

Figure 6-2. To magnify a range of cells, select them, as shown here, and then choose View → Zoom → Zoom to Selection to have Excel expand the range to fill the entire window, as shown in Figure 6-3.

TIP

If you're using a mouse with a scroll wheel, you can zoom with the wheel. Just hold down the Ctrl key, and roll the scroll wheel up (to zoom in) or down (to zoom out).

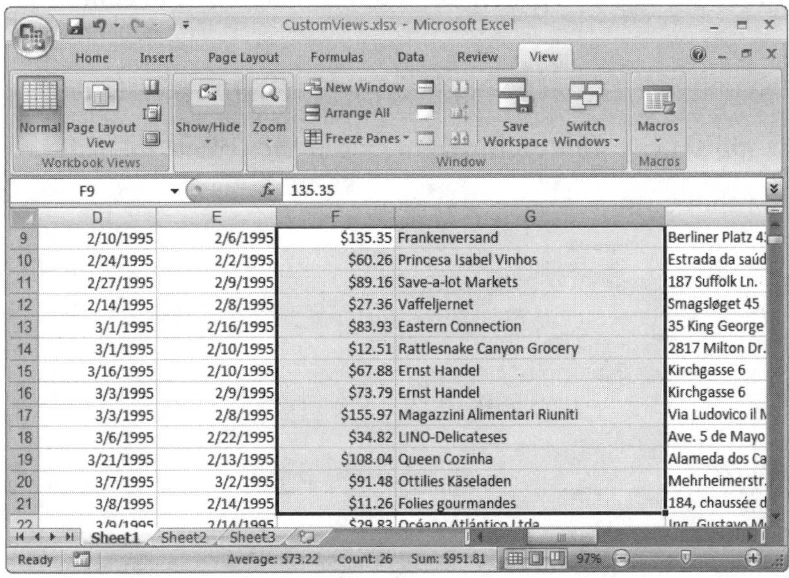

Figure 6-3. The zoom slider (lower-right corner) shows that Excel automatically zoomed your data from 57 percent (to 97 percent in this figure).

Viewing Distant Parts of a Spreadsheet at Once

Zooming is an excellent way to survey a large expanse of data or focus on just the important cells, but it won't help if you want to simultaneously view cells that aren't near each other. For example, if you want to focus on both row 1 and row 138 at the same time, then zooming won't help. Instead, try splitting your Excel window into multiple *panes*—separate frames that each provide a different view of the same worksheet. You can split a worksheet into two or four panes, depending on how many different parts you want to see at once. When you split a worksheet, each pane contains an identical replica of the entire worksheet. When you make a change to the worksheet in one pane, Excel automatically applies the same change in the other panes. The beauty of panes is that you can look at different parts of the same worksheet at once.

You can split a window horizontally or vertically (or both). When you want to compare different *rows* in the same worksheet, use a horizontal split. To compare different *columns* in the same worksheet, use a vertical split. And if you want to be completely crazy and see four different parts of your worksheet at once, then you can use a horizontal and a vertical split—but that's usually too confusing to be much help.

Excel gives you two ways to split the windows. Here's the easy way:

1. **Find the splitter controls on the right side of the screen.**

   Figure 6-4 shows you where to find them.

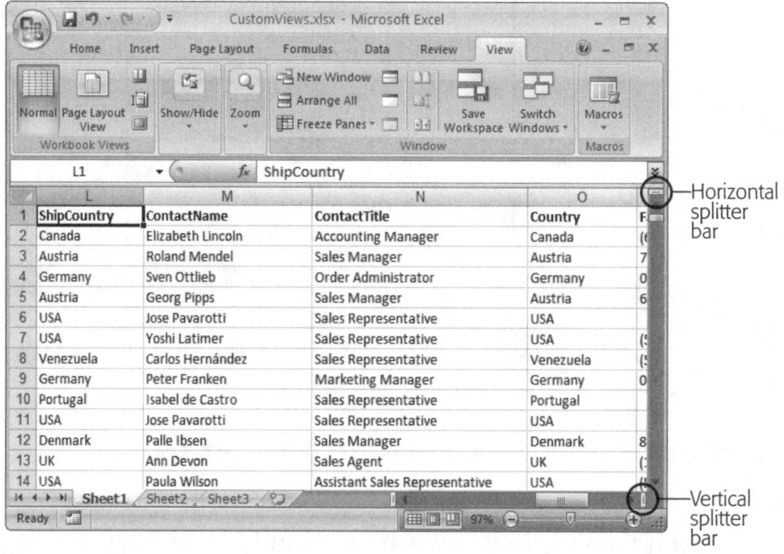

Figure 6-4. Every Excel window contains both horizontal and vertical splitter controls.

2. **Drag either control to split the window into two panes. As you drag, Excel displays a gray bar showing where it'll divide the window. Release the splitter control when you're happy with the layout. (At this point, you don't need to worry about whether you can actually view the data you want to compare; you're simply splitting up the window.)**

   If you want to split the window into an upper and lower portion, drag the horizontal control down to the location where you want to split the window.

   If you want to split the window into a left and right portion, drag the vertical control leftwards—to the location where you want to split the window.

NOTE

If for any reason you *do* want to split the window into four panes, use both controls. The order you follow isn't important.

If you don't like the layout you've created, simply move the splitter bars by dragging them just as you did before.

3. **Within each pane, scroll to the cells you want to see.**

   For example, if you have a 100-row table that you split horizontally in order to compare the top five rows and the bottom five, scroll to the top of the upper pane, and then scroll to the bottom of the lower pane. (Again, the two panes are replicas of each other; Excel is just showing you different parts of the same worksheet.)

Using the scroll bars in panes can take some getting used to. When the window is split in two panes, Excel synchronizes scrolling between both panes in *one direction*. For example, if you split the window into top and bottom halves, Excel gives you just one *horizontal* scroll bar (at the bottom of the screen), which controls both panes (Figure 6-5). Thus, when you scroll to the left or right, Excel moves both panes horizontally. On the other hand, Excel gives you separate *vertical* scroll bars for each pane, letting you independently move up and down within each pane.

TIP

If you want the data in one pane—for example, column titles—to remain in place, you can freeze that pane. The next section tells you how.

The reverse is true with a vertical split; in this case, you get one vertical scroll bar and two horizontal bars, and Excel synchronizes both panes when you move up or down. With four panes, life gets a little more complicated. In this case, when you scroll left or right, the frame that's just above or just below the current frame moves, too. When you scroll up or down, the frame that's to the left or to the right moves with you. Try it out.

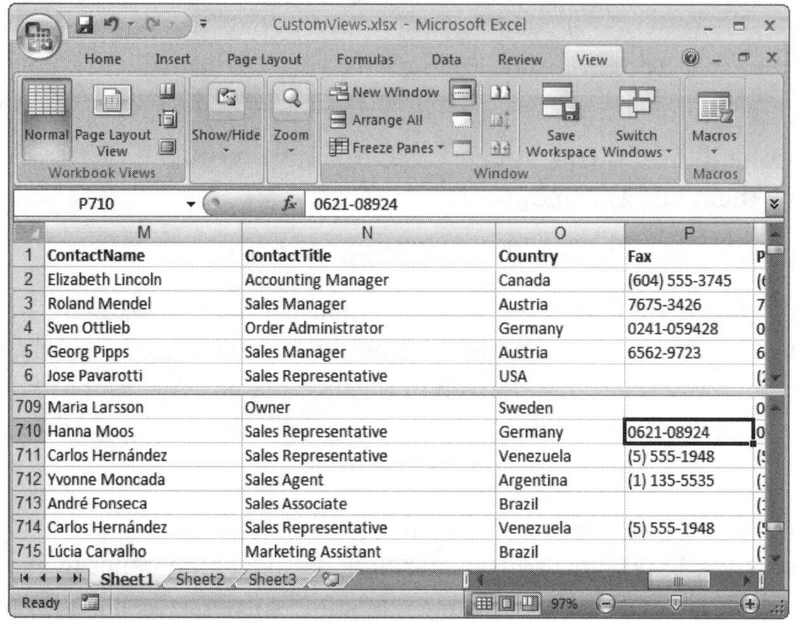

Figure 6-5. Here you can see the data in rows 1 through 6 and rows 709 through 715 at the same time. As you move from column to column, both panes move in sync, letting you see, for instance, the phone number information in both panes at once. (You can scroll up or down separately in each pane.)

NOTE

If you want to remove your panes, then just drag the splitter bars back to the edges of the window, or double-click it.

You can also create panes by using the ribbon command View → Window → Split. When you do, Excel carves the window into four equal panes. You can change the pane sizes as described above, or use View → Window → Split again to return to normal.

NOTE

If you use Excel's worksheet navigation tools—like the Go To and Find commands—*all* your panes move to the newly found spot. For example, if you use the Find command in one pane to scroll to a new cell, the other panes display the same cell.

GEM IN THE ROUGH

Filling the Screen with Cells

If you really want to see the maximum number of cells at once, Excel provides a little-known feature that strips away the ribbon, the formula bar, and all other extraneous screen elements, making more room for cells. To make the switch, choose View → Workbook View → Full Screen. To return things to the way they were, right-click anywhere on the worksheet grid, and then choose Close Full Screen.

Most people find that Full Screen mode is just a little too drastic. Another good option is to collapse the ribbon, which reclaims a significant portion of screen real estate. To do so, in the ribbon, double-click any tab title. Excel hides the ribbon surface, but leaves just the tab titles above your worksheet. Even when the ribbon is collapsed, you can still use it—just click a tab title (which pops that tab back into view), and then click the command you want. The ribbon disappears again as soon as you're done. If you're an unredeemed keyboard lover, then you can use the ribbon in the same way whether it's collapsed or expanded. Just press Alt, and then follow the KeyTips (page 7). And if you get tired of the collapsed ribbon, you can double-click any tab title or press Ctrl+F1 to show the full ribbon once again.

Freezing Columns or Rows

Excel has another neat trick up its sleeve to help you manage large worksheets: *freezing*. Freezing is a simpler way to make sure a specific set of rows or columns remains visible at all times. When you freeze data, it remains fixed in place in the Excel window, even as you move to another location in the worksheet in a different pane. For example, say you want to keep visible the first row that contains column titles. When you freeze that row, you can always tell what's in each column—even when you've scrolled down several screenfuls. Similarly, if your first column holds identifying labels, you may want to freeze it so that when you scroll off to the right, you don't lose track of what you're looking at.

TIP

Excel lets you print out worksheets with a particular row or column fixed in place. Page 205 tells you how.

You can freeze rows at the top of your worksheet, or columns at the left of your worksheet, but Excel does limit your freezing options in a few ways:

- **You can freeze rows or columns only in groups.** That means you can't freeze column A and C without freezing column B. (You can, of course, freeze just one row or column.)
- **Freezing always starts at column A (if you're freezing columns) or row 1 (if you're freezing rows).** That means that if you freeze row 13, Excel also freezes all the rows above it (1 through 12) at the top of your worksheet.
- **If a row or column isn't visible and you freeze it, you can't see it until you unfreeze it.** For example, if you scroll down so that row 100 appears at the top of the worksheet grid, and then freeze the top 100 rows, you can't see rows 1 to 99 anymore. This may be the effect you want, or it may be a major annoyance.

NOTE

As far as Excel is concerned, frozen rows and columns are a variation on panes (described earlier). When you freeze data, Excel creates a vertical pane for columns or a horizontal pane for rows. It then fixes that pane so you can't scroll through it.

To freeze a row or set of rows at the top of your worksheet, just follow these steps:

1. **Make sure the row or rows you want to freeze are visible and at the top of your worksheet.**

   For example, if you want to freeze rows 2 and 3 in place, make sure they're visible at the top of your worksheet. Remember, rows are frozen starting at row 1. That means that if you scroll down so that row 1 isn't visible, and you freeze row 2 and row 3 at the top of your worksheet, then Excel also freezes row 1—and keeps it hidden so you can't scroll up to see it.

2. **Move to the first row you want *unfrozen*, and then move left to column A.**

   At this point, you're getting into position so that Excel knows where to create the freeze.

3. **Select View → Freeze Panes → Freeze Panes.**

   Excel splits the worksheet, but instead of displaying a gray bar (as it does when you create panes), it uses a solid black line to divide the frozen rows from the rest of the worksheet. As you scroll down the worksheet, the frozen rows remain in place.

   To unfreeze the rows, just select View → Freeze Panes → Unfreeze Panes.

Freezing columns works the same way:

1. **Make sure the column or columns you want to freeze are visible and at the left of your worksheet.**

   For example, if you want to freeze columns B and C in place, make sure they're visible at the edge of your worksheet. Remember, columns are frozen starting at column A. That means that if you scroll over so that column A isn't visible, and you freeze columns B and C on the left side of your worksheet, Excel also freezes column A—and keeps it hidden so you can't scroll over to see it.

2. **Move to the first column you want *unfrozen*, and then move up to row 1.**

   At this point, you're getting into position so that Excel knows where to create the freeze.

3. **Select View → Freeze Panes → Freeze Panes.**

   Excel splits the worksheet, but instead of displaying a gray bar (as it does when you create panes), Excel uses a solid black line to divide the frozen columns from the rest of the worksheet. As you scroll across the worksheet, the frozen columns remain in place.

   To unfreeze the columns, select View → Freeze Panes → Unfreeze Panes.

TIP

If you're freezing just the first row or the leftmost column, then there's no need to go through this whole process. Instead, you can use the handy View → Freeze Panes → Freeze Top Row or View → Freeze Panes → Freeze First Column.

You can also freeze columns and rows *at the same time*, which is useful when you have identifying information that you need to keep visible both on the left and the top of your worksheet. Figure 6-6 shows an example.

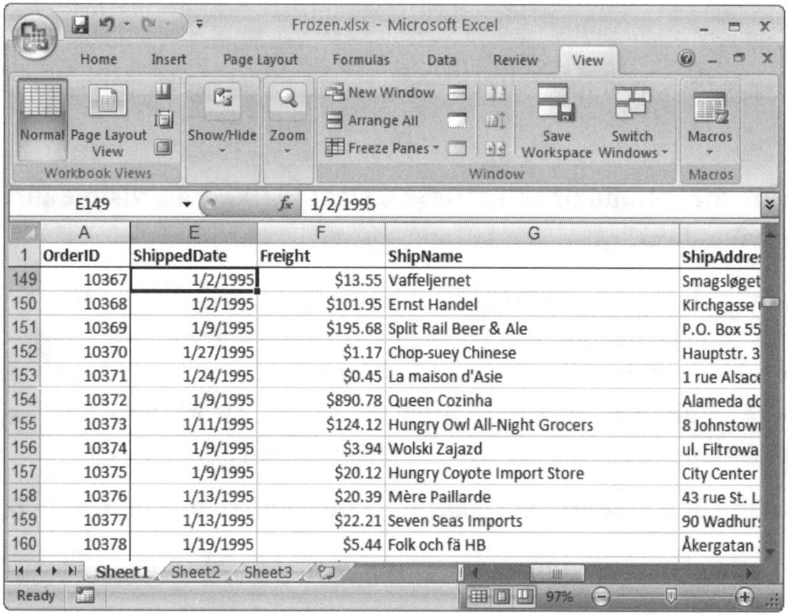

Figure 6-6. Here, both column A and row 1 are frozen, and thus always remain visible. The easiest way to create these frozen regions is to scroll to the top of the worksheet, position the active cell at B2, and choose View → Freeze Panes → Freeze Panes. Excel then automatically freezes the rows above and the columns to the left in separate panes.

TIP

You can also create a horizontal or vertical pane by using one of the splitter bars, and then freezing that pane. Just drag the splitter bar to the appropriate position, and select View → Freeze Panes → Freeze Panes.

Hiding Data

In some cases your problem isn't that you need to keep data visible, but that you need to *hide* it. For example, say you have a column of numbers that you need only for a calculation but don't want to see when you edit or print the sheet. Excel provides the perfect solution: *hiding* rows and columns. Hiding doesn't delete information, it just temporarily tucks it out of view. You can restore hidden information any time you need it.

Technically, hiding a row or column is just a special type of resizing. When you instruct Excel to hide a column, it simply shrinks the column down to a width of 0. Similarly, when you hide a row, Excel compresses the row height.

You can hide data a few ways:

- To hide a column, right-click the column header (the letter button on the top of the column), and then choose Hide. Or, put your cursor in any row in that column, and then select Home → Cells → Format → Hide & Unhide → Hide Columns.
- To hide a row, right-click the row header (the number button at the left of the row), and then choose Hide. Or, put your cursor in any column in that row, and then select Home → Cells → Format → Hide & Unhide → Hide Rows.
- To hide multiple rows or columns, just select all the ones you want to disappear before choosing Hide.

To unhide a column or row, select the *range* that includes the hidden cells. For example, if you hid column B, select columns A and C by dragging over the numeric row headers. Then choose Home → Cells → Format → Hide & Unhide → Unhide Columns (or Unhide Rows). Or just right-click the selection, and then choose Unhide. Either way, Excel makes the missing columns or rows visible and then highlights them so you can see which information you've restored.

TIP

To unhide all columns (or rows) in a worksheet, select the entire worksheet (by clicking the square in the top-left corner of the grid), and then select Home → Cells → Format → Hide & Unhide → Unhide Columns (or Unhide Rows).

Forgetting that you've hidden data is as easy as forgetting where you put your keys. While Excel doesn't include a hand-clapper to help you locate your cells, it does indicate that some of your row numbers or column letters are missing, as shown in Figure 6-7.

	A	O	P	Q	R	
1	OrderID	Country	Fax	Phone	PostalCode	Re
2	10389	Canada	(604) 555-3745	(604) 555-4729	T2F 8M4	BC
3	10390	Austria	7675-3426	7675-3425	8010	
4	10391	Germany	0241-059428	0241-039123	52066	
5	10392	Austria	6562-9723	6562-9722	5020	
6	10393	USA		(208) 555-8097	83720	ID
7	10394	USA	(503) 555-2376	(503) 555-6874	97827	OR
8	10395	Venezuela	(5) 555-1948	(5) 555-1340	5022	Tác

Sheet1 Sheet2 Sheet3

Figure 6-7. This worksheet jumps directly from column A to column O, which tells you that B through N are hidden.

Saving View Settings

If you regularly tweak things like the zoom, visible columns, and the number of panes, you can easily spend more time adjusting your worksheet than editing it. Fortunately, Excel lets you save your view settings with *custom views*. Custom views let you save a combination of view settings in a workbook. You can store as many custom views as you want. When you want to use a particular view you've created, simply select it from a list and Excel applies your settings.

Custom views are particularly useful when you frequently switch views for different tasks, like editing and printing. For example, if you like to *edit* with several panes open and all your data visible, but you like to *print* your data in one pane with some columns hidden, custom views let you quickly switch between the two layouts.

Note

You can't save a custom view for one worksheet and apply it to another.

Custom views can save the following settings:

- The location of the active cell. (In other words, your position in the worksheet. For example, if you've scrolled to the bottom of a 65,000-row spreadsheet, then the custom view returns you to the active cell in a hurry.)
- The currently selected cell (or cells).
- Column widths and row heights, including hidden columns and rows.
- Frozen panes (page 183).
- View settings, like the zoom percentage, which you set using the ribbon's View tab.
- Print settings, like the page margins.
- Filter settings, which affect what information Excel shows in a data list (see Chapter 8).

To create a custom view, follow these steps:

1. **Adjust an open worksheet for your viewing pleasure.**

   Set the zoom, hide or freeze columns and rows, and move to the place in the worksheet where you want to edit.

2. **Choose View → Workbook Views → Custom View.**

   The Custom Views dialog box appears, showing you a list of all the views defined for this workbook. If you haven't created any yet, this list is empty.

3. **Click the Add button.**

   The Add View dialog box appears.

4. **Type in a name for your custom view.**

   You can use any name, but consider something that'll remind you of your view settings (like "50 percent Zoom"), or the task that this view is designed for (like "All Data at a Glance"). A poor choice is one that won't mean anything to you later ("View One" or "Zoom with a View").

The Add View dialog box also gives you the chance to specify print settings or hidden rows and columns that Excel *shouldn't* save as part of the view. Turn off the appropriate checkboxes if you don't want to retain this information. Say you hide column A, but you clear the "Hidden rows, columns, and filter settings" checkbox because you don't want to save this as part of the view. The next time you restore the view, Excel won't make any changes to the visibility of column A. If it's hidden, it stays hidden; if it's visible, it stays visible. On the other hand, if you want column A to always be hidden when you apply your new custom view, then keep the "Hidden rows, columns, and filter settings" checkbox turned on when you save it.

After you've typed your view name and dealt with the inclusion settings, click OK to create your new view. Excel adds your view to the list.

5. **Click Close.**

   You're now ready to use your shiny new view or add another (readjust your settings and follow this procedure again).

Applying your views is a snap. Simply select View → Workbook Views → Custom Views to return to the Custom Views dialog box (Figure 6-8), and then select your view from the list and click Show. Because Excel stores views with the workbook, they'll always be available when you open the file, even if you take that file to another computer.

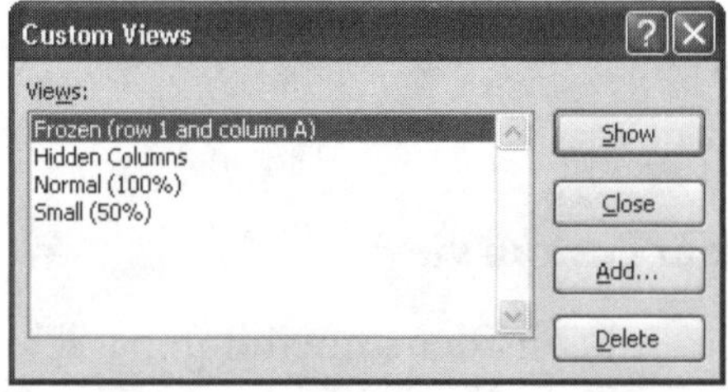

Figure 6-8. You can use this dialog box to show or delete existing views or to create new ones (click Add, and then follow the procedure from step 4, above).

TIP

For some examples of custom views in action, visit this book's "Missing CD" page at *www.missingmanuals.com* and download CustomViews.xls, a sample spreadsheet with an array of custom views already set up.

Printing

Printing in Excel is pretty straightforward—as long as your spreadsheet fits on a normal 8.5 × 11-inch piece of paper. If you're one of the millions of spreadsheet owners who don't belong to that club, welcome to the world of Multiple Page Disorder: the phenomenon in which pages and pages of apparently unrelated and noncontiguous columns start spewing from your printer. Fortunately, Excel comes with a slew of print-tweaking tools designed to help you control what you're printing. First off, though, it helps to understand the default settings Excel uses when you click the print button.

NOTE

You can change most of the settings listed; this is just a list of what happens if you *don't* adjust any settings before printing a spreadsheet.

- In the printout, Excel uses all the formatting characteristics you've applied to the cells, including fonts, fills, and borders. However, Excel's gridlines, row headers, and column headers *don't* appear in the printout.
- If your data is too long (all the rows won't fit on one page) or too wide (all the columns won't fit), Excel prints the data on multiple pages. If your data is both too long *and* too wide, Excel prints in the following order: all the rows for the first set of columns that fit on a printed page, then all the rows for the next set of columns that fit, and so on (this is known as "down, then over"). When printing on multiple pages, Excel never prints *part* of an individual column or row.
- Excel prints your file in color if you use colors and you've got a color printer.
- Excel sets margins to 0.75 inches at the top and bottom of the page, and 0.7 inches on the left and right sides of the page. Ordinarily, Excel doesn't include headers and footers (so you don't see any page numbers).
- Excel doesn't include hidden rows and columns in the printout.

How to Print an Excel File

Printing a worksheet is similar to printing in any other Windows application. Follow these steps:

1. **Choose Office button → Print.**

   The Print dialog box appears, as shown in Figure 6-9.

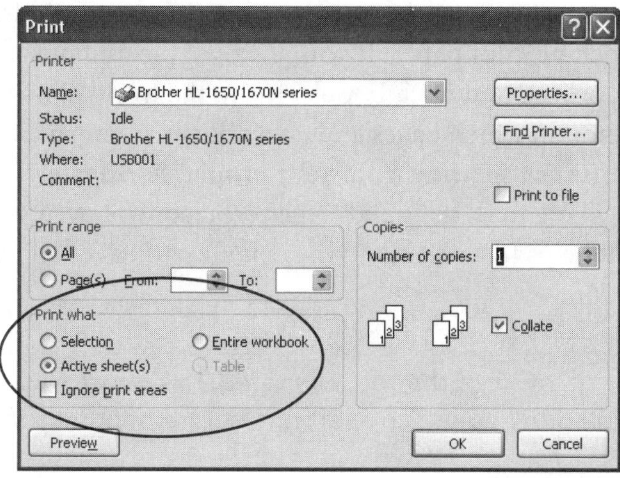

Figure 6-9. The Excel Print dialog box looks more or less like the Print dialog box in other Windows applications. The key difference is the "Print what" box, which lets you choose to print the current worksheet, all worksheets, or a selected range of cells.

2. **Select a printer from the drop-down list.**

   When the Print dialog box first appears, Excel automatically selects your default printer. If you have more than one printer installed, and you want to use a different printer, then you need to select this printer from the Name pull-down menu. You can also adjust printer settings by clicking the Properties button. Every printer has its own set of options here, but common Properties settings include print quality and paper handling (like double-sided printing for those lucky enough to have a printer that supports it).

3. **Choose what you want to print from the "Print what" box.**

   The standard option, "Active sheet(s)," prints the current worksheet. If you select "Entire workbook," Excel prints all the worksheets in your file. Finally, to print out just a portion of a worksheet, select a range of cells, columns, or rows, and then choose Selection.

   If you've set a print area on your worksheet (see the box "Printing Parts of a Spreadsheet" on page 194), you can choose "Ignore print areas" to print the full worksheet, not just the print area.

4. **Use the "Print range" box to limit the number of pages that Excel prints.**

   If you choose All in the "Print range" box, Excel prints as many pages as it needs to output all the data you've chosen in the "Print what" box. Alternately, you can choose a range of pages using the Page(s) option. For example, you can choose to print only the first three pages by printing pages from 1 to 3. You can also print just the fourth page by printing from 4 to 4.

NOTE

In order to use the "Print range" box effectively, you need to know how many pages you need to print your worksheet and what data will appear on each page. Excel's Page Layout view (page 195), is just the ticket.

5. **Use the "Number of copies" box to print multiple copies of your data.**

   If you want to print more than one identical copy of your data, change the "Number of copies" text box accordingly. The Collate option determines whether Excel duplicates each page separately. For example, if you print 10 pages and Collate isn't turned on, Excel prints 10 copies of page 1, 10 copies of page 2, and so on. If Collate *is* turned on, Excel prints the entire 10-page document, and then prints out another copy, and so on. You'll still end up with 10 copies of each page, plus, for added convenience, they'll be grouped together.

6. **Click OK to send the spreadsheet to the printer.**

   Excel prints your document using the settings you've selected.

If you're printing a very large worksheet, Excel shows a Printing dialog box for a few seconds as it sends the pages to the printer. If you decide to cancel the printing process—and you're quick enough—you can click the Cancel button in this Printing dialog box to stop the operation. If you don't possess the cat-like reflexes you once did, you can also open your printer queue to cancel the process. Look for your printer icon in the notification area at the bottom-right of your screen, and double-click that icon to open a print window. Then, select the offending print job in the list, and then press Delete (or choose Document → Cancel from the print window's menu). Some printers also provide their own cancel button that lets you stop a print job even after it's left your computer.

GEM IN THE ROUGH

Printing Parts of a Spreadsheet

When working with large worksheets, you'll often want to print only a small portion of your total data. Excel gives you several ways to limit your printout. You can hide the rows or columns you aren't interested in, or you can select the cells you want to print, and, in the Print dialog box's "Print what" box, choose Selection. But if you frequently need to print the same area, you're better off defining and using a *print area*.

A print area designates a portion of your worksheet as the only region that Excel will print. (The one exception is if you choose Selection from the "Print what" box, in which case Excel prints the selected cells, not the print area.) Once you define a print area, Excel retains it until you remove it. That means you can make changes, save, close, and open your spreadsheet, and the same print area remains in place.

To set a print area, select the rows, columns, or group of cells, and then choose Page Layout → Page Setup → Print Area → Set Print Area. The portion of the worksheet that you've highlighted now has a thin dashed outline, indicating that this is the only region Excel will print. You can only have one print area at a time, and setting a new one always clears the previous one. To remove your print area so that you can print the entire worksheet, choose Page Layout → Page Setup → Print Area → Clear Print Area.

Quick Printing

If you know that the currently selected printer is the one you want to use, and you don't want to change any other print settings, you can skip the Print dialog box altogether using the popular (but slightly dangerous) Quick Print feature. Just choose Office button → Print → Quick Print to create an instant printout, with no questions asked.

The Quick Print feature's so commonly used that many Excel experts add it to the Quick Access toolbar so it's always on hand. If you want to do this, hover over the Office button → Print → Quick Print command, right-click it, and then choose Add To Quick Access Toolbar. (The Appendix has more about customizing the Quick Access toolbar.)

Previewing Your Printout

When you're preparing to print that 142-page company budget monstrosity, there's no reason to go in blind. Instead, prudent Excel fans use Page Layout view to check out what their printouts look like *before* they appear on paper. The tool is especially helpful if you've run rampant with formatting, or you want to tweak a variety of page layout settings, and you want to see what the effects will be before clicking Print.

To see the Page Layout view for a worksheet, choose View → Workbook Views → Page Layout View. Or, for an even quicker alternative, use the tiny Page Layout View button in the status bar, which appears immediately to the left of the zoom slider. Either way, you see a nicely formatted preview (Figure 6-10).

How does Page Layout view differ from Normal view? You'll see several differences, including:

- Page Layout view paginates your data. You see exactly what fits on each page, and how many pages your printout requires.
- Page Layout view reveals any headers and footers you've set as part of the page setup. These details don't appear in the Normal worksheet view.
- Page Layout view shows the margins that Excel will use for your pages.

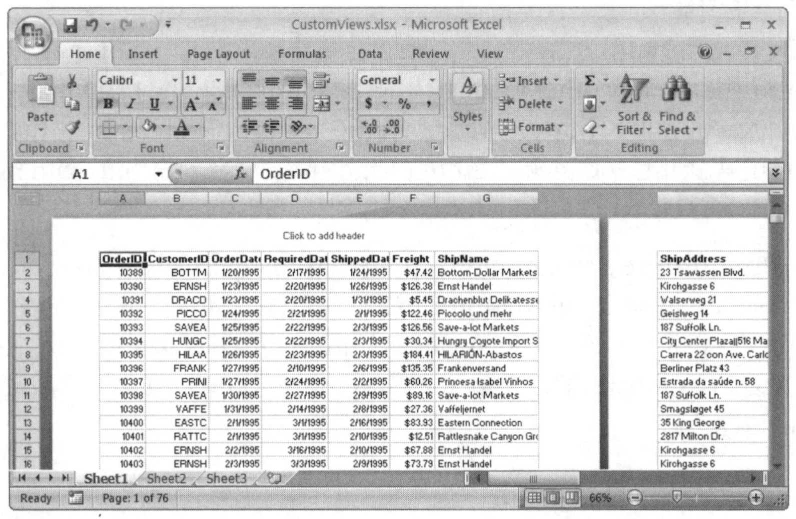

Figure 6-10. The Page Layout view shows the first (and part of the second) page of this worksheet's 76 printed pages. This worksheet has 19 columns, but since they're wider than the width of a single printed page, the first page includes only the leftmost seven columns, as shown here. You can scroll to the right to see the additional columns that'll turn up on other pages, or scroll down to see more rows.

- Page Layout view doesn't show anything that Excel won't print (like the letters at the top of each column). The only exception is the cell gridlines, which are shown to help you move around your worksheet.
- Page Layout view includes a bit of text in the Status bar that tells you where you are, page-wise, in a large spreadsheet. For example, you might see the text "Page: 5 of 26."

NOTE

Don't confuse Page Layout view with an ordinary print preview. A print preview provides a fixed "snapshot" of your printout. You can look, but you can't touch. Page Layout view is vastly better because it shows what your printout will look like *and* it lets you edit data, change margins, set headers and footers, create charts, draw pictures—you get the idea. In fact, you can do everything you do in Normal view mode in Page Layout view. The only difference is you can't squeeze quite as much data into the view at once.

If you aren't particularly concerned with your margin settings, you can hide your margins in Page Layout view so you can fit more information into the Excel window. Figure 6-11 shows you how.

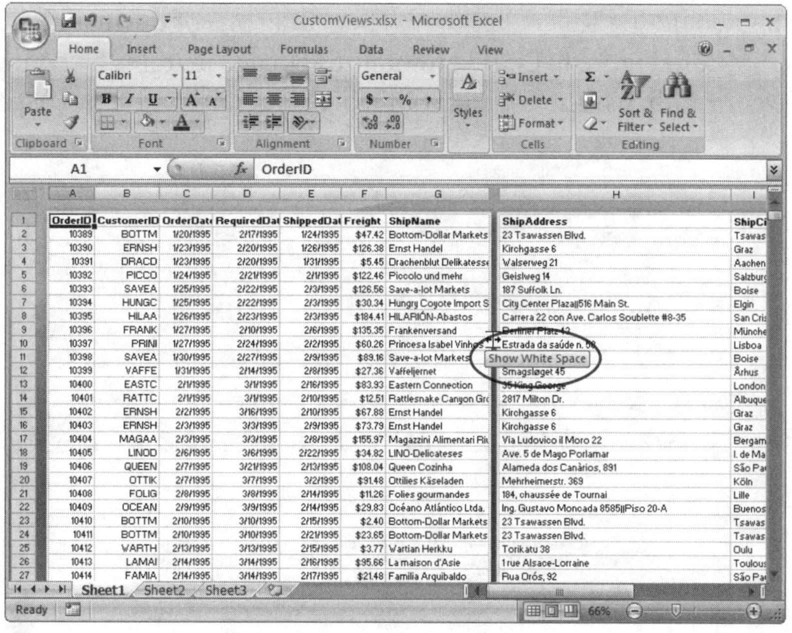

Figure 6-11. Move your mouse between the pages and your mouse pointer changes into this strange two-arrow beast. You can then click to hide the margins in between pages (as shown here), and click again to show them (as shown in Figure 6-10). Either way, you see an exact replica of your printout. The only difference is whether you see the empty margin space.

Here are some of the tasks you may want to perform in Page Layout view:

- If the print preview meets with your approval, choose Office button → Print to send the document to the printer.
- To tweak print settings and see the effect, choose the Page Layout tab in the ribbon and start experimenting. You'll learn more about these settings on page 201.
- To move from page to page, you can use the scroll bar at the side of the window, or you can use the keyboard (like Page Up, Page Down, and the arrow keys).

When you reach the edge of your data, you see shaded pages with the text “Click to add data” superimposed. If you want to add information further down the worksheet, just click one of these pages and start typing.

- To adjust the page margins, first make sure the ruler is visible by turning on the View → Show/Hide → Ruler checkbox. Then, drag one of the margin lines on the ruler, as shown in Figure 6-12. If you want to set page margins by typing in the exact margin width, use the Page Layout tab of the ribbon instead (page 201).

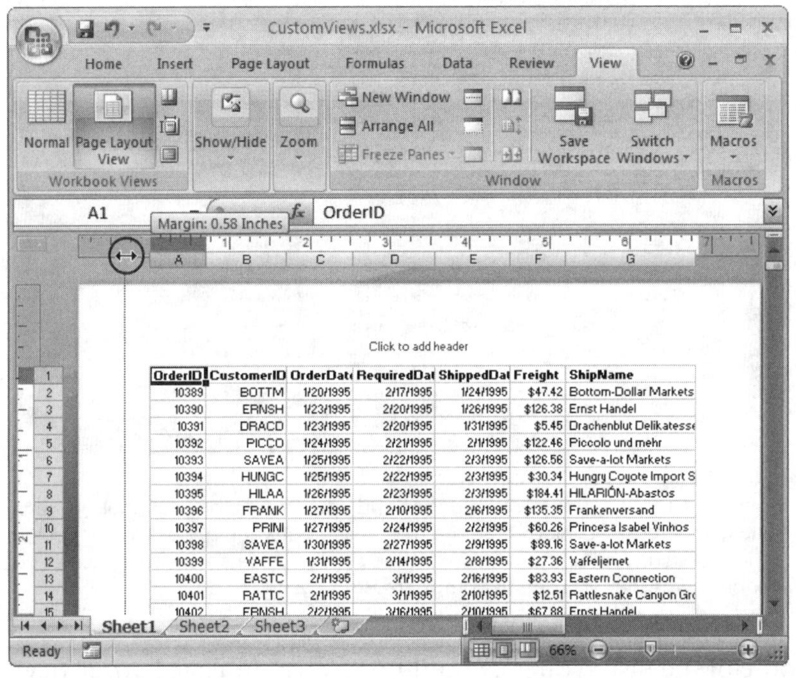

Figure 6-12. The Page Layout view lets you set margins by dragging the margin edge with your mouse. Here, the left margin (circled) is about to be narrowed down to 0.58 inches. If you're also using a header or footer (page 199), make sure you don't drag the page margin above the header or below the footer. If you do, then your header or footer will overlap your worksheet's data.

- When you're ready to return to the Normal worksheet view, choose View → Workbook Views → Normal (or just click the Status bar's tiny Normal View button).

Creating Headers and Footers

A *header* is a bit of text that's printed at the top of every page in your printout. A *footer* is a bit of text that's printed at the bottom of every page. You can use one, both, or neither in a printout.

Ordinarily, every new workbook starts out without a header or footer. However, Page Layout view gives you an easy way to add either one (or both). Just scroll up to the top of any page to create a header (or the bottom to create a footer), and then look for the box with the text "Click to add header" or "Click to add footer". Click inside this box, and you can type the header or footer text you want.

NOTE

You won't see the header or footer boxes if you've drastically compressed your margins. That's because the header and footer don't fit. To get them back, resize the margins so that they're larger. When you're finished adding the header or footer, you can try adjusting the margins again to see just how small you can get them.

Of course, a good header or footer isn't just an ordinary piece of text. Instead, it contains information that changes dynamically, like the file name, current page, or the date you printed it. You can get these pieces of information using specialized header and footer *codes*, which are distinguished by their use of square brackets. For example, if you enter the code *[Page]* into a footer, then Excel replaces it with the current page number. If you use the code *[Date]*, then Excel substitutes the current date (when you fire off your printout). Of course, no one wants to memorize a long list of cryptic header and footer codes. To help you get these important details right, Excel adds a new tab to the ribbon named Header & Footer Tools | Design (Figure 6-13) when you edit a header or footer.

The quickest way to get a header or footer is to go to the Header & Footer Tools | Design → Header & Footer section (shown in Figure 6-13), and then choose one of the Header or Footer list's ready-made options. Some of the options you can use for a header or footer include:

- Page numbering (for example, Page 1 or Page 1 of 10)
- Worksheet name (for example, Sheet 1)

- File name (for example, myfile.xlsx or C:\MyDocuments\myfile.xlsx)
- The person who created the document, and the date it was created
- A combination of the above information

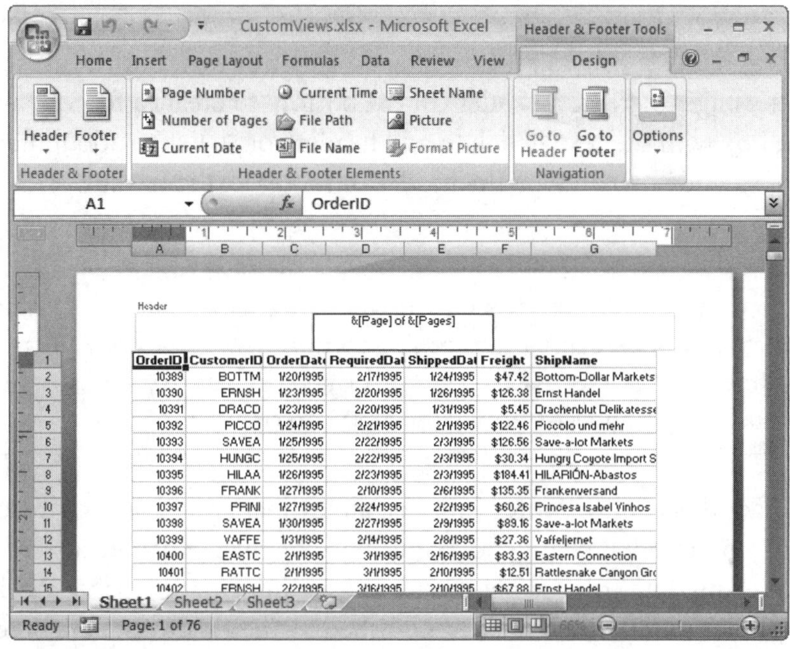

Figure 6-13. The Header & Footer Tools | Design tab is chock-full of useful ingredients you can add to a header or footer. Click a button in the Header & Footer Elements section to insert a special Excel code that represents a dynamic value, like the current page.

Oddly enough, the header and footer options are the same. It's up to you to decide whether you want page numbering at the bottom and a title at the top, or vice versa.

If none of the standard options matches what you need, you can edit the automatic header or footer, or you can create your own from scratch. Start typing in the header or footer box, and use the buttons in the Header & Footer Elements section to paste in the code you need for a dynamic value. And if you want to get more creative, switch to the Home tab of the ribbon, and then use the formatting buttons to change the font, size, alignment, and color of your header or footer.

Finally, Excel gives you a few high-powered options in the Header & Footer Tools | Design → Options section. These include:

- **Different First Page.** This option lets you create one header and footer for the first page, and use a different pair for all subsequent pages. Once you've checked this option, fill in the first page header and footer on the first page, and then head to the second page to create a new header and footer that Excel can use for all subsequent pages.
- **Different Odd & Even pages.** This option lets you create two different headers (and footers)—one for all even-numbered pages and one for all odd-numbered pages. (If you're printing a bunch of double-sided pages, you can use this option to make sure the page number appears in the correct corner.) Use the first page to fill in the odd-numbered header and footer, and then use the second page to fill in the even-numbered header and footer.
- **Scale with Document.** If you select this option, then when you change the print scale to fit in more or less information on your printout, Excel adjusts the headers and footers proportionately.
- **Align with Page Margins.** If you select this option, Excel moves the header and footer so that they're centered in relation to the margins. If you don't select this option, Excel centers them in relation to the whole page. The only time you'll notice a difference is if your left and right margins are significantly different sizes.

All these settings affect both headers and footers.

Customizing Print Settings

Excel's standard print settings are fine if you've got a really small amount of data in your worksheet. But most times, you'll want to tweak these settings so that you can easily read what you print. The Page Layout tab of the ribbon is your control center (Figure 6-14). It lets you do everything from adding headers and footers to shrinking the size of your data so you can cram more information onto a single printed page.

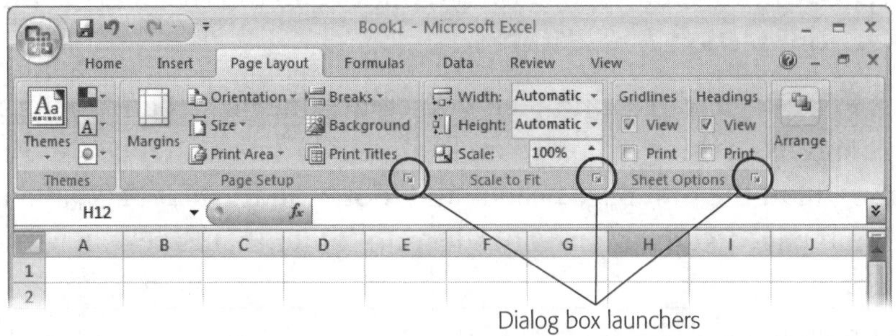

Figure 6-14. The Page Layout tab's most important print-related sections are Page Setup (which lets you change orientation and margin settings), Scale to Fit (which lets you cram more information into your printed pages), and Sheet Options (which lets you control whether gridlines and column headers appear on the printout). To get even more settings, you can click the dialog box launcher (circled), which pops up a full-fledged Page Setup dialog box.

Margins

The Page Layout → Page Setup → Margins list (Figure 6-15) lets you adjust the size of your printed page's *margins* (the space between your worksheet data and the edge of the page). All you need to do is pick one of the preset options. The margin numbers indicate the distance between the item indicated (for example, the top of the page, or the footer on the bottom) and the edge of the paper.

Note

The units Excel uses for margins depend on the regional settings on your computer (which you can adjust through the Control Panel's Regional and Language Options icon). Unfortunately, Excel doesn't indicate the type of units in the Page Setup dialog box, and it doesn't give you any choice to override your regional settings and use different units.

Logically enough, when you reduce the size of your margins, you can accommodate more information. However, you can't *completely* eliminate your margins. Most printers require at least a little space (usually no less than .25 inches) to grip onto the page, and you won't be able to print on this part (the very edge of the page). If you try to make the margins too small, Excel won't inform you of the problem; instead,

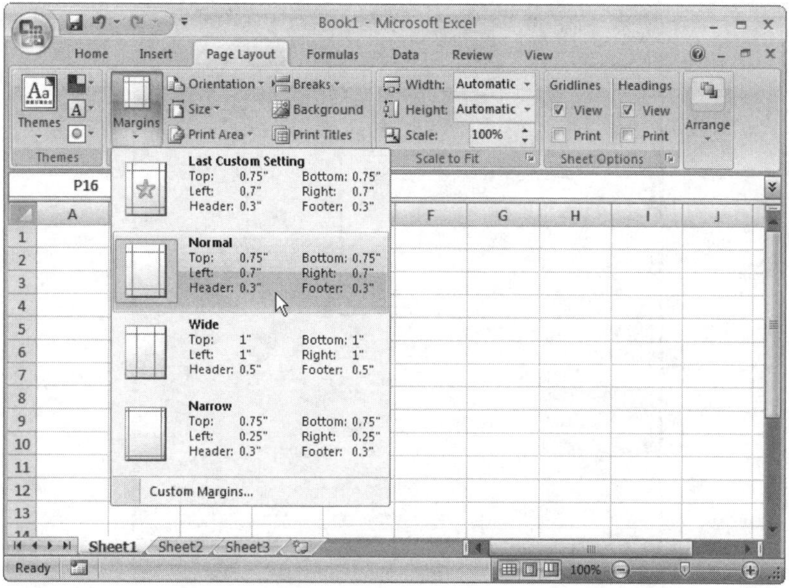

Figure 6-15. You can choose a helpful margin preset (Normal, Wide, or Narrow), or choose Custom Margins to fine-tune your margins precisely, as shown in Figure 6-16.

it'll just stick with the smallest margin your current printer allows. This behavior is different from that of other Microsoft Office applications (like Word). To see this in action, try setting your margins to 0, and then look at the result in the print preview window. You'll see there's still a small margin left between your data and the page borders.

TIP

A good rule of thumb is to adjust margins symmetrically (printouts tend to look nicest that way). Thus, if you shrink the left margin to 0.5, make the same change to the right margin. Generally, if you want to fit more data and you don't need any header or footer space, then you can safely reduce all your margins to 0.5. If you really want to cram in the maximum amount of data you can try 0.25, but that's the minimum margin that most printers allow.

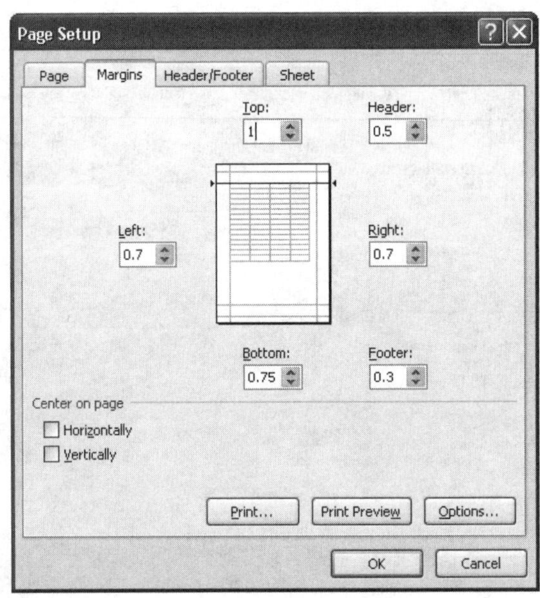

Figure 6-16. Excel allocates space at the top and bottom of your printout for a header or footer. In this example, the header margin is set to 0.5, which means that any header information will appear half an inch below the top of the page. The top margin's set to 1, meaning the worksheet data will appear one inch below the top of the page. When adjusting either of these settings, be careful to make sure the top margin's always larger than the header margin; otherwise, your worksheet's data will print on top of your header.

When you have only a few rows or columns of information, you may want to use one of the "Center on page" options at the bottom of the tab. Select Horizontally to center your columns between the left and right margins. Select Vertically to center your data between the top and bottom of the page.

Paper size and orientation

Orientation is the all-time most useful print setting. This setting lets you control whether you're printing on pages that are upright (in portrait mode) or turned horizontally on their sides (in landscape mode). If Excel is splitting your rows across multiple pages when you print your worksheet, it makes good sense to switch to landscape orientation. That way, Excel prints your columns across a page's long edge, which accommodates more columns (but fewer rows per page).

If you're fed up with trying to fit all your data on an ordinary sheet no matter which way you turn it, you may be tempted to try using a longer sheet of paper. You can then tell Excel what paper you've decided to use by choosing it from the Paper Size menu. (Of course, the paper needs to fit into your printer.) Letter is the standard 8.5 × 11-inch sheet size, while Legal is another common choice—it's just as wide but comes in a bit longer at 8.5 × 14 inches.

NOTE

When using different types of paper, remember to place the paper in your printer *before* you start the print job.

Sheet settings

Margins and orientation are the most commonly adjusted print settings. However, Excel has a small family of additional settings hidden on the Page Setup dialog box's Sheet tab. To see these, go to the Page Layout → Page Setup section of the ribbon, and click the dialog box launcher (the tiny square-with-an-arrow icon in the bottom-right corner). The Page Setup dialog box appears, as shown in Figure 6-17.

The Sheet tab includes the following settings:

- **Print area** lets you specify the range of cells you want to print. While this tool definitely gets the job done, it's easier to use the Print Area tool (described in the box on page 194). Some people find the Print dialog box's Selection setting (page 193) also a more efficient method.
- **Print titles** lets you print specific rows at the top of every page, or specific columns on the left side of every page. For example, you could use this setting to print column titles on the top of every page.
- **Gridlines** prints the grid of lines separating columns and rows that you see on your worksheet.
- **Row and column headings** prints the column headers (which contain the column letters) at the top of each page and the row headers (with the row numbers) on the left side of each page.
- **Black and white** tells Excel to render all colors as a shade of gray, regardless of your printer settings.

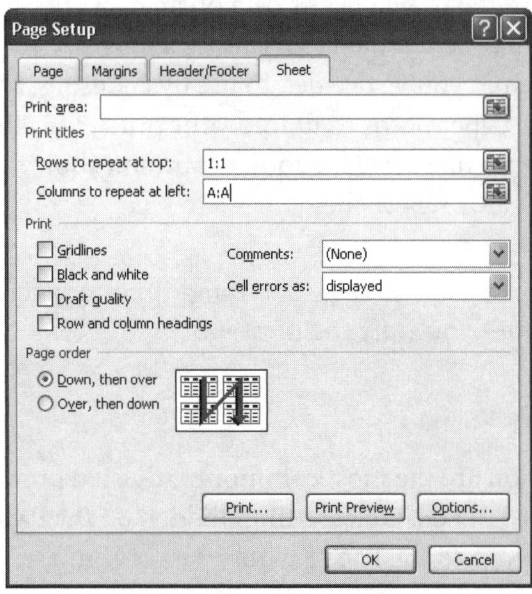

Figure 6-17. The Page, Margins, and Header/Footer tabs provide options that are easier to configure than using the Page Layout ribbon tab. However, the Sheet tab includes a few options that you can't find anywhere else. In this example, Excel uses the "Print titles" section to ensure that every page in this printout will display the first row of the spreadsheet as well as the first column.

- **Draft quality** tells Excel to use lower-quality printer settings to save toner and speed up printing, assuming your printer has these features, of course.
- **Comments** lets you print the comments that you've added to a worksheet. Excel can either append them to the cells in the printout or add them at the end of the printout, depending on the option you select.
- **Cell errors** lets you configure how Excel should print a cell if it contains a formula with an error. You can choose to print the error that's shown (the standard option), or replace the error with a blank value, two dashes (--), or the error code #N/A (meaning not available). You'll learn much more about formulas in Chapter 7.
- **Page order** sets the way Excel handles a large worksheet that's too wide and too long for the printed page's boundaries. When you choose "Down, then over" (the standard option), Excel starts by printing all the rows in the first batch of columns. Once it's finished this batch, Excel then moves on to the next set of

columns, and prints those columns for all the rows in your worksheet, and so on. When you chose "Over, then down," Excel moves across your worksheet first. That means it prints all the columns in the first set of rows. After it's printed these pages, it moves to the next set of rows, and so on.

Controlling Pagination

Sooner or later it will happen to you—you'll face an intimidatingly large worksheet that, when printed, is hacked into dozens of apparently unconnected pages. You could spend a lot of time assembling this jigsaw printout (using a bulletin board and lots of tape), or you could take control of the printing process and tell Excel exactly where to split your data into pages. In the following sections, you'll learn several techniques to do just that.

Page Breaks

One of Excel's often overlooked but surprisingly handy features is *manual page breaks*. The idea is you tell Excel explicitly where to start a new page. You can tell Excel to start a new page between subsequent tables on a worksheet (rather than print a page that has the end of the first one and the beginning of the next).

To insert a page break, move to the leftmost column (column A), and then scroll down to the first cell that you want to appear on the new page. Then, choose Page Layout → Page Setup → Breaks → Insert Page Break. You see a dotted line that indicates the dividing lines in between pages (Figure 6-18).

TIP

There's no limit to how many page breaks you can add to a worksheet—if you have a dozen tables that appear one after the other, you can place a page break after each one to make sure they all start on a new page.

You can also insert page breaks to split your worksheet vertically into pages. This is useful if your worksheet is too wide to fit on one page, but you want to control exactly where the page break will fall. To do so, move to the first row, scroll to the column where the new page should begin, and then choose Page Layout → Page Setup → Breaks → Insert Page Break.

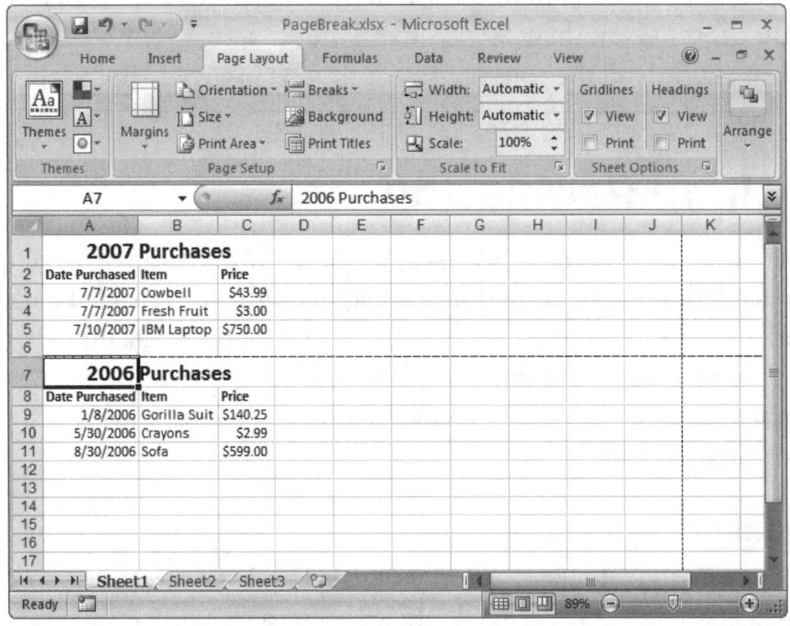

Figure 6-18. Using a page break, you can make sure the second table ("2006 Purchases") always begins on a new page. The dotted line shows where one page ends and the new page starts. When you add a page break, you see a dotted line for it, and you see a dotted line that shows you where additional page breaks naturally fall, based on your margins, page orientation, and paper size settings.

You can remove page breaks one at a time by moving to an adjacent cell and choosing Page Layout → Page Setup → Breaks → Remove Page Break. Or you can clear them all using Page Layout → Page Setup → Breaks → Reset All Page Breaks.

Scaling

Page breaks are a nifty feature for making sure your printouts are paginated just the way you want them. However, they can't help you fit more information on a page. They simply allow you to place page breaks earlier than they would ordinarily occur, so they fall in a more appropriate place.

If you want to fit more on a page, you need to shrink your information down to a smaller size. Excel includes a scaling feature that lets you take this step easily without forcing you to reformat your worksheet.

Scaling lets you fit more rows and columns on a page, by shrinking everything proportionally. For example, if you reduce scaling to 50 percent, you fit twice as many columns and rows on a page. (Keep in mind that the font size in the printout will be smaller, and it may be hard to read.) Conversely, you can use scaling to enlarge your data.

To change the scaling percentage, just type a new percentage into the Page Layout → Scale to Fit → Scale box. The data still appears just as big on your worksheet, but Excel shrinks or expands it in the printout. To gauge the effect, you can use the Page Layout view to preview your printout, as described on page 195.

Rather than fiddling with the scaling percentage (and then seeing what its effect is on your worksheet by trial and error), you may want to force your data to fit into a fixed number of pages. To do this, you set the values in the Page Layout → Scale to Fit → Width box and the Page Layout → Scale to Fit → Height box. Excel performs a few behind-the-scenes calculations and adjusts the scaling percentage accordingly. For example, if you choose one page tall and one page wide, Excel shrinks your entire worksheet so that everything fits into one page. This scaling is tricky to get right (and can lead to hopelessly small text), so make sure you review your worksheet in the Page Layout view before you print it.

TIP

Page Break Preview mode, described below, gives you yet another way to squeeze more data onto a single page.

Page Break Preview: A Bird's-Eye View of Your Worksheet

You don't have to be a tree-hugging environmentalist to want to minimize the number of pages you print out. Enter the Page Break Preview, which gives you a bird's-eye view of how an entire worksheet's going to print. Page Break Preview is particularly useful if your worksheet is made up of lots of columns. That's because Page Break Preview zooms out so you can see a large amount of data at once, and it uses thick blue dashed lines to show you where page breaks will occur, as shown in Figure 6-19. In addition, the Page Break Preview numbers every page, placing the label "Page X" (where "X" is the page number) in large gray lettering in the middle of each page.

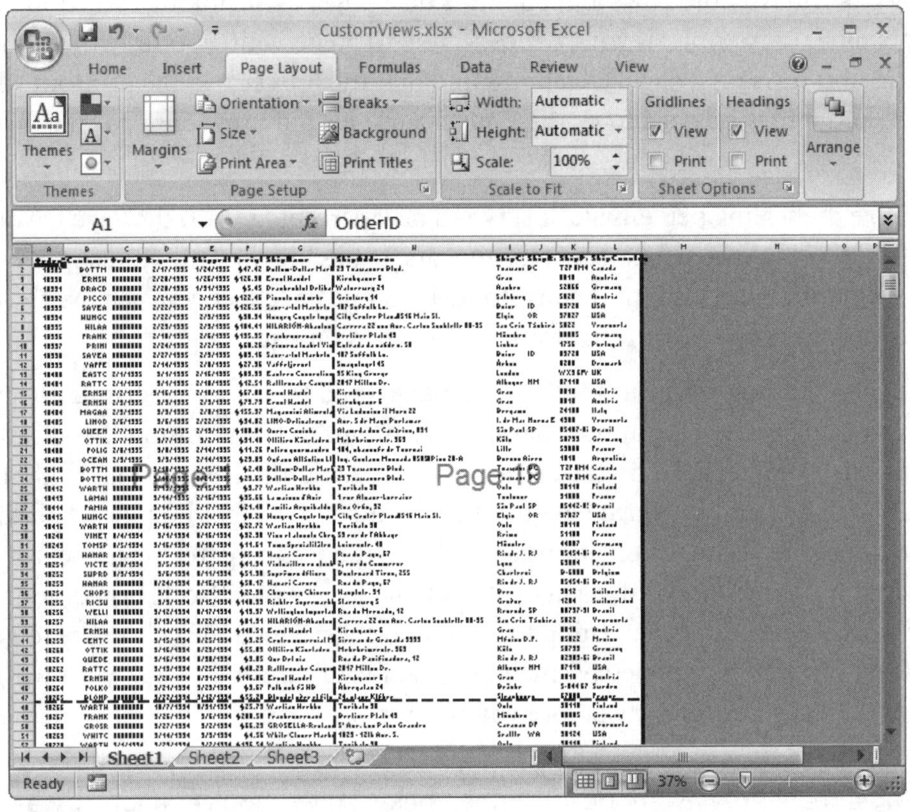

Figure 6-19. This example shows a large worksheet in Page Break Preview mode. The worksheet is too wide to fit on one page (at least in portrait orientation), and the thick dotted line indicates that the page breaks after column G and after row 47. (Excel never breaks a printout in the middle of a column or row.)

To preview the page breaks in your data, select View → Workbook Views → Page Break Preview, or use the tiny Page Break Preview button in the status bar. A window appears, informing you that you can use Page Break Preview mode to move page breaks. You can choose whether you want to see this message again; if not, turn on the "Do not show this dialog again" checkbox before clicking OK.

Once you're in Page Break Preview mode, you can do all of the things you do in Normal view mode, including editing data, formatting cells, and changing the zoom percentage to reveal more or fewer pages. You can also click the blue dashed lines that represent page breaks, and drag them to include more or less rows and columns in your page.

Excel lets you make two types of changes using page breaks:

- **You can make *less* data fit onto a page.** To do so, drag the bottom page break up or the left-side page break to the right. Usually, you'll perform these steps if you notice that a page break occurs in an awkward place, like just before a row with some kind of summary or subtotal.
- **You can make *more* data fit onto a page.** To do so, drag the bottom page break down or the left-side page break to the left.

Of course, everyone wants to fit more information onto their printouts, but there's only so much space on the page. So what does Excel do when you expand a page by dragging the page break? It simply adjusts the scaling setting you learned about earlier (on page 208). The larger you make the page, the smaller the Scaling percentage setting becomes. That means your printed text may end up too tiny for you to read. (The text on your computer's display doesn't change, however, so you don't have any indication of just how small your text has become until you print out your data, or take a look at it in Page Layout view.)

NOTE

Scaling affects all the pages in your printout. That means when you drag one page break to expand a page, you actually end up compressing *all* the pages in your workbook. However, the page *breaks* don't change for other pages, which means you may end up with empty, unused space on some of the pages.

The best advice: If your goal is merely to fit more information into an entire printout, change the scaling percentage manually (page 209) instead of using the Page Break Preview. On the other hand, if you need to squeeze just a little bit more data onto a specific page, use the Page Break Preview.

PART TWO: WORKSHEET POWER

7 BUILDING BASIC FORMULAS

- Creating a Basic Formula
- Formula Shortcuts
- Copying Formulas

MOST EXCEL FANS DON'T TURN TO THE WORLD'S LEADING spreadsheet software just to create nicely formatted tables. Instead, they rely on Excel's industrial-strength computing muscle, which lets you reduce reams of numbers to neat subtotals and averages. Performing these calculations is the first step to extracting meaningful information out of raw data.

Excel provides a number of different ways to build formulas, letting you craft them by hand or point-and-click them into existence. In this chapter, you'll learn about all of these techniques. You'll start by examining the basic ingredients that make up any formula, and then take a close look at the rules Excel uses when evaluating a formula.

Creating a Basic Formula

First things first: what exactly do formulas do in Excel? A *formula* is a series of mathematical instructions that you place in a cell in order to perform some kind of calculation. These instructions may be as simple as telling Excel to sum up a column of numbers, or they may incorporate advanced statistical functions to spot trends and make predictions. But in all cases, all formulas share the same basic characteristics:

- You enter each formula into a single cell.
- Excel calculates the result of a formula every time you open a spreadsheet or change the data a formula uses.
- Formula results are usually numbers, although you can create formulas that have text or Boolean (true or false) results.
- To view any formula (for example, to gain some insight into how Excel produced a displayed result), you have to move to the cell containing the formula, and then look in the *formula bar* (see Figure 7-1). The formula bar also doubles as a handy tool for editing your formulas.
- Formulas can evaluate a combination of numbers you input (useful when you want to use Excel as a handy calculator) or, more powerfully, the contents of other cells.

One of the simplest formulas you can create is this one:

```
=1+1
```

The equal sign is how you tell Excel that you're entering a formula (as opposed to a string of text or numbers). The formula that follows is what you want Excel to calculate. Note that the formula doesn't include the *result*. When creating a formula in Excel, you write the question, and then Excel coughs up the answer, as shown in Figure 7-1.

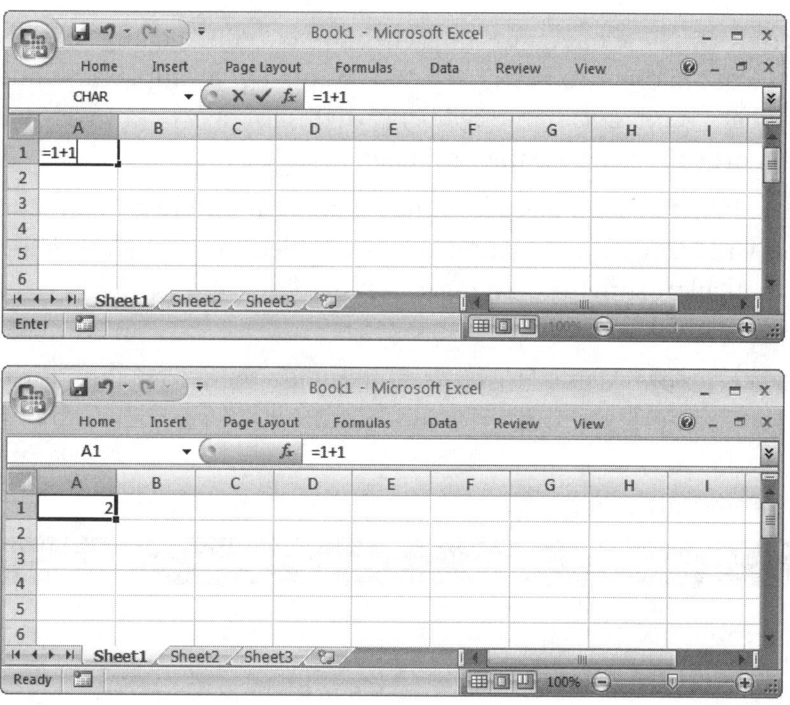

Figure 7-1. Top: This simple formula begins its life when you enter it into a cell. The checkmark and X buttons to the left of the formula bar let you quickly complete or cancel, respectively, your formula.

Bottom: Or you can press Enter, and Excel displays the result in the cell. The formula bar always displays the complete formula (=1+1). In formula lingo, this particular example consists of two literal values (1 and 1) and one arithmetic operator (+).

All formulas use some combination of the following ingredients:

- **The equal sign** (=). Every formula must begin with the equal sign. It signals to Excel that the cell contains a formula, not just ordinary text.

- **The simple operators.** These ingredients include everything you fondly remember from high school math class, including addition (+), subtraction (–), multiplication (*), division (/), and exponentiation (^). Table 7-1 lists these ingredients, also known as *arithmetic operators.*
- **Numbers.** These ingredients are known as constants or *literal values*, because they never change (unless you edit the formula).
- **Cell references.** These references point to another cell, or a range of cells, that you need data from in order to perform a calculation. For example, say you have a list of 10 numbers. A formula in the cell beneath this list may refer to all 10 of the cells above it in order to calculate their average.
- **Functions.** Functions are specialized formulas built into Excel that let you perform a wide range of calculations. For example, Excel provides dedicated functions that calculate sums and averages, standard deviations, yields, cosines and tangents, and much more.
- **Spaces.** Excel ignores these. However, you can use them to make a formula easier to read. For example, you can write the formula *=3*5 + 6*2* instead of *=3*5+6*2*.

Table 7-1. Excel's Arithmetic Operators

Operator	Name	Example	Result
+	Addition	=1+1	2
-	Subtraction	=1-1	0
*	Multiplication	=2*2	4
/	Division	=4/2	2
^	Exponentiation	=2^3	8
%	Percent	=20%	0.20

NOTE

The percentage (%) operator divides a number by 100.

Excel's Order of Operations

For computer programs and human beings alike, one of the basic challenges when it comes to reading and calculating formula results is figuring out the *order of operations*—mathematician-speak for deciding which calculations to perform first when there's more than one calculation in a formula. For example, given the formula:

```
=10 - 8 * 7
```

the result, depending on your order of operations, is either 14 or –46. Fortunately, Excel abides by what's come to be accepted among mathematicians as the standard rules for order of operations, meaning it doesn't necessarily process your formulas from left to right. Instead, it evaluates complex formulas piece-by-piece in this order:

1. **Parentheses (any calculations within parentheses are always performed first)**
2. **Percent**
3. **Exponents**
4. **Division and Multiplication**
5. **Addition and Subtraction**

Note

When Excel encounters formulas that contain operators of equal *precedence* (that is, the same order of operation priority level), it evaluates these operators from left to right. However, in basic mathematical formulas, this has no effect on the result.

For example, consider the following formula:

```
=5 + 2 * 2 ^ 3 - 1
```

To arrive at the answer of 20, Excel first performs the exponentiation (2 to the power of 3):

```
=5 + 2 * 8 - 1
```

and then the multiplication:

```
=5 + 16 - 1
```

and then the addition and subtraction:

```
=20
```

To control this order, you can add parentheses. For example, notice how adding parentheses affects the result in the following formulas:

```
5 + 2 * 2 ^ (3 - 1) = 13
(5 + 2) * 2 ^ 3 - 1 = 55
(5 + 2) * 2 ^ (3 - 1) = 28
5 + (2 * (2 ^ 3)) - 1 = 20
```

You must always use parentheses in pairs (one open parenthesis for every closing parenthesis). If you don't, then Excel gets confused and lets you know you need to fix things, as shown in Figure 7-2.

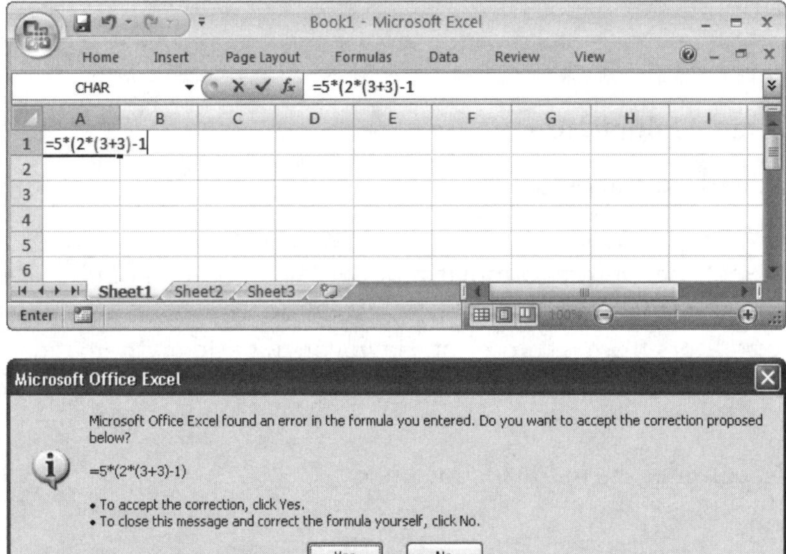

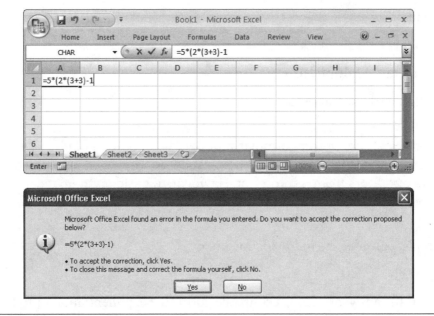

Figure 7-2. Top: If you create a formula with a mismatched number of opening and closing parentheses (like this one), Excel won't accept it.

Bottom: Excel offers to correct the formula by adding the missing parentheses at the end. You may not want this addition, though. If not, cancel the suggestion, and edit your formula by hand. Excel helps a bit by highlighting matched sets of parentheses. For example, as you move to the opening parenthesis, Excel automatically bolds both the opening and closing parentheses in the formula bar.

TIP

Remember, when you're working with a lengthy formula, you can expand the formula bar to see several lines at a time. To do so, click the down arrow at the far right of the formula bar (to make it three lines tall), or drag the bottom edge of the formula bar to make it as many lines large as you'd like.

Cell References

Excel's formulas are handy when you want to perform a quick calculation. But if you want to take full advantage of Excel's power, then you're going to want to use formulas to perform calculations on the information that's already in your worksheet. To do that you need to use *cell references*—Excel's way of pointing to one or more cells in a worksheet.

For example, say you want to calculate the cost of your Amazonian adventure holiday, based on information like the number of days your trip will last, the price of food and lodging, and the cost of vaccination shots at a travel clinic. If you use cell references, then you can enter all this information into different cells, and then write a formula that calculates a grand total. This approach buys you unlimited flexibility because you can change the cell data whenever you want (for example, turning your three-day getaway into a month-long odyssey), and Excel automatically refreshes the formula results.

Cell references are a great way to save a *ton* of time. They come in handy when you want to create a formula that involves a bunch of widely scattered cells whose values frequently change. For example, rather than manually adding up a bunch of subtotals to create a grand total, you can create a grand total formula that uses cell references to point to a handful of subtotal cells. They also let you refer to large groups of cells by specifying a *range*. For example, using the cell reference lingo you'll learn on page 227, you can specify all the cells in the first column between the 2nd and 100th rows.

Every cell reference points to another cell. For example, if you want a reference that points to cell A1 (the cell in column A, row 1), use this cell reference:

```
=A1
```

In Excel-speak, this reference translates to "get the value from cell A1, and insert it in the current cell." So if you put this formula in cell B1, then it displays whatever value's currently in cell A1. In other words, these two cells are now linked.

Cell references work within formulas just as regular numbers do. For example, the following formula calculates the sum of two cells, A1 and A2:

```
=A1+A2
```

Provided both cells contain numbers, you'll see the total appear in the cell that contains the formula. If one of the cells doesn't contain numeric information, then you'll see a special error code instead that starts with a # symbol. Errors are described in more detail on page 228.

GEM IN THE ROUGH

Excel As a Pocket Calculator

Sometimes you need to calculate a value before you enter it into your worksheet. Before you reach for your pocket calculator, you may like to know that Excel lets you enter a formula in a cell, and then use the result in that same cell. This way, the formula disappears and you're left with the result of the calculated value.

Start by typing your formula into the cell (for example *=65*88*). Then, press F2 to put the cell into edit mode. Next, press F9 to perform the calculation. Finally, just hit Enter to insert this value into the cell.

Remember, when you use this technique, you replace your formula with the calculated value. If your calculation is based on the values of other cells, then Excel won't update the result if you change those other cells' values. That's the difference between a cell that has a value, and a cell that has a formula.

How Excel Formats Cells That Contain Cell References

As you learned in Chapter 5, the way you format a cell affects how Excel displays the cell's value. When you create a formula that references other cells, Excel attempts to simplify your life by applying automatic formatting. It reads the number format that the *source cells* (that is, the cells being referred *to*) use, and applies that to the cell with the formula. If you add two numbers and you've formatted both with the

Currency number format, then your result also has the Currency number format. Of course, you're always free to change the formatting of the cell after you've entered the formula.

Usually, Excel's automatic formatting is quite handy. Like all automatic features, however, it's a little annoying if you don't understand how it works when it springs into action. Here are a few points to consider:

- Excel copies only the number format to the formula cell. It ignores other details, like fonts, fill colors, alignment, and so on. (Of course, you can manually copy formats using the Format Painter, as discussed on page 167.)
- If your formula uses more than one cell reference, and the different cells use different number formats, Excel uses its own rules of precedence to decide which number format to use. For example, if you add a cell that uses the Currency number format with one that uses the Scientific number format, then the destination cell has the Scientific number format. Sadly, these rules aren't spelled out anywhere, so if you don't see the result you want, it's best to just set your own formatting.
- If you change the formatting of the source cells *after* you've entered the formula, it won't have any effect on the formula cell.
- Excel copies source cell formatting only if the cell that contains the formula uses the General number format (which is the format that all cells begin with). If you apply another number format to the cell *before* you enter the formula, then Excel doesn't copy any formatting from the source cells. Similarly, if you change a formula to refer to new source cells, then Excel doesn't copy the format information from the new source cells.

Functions

A good deal of Excel's popularity is due to the collection of *functions* it provides. Functions are built-in, specialized algorithms that you can incorporate into your own formulas to perform powerful calculations. Functions work like miniature computer programs—you supply the data, and the function performs a calculation and gives you the result.

In some cases, functions just simplify calculations that you could probably perform on your own. For example, most people know how to calculate the average of several values, but when you're feeling a bit lazy, Excel's built-in AVERAGE( ) function automatically gives you the average of any cell range.

NOTE

Excel provides a detailed function reference that lists all the functions you can use (and how to use them). This function reference doesn't exactly make for light reading, though; for the most part, it's written in IRS-speak. You'll learn more about using this reference in "Using the Insert Function Button to Quickly Find and Insert Functions" on page 238.

Every function provides a slightly different service. For example, one of Excel's statistical functions is named COMBIN( ). It's a specialized tool used by probability mathematicians to calculate the number of ways a set of items can be combined. Although this sounds technical, even ordinary folks can use COMBIN( ) to get some interesting information. You can use the COMBIN( ) function, for example, to count the number of possible combinations there are in certain games of chance.

The following formula uses COMBIN( ) to calculate how many different five-card combinations there are in a standard deck of playing cards:

```
=COMBIN(52,5)
```

Functions are always written in all-capitals. (More in a moment on what those numbers inside the parentheses are doing.) However, you don't need to worry about the capitalization of function names because Excel automatically capitalizes the function names that you type in (provided it recognizes them).

Using a function in a formula

Functions alone don't actually *do* anything in Excel. Functions need to be part of a formula to produce a result. For example, COMBIN( ) is a function name. But it actually *does* something—that is, give you a result—only when you've inserted it into a formula, like so: *=COMBIN(52,5)*.

Whether you're using the simplest or the most complicated function, the *syntax*—or, rules for including a function within a formula—is always similar. To use a function, start by entering the function name. Excel helps you out by showing a pop-up list with possible candidates as you type, as shown in Figure 7-3. This handy feature is new to Excel 2007, and it's called Formula AutoComplete.

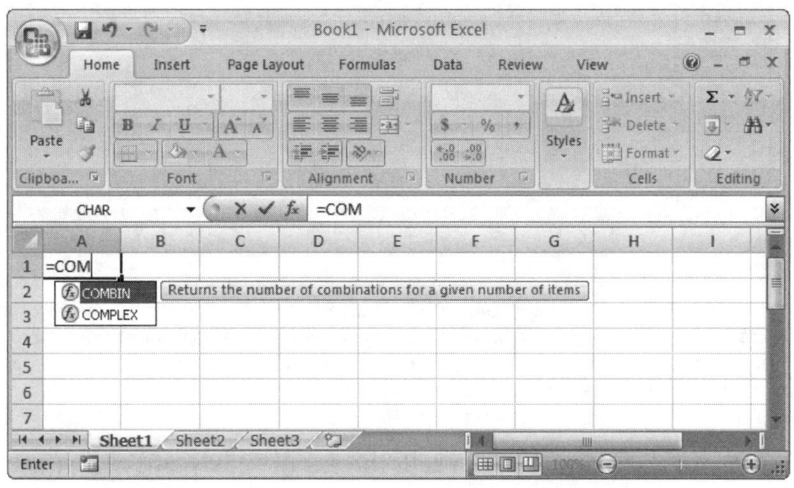

Figure 7-3. After you type =COM, Excel helpfully points out that it knows only two functions that start that way: COMBIN( ) and COMPLEX( ). If your fingers are getting tired, then use the arrow keys to pick the right one out of the list, and then click Tab to pop it into your formula. (Or, you can just double-click it with the mouse.)

After you type the function name, add a pair of parentheses. Then, inside the parentheses, put all the information the function needs to perform its calculations.

In the case of the COMBIN( ) function, Excel needs two pieces of information, or *arguments*. The first is the number of items in the set (the 52-card deck), and the second's the number of items you're randomly selecting (in this case, 5). Most functions, like COMBIN( ), require two or three arguments. However, some functions can accept many more, while a few don't need any arguments at all. Once again, Formula AutoComplete guides you by telling you what arguments you need, as shown in Figure 7-4.

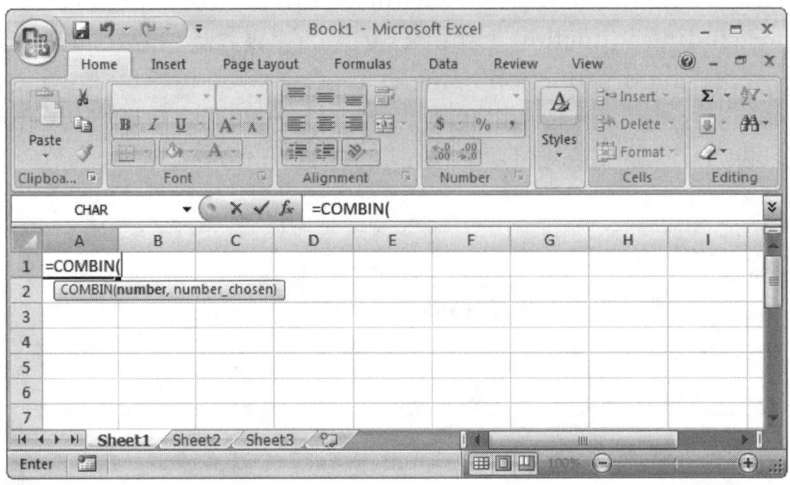

Figure 7-4. When you type the opening parentheses after a function name, Excel automatically displays a tooltip indicating what arguments the function requires. The argument you're currently entering is shown bolded in the tooltip. The argument names aren't crystal clear, but if you already know how the function works, they're usually enough to jog your memory.

Once you've typed this formula into a cell, the result (2598960) appears in your worksheet. In other words, there are 2,598,960 different possible five-card combinations in any deck of cards. Rather than having to calculate this fact using probability theory—or, heaven forbid, trying to count out the possibilities manually—the COMBIN( ) function handled it for you.

Note

Even if a function doesn't take any arguments, you still need to supply an empty set of parentheses after the function name. One example is the RAND( ) function, which generates a random fractional number. The formula =RAND( ) works fine, but if you forget the parentheses and merely enter *=RAND*, then Excel displays an error message *(#NAME?)* that's Excelian for: "Hey! You got the function's name wrong." See Table 7-2 on page 231 for more information about Excel's error messages.

Using cell references with a function

One of the particularly powerful things about functions is that they don't necessarily need to use literal values in their arguments. They can also use cell references. For example, you could rewrite the five-card combination formula (mentioned previously) so that it specifies the number of cards that'll be drawn from the deck based on a number that you've typed in somewhere else in the spreadsheet. Assuming this information's entered into cell B2, the formula would become:

```
=COMBIN(52,B2)
```

Building on this formula, you can calculate the probability (albeit astronomically low) of getting the exact hand you want in one draw:

```
=1/COMBIN(52,B2)
```

You could even multiply this number by 100 or use the Percent number style to see your percentage chance of getting the cards you want.

Using cell ranges with a function

In many cases, you don't want to refer to just a single cell, but rather a *range* of cells. A range is simply a grouping of multiple cells. These cells may be next to each other (say, a range that includes all the cells in a single column), or they could be scattered across your worksheet. Ranges are useful for computing averages, totals, and many other calculations.

To group together a series of cells, use one of the two following reference operators:

- **The comma (,) separates more than one cell.** For example, the series *A1, B7, H9* is a cell range that contains three cells. The comma's known as the *union operator*. You can add spaces before or after a comma, but Excel just ignores or removes them (depending on its mood).
- **The colon (:) separates the top-left and bottom-right corners of a block of cells.** You're telling Excel: "Hey, use *this* block of cells in my formula." For example, *A1:A5* is a range that includes cells A1, A2, A3, A4, and A5. The range *A2:B3* is a grid that contains cells A2, A3, B2, and B3. The colon is the *range operator*—by far the most powerful way to select multiple cells.

TIP

As you might expect, Excel lets you specify ranges by selecting cells with your mouse, instead of typing in the range manually. You'll see this trick later in this chapter on page 234.

You can't enter ranges directly into formulas that just use the simple operators. For example, the formula *=A1:B1+5* doesn't work, because Excel doesn't know what to do with the range A1:B1. (Should the range be summed up? Averaged? Excel has no way of knowing.) Instead, you need to use ranges with functions that know how to use them. For instance, one of Excel's most basic functions is named SUM( ); it calculates the total for a group of cells. To use the SUM( ) function, you enter its name, an open parenthesis, the cell range you want to add up, and then a closed parenthesis.

Here's how you can use the SUM( ) function to add together three cells, A1, A2, and A3:

```
=SUM(A1,A2,A3)
```

And here's a more compact syntax that performs the same calculation using the range operator:

```
=SUM(A1:A3)
```

A similar SUM( ) calculation's shown in Figure 7-5. Clearly, if you want to total a column with hundreds of values, then it's far easier to specify the first and last cell using the range operator rather than including each cell reference in your formula!

Formula Errors

If you make a syntax mistake when entering a formula (such as leaving out a function argument or including a mismatched number of parentheses), Excel lets you know right away. Moreover, like a stubborn school teacher, Excel won't accept the formula until you've corrected it. It's also possible, though, to write a perfectly legitimate formula that doesn't return a valid answer. Here's an example:

```
=A1/A2
```

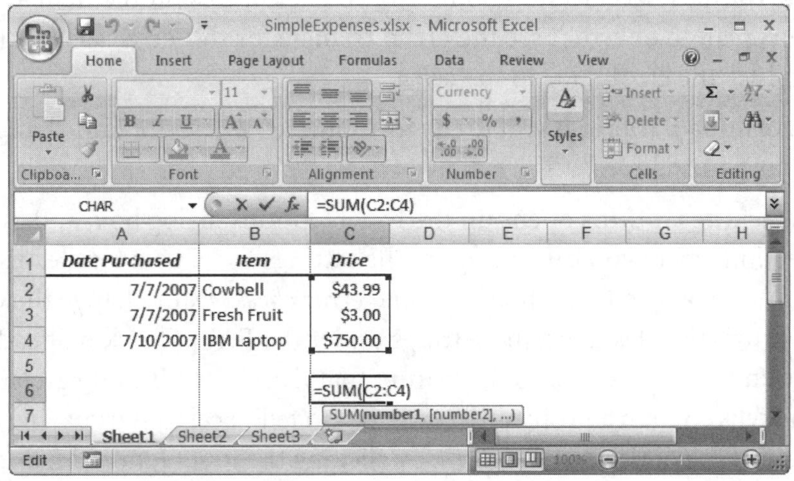

Figure 7-5. Using a cell range as the argument in the SUM( ) function is a quick way to add up a series of numbers in a column. Note that when you enter or edit a formula, Excel highlights all the cells that formula uses with different colored borders. In this example, you see the range of cells C2, C3, and C4 in a blue box.

If both A1 and A2 have numbers, this formula works without a hitch. However, if you leave A2 blank, or if you enter text instead of numbers, then Excel can't evaluate the formula, and it reminds you with an error message.

Excel lets you know about formula errors by using an *error code* that begins with the number sign (#) and ends with an exclamation point (!), as shown in Figure 7-6. In order to remove this error, you need to track down the problem and resolve it, which may mean correcting the formula or changing the cells it references.

When you click the exclamation mark icon next to an error, you see a menu of choices (as shown in Figure 7-6):

- **Help On This Error** pops open Excel's online help, with a (sometimes cryptic) description of the problem and what could have caused it.
- **Show Calculation Steps** pops open the Evaluate Formula dialog box, where you can work your way through a complex formula one step at a time.

- **Ignore Error** tells Excel to stop bothering you about this problem, in any worksheet you create. You won't see the green triangle for this error again (although you'll still see the error code in the cell).
- **Edit in Formula Bar** brings you to the formula bar, where you can change the formula to fix a mistake.
- **Error Checking Options** opens up the Excel Options dialog box, and brings you to the section where you can configure the settings Excel uses for alerting you about errors. You can turn off *background error checking,* or change the color of the tiny error triangles using the settings under the Error Checking heading. (Background error checking is the feature that flags cells with tiny green triangles when the cells contain a problem.) You can also tell Excel to start paying attention to errors you previously told it ignore by clicking the Reset Ignored Errors button.

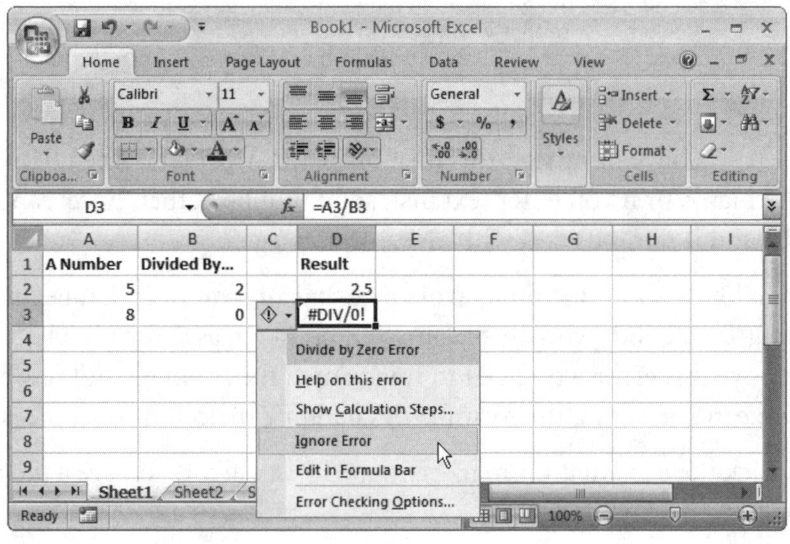

Figure 7-6. When Excel spots an error, it inserts a tiny green triangle into the cell's top-left corner. When you move to the offending cell, Excel displays an exclamation mark icon next to it (a smart tag). Hover over the exclamation mark to view a description of the error (which appears in a tooltip), or click the exclamation icon to see a list of menu options.

Table 7-2 lists most of the error codes that Excel uses.

Table 7-2. Excel's Error Codes

Error Code	Description
#VALUE!	You used the wrong type of data. Maybe your function expects a single value and you submitted a whole range. Or, more commonly, you might have used a function or created a simple arithmetic formula with a cell that contains text instead of numbers.
#NAME?	Excel can't find the name of the function you used. This error code usually means you misspelled a function's name, although it can indicate you used text without quotation marks or left out the empty parentheses after the function name.
#NUM!	There's a problem with one of the numbers you're using. For example, this error code appears when a calculation produces a number that's too large or too small for Excel to deal with.
#DIV/0	You tried to divide by zero. This error code also appears if you try to divide by a cell that's blank, because Excel treats a blank cell as though it contains the number 0 for the purpose of simple calculations with the arithmetic operators. (Some functions, like AVERAGE( ), are a little more intelligent and ignore blank cells.)
#REF!	Your cell reference is invalid. This error most often occurs if you delete or paste over the cells you were using, or if you try to copy a cell from one worksheet to another.
#N/A	The value isn't available. This error can occur if you try to perform certain types of lookup or statistical functions that work with cell ranges. For example, if you use a function to search a range and it can't find what you need, you may get this result. Sometimes people enter a #N/A value manually in order to tell Excel to ignore a particular cell when creating charts and graphs. The easiest way to do this is to use the NA( ) function (rather than entering the text *#N/A*).
########	This code isn't actually an error condition—in all likelihood, Excel has successfully calculated your formula. However, the formula can't be displayed in the cell using the current number format. To solve this problem, you can widen the column, or possibly change the number format if you require a certain number of fixed decimal places.

Logical Operators

So far, you've seen the basic arithmetic operators (which are used for addition, subtraction, division, and so on) and the cell reference operators (used to specify one or more cells). There's one final category of operators that's useful when creating formulas: *logical operators.*

Logical operators let you build conditions into your formulas so the formulas produce different values depending on the value of the data they encounter. You can use a condition with cell references or literal values.

For example, the condition A2=A4 is true if cell A2 contains the same value as cell A4. On the other hand, if these cells contain different values (say 2 and 3), then the formula generates a false value. Using conditions is a stepping stone to using conditional logic. Conditional logic lets you perform different calculations based on different scenarios.

For example, you can use conditional logic to see how large an order is, and provide a discount if the total order cost's over $5,000. Excel *evaluates* the condition, meaning it determines if the condition's true or false. You can then tell Excel what to do based on that evaluation.

Table 7-3 lists all the logical operators you can use to build formulas.

Table 7-3. Logical Operators

Operator	Name	Example	Result
=	Equal to	1=2	FALSE
>	Greater than	1>2	FALSE
<	Less than	1<2	TRUE
>=	Greater than or equal to	1>=1	TRUE
<=	Less than or equal to	1<=1	TRUE
<>	Not equal to	1<>1	FALSE

You can use logical operators to build standalone formulas, but that's not particularly useful. For example, here's a formula that tests whether cell A1 contains the number 3:

```
=(A2=3)
```

The parentheses aren't actually required, but they make the formula a little bit clearer, emphasizing the fact that Excel evaluates the condition first, and then displays the result in the cell. If you type this formula into the cell, then you see either the uppercase word TRUE or FALSE, depending on the content in cell A2.

On their own, logical operators don't accomplish much. However, they really shine when you start combining them with other functions to build conditional logic. For example, you can use the SUMIF( ) function, which totals the value of certain rows, depending on whether the row matches a set condition. Or you can use the IF( ) function to determine what calculation you should perform.

The IF( ) function has the following function description:

```
IF(condition, [value_if_true], [value_if_false])
```

In English, this line of code translates to: If the condition is true, display the second argument in the cell; if the condition is false, display the third argument.

Consider this formula:

```
=IF(A1=B2, "These numbers are equal", "These numbers are not equal")
```

This formula tests if the value in cell A1 equals the value in cell B2. If this is true, you'll see the message "These numbers are equal" displayed in the cell. Otherwise, you'll see "These numbers are not equal."

NOTE

If you see a quotation mark in a formula, it's because that formula uses text. You must surround all literal text values with quotation marks. (Numbers are different: You can enter them directly into a formula.)

People often use the IF( ) function to prevent Excel from performing a calculation if some of the data is missing. Consider the following formula:

```
=A1/A2
```

This formula causes a divide-by-zero error if A2 contains a 0 value. Excel then displays an error code in the cell. To prevent this from occurring, you can replace this formula with the conditional formula shown here:

```
=IF(A2=0, 0, A1/A2)
```

This formula checks if cell A2 is empty or contains a 0. If so, the condition is true, and the formula simply gives you a 0. If it isn't, the condition is false, and Excel performs the calculation A1/A2.

Formula Shortcuts

So far, you've learned how to build a formula by entering it manually. That's a good way to start out because it forces you to understand the basics of formula writing. But writing formulas by hand is a drag; plus, it's easy to type in the wrong cell address. For example, if you type A2 instead of A3, you can end up with incorrect data, and you won't necessarily notice your mistake.

As you become more comfortable with formulas, you'll find that Excel gives you a few tools—like point-and-click formula creation and the Insert Function button—to speed up your formula writing and reduce your mistakes. You'll learn about these features in the following sections.

Note

In previous versions of Excel, the Insert Function dialog box was almost exactly the same, except it was known as the Function wizard.

Point-and-Click Formula Creation

Instead of entering a formula by typing it out letter-by-letter, Excel lets you create formulas by clicking the cells you want to use. For example, consider this simple formula that totals the numbers in two cells:

```
=A1+A2
```

To build this formula by clicking, just follow these steps:

1. **Move to the cell where you want to enter the formula.**

   This cell's where the result of your formula's calculation will appear. While you can pick any cell on the worksheet, A3 works nicely because it's directly below the two cells you're adding.

2. **Press the equal sign (=) key.**

   The equal sign tells Excel you're going to enter a formula.

3. **Move to the first cell you want to use in your formula (in this case, A1).**

   You can move to this first cell by pressing the up arrow key twice, or by clicking it with the mouse. You'll notice that moving to another cell doesn't cancel your edit, as it would normally, because Excel recognizes that you're building a formula. When you move to the new cell, the cell reference appears automatically in the formula (which Excel displays in cell A3, as well as in the formula bar just above your worksheet). If you move to another cell, Excel changes the cell reference accordingly.

4. **Press the + key.**

   Excel adds the + sign to your formula so that it now reads *=A1+*.

5. **Finish the formula by moving to cell A2 and pressing Enter.**

   Again, you can move to A2 either by pressing the up arrow key or by clicking the cell directly. Remember, you can't just finish the formula by moving somewhere else; you need to press Enter to tell Excel you're finished writing the formula. Another way to complete your edit is to click the checkmark that appears on the formula bar, to the left of the current formula. Even experienced Excel fans get frustrated with this step. If you click another cell before you press Enter, then you won't move to the cell—instead, Excel inserts the cell into your formula.

TIP

You can use this technique with any formula. Just type in the operators, function names, and so on, and use the mouse to select the cell references. If you need to select a range of cells, then just drag your mouse until the whole group of cells is highlighted. You can practice this technique with the SUM( ) function. Start by typing *=SUM(* into the cell, and then selecting the range of cells you want to add. Finish by adding a final closing parenthesis and pressing Enter.

Point-and-Click Formula Editing

You can use a similar approach to edit formulas, although it's slightly trickier:

1. **Move to the cell that contains the formula you want to edit, and put it in edit mode by double-clicking it or pressing F2.**

Excel highlights all the cells that this formula uses with a colored outline. Excel's even clever enough to use a helpful color-coding system. Each cell reference uses the same color as the outline surrounding the cell it's referring to. This can help you pick out where each reference is.

2. **Click the outline of the cell you want to change. (Your pointer changes from a fat plus sign to a four-headed arrow when you're over the outline.) With the mouse button still held down, drag this outline over to the new cell (or cells) you want to use.**

   Excel updates the formula automatically. You can also expand and shrink cell range references. To do so, put the formula-holding cell into edit mode, and then click any corner of the border that surrounds the range you want to change. Next, drag the border to change the size of the range. If you want to move the range, then click any part of the range border and drag the outline in the same way as you would with a cell reference.

3. **Press Enter or click the formula bar checkmark to accept your changes.**

   That's it.

FREQUENTLY ASKED QUESTION

Showing and Printing Formulas

How in the world do I print out formulas that appear in my cells?

When you print a worksheet, Excel prints the calculated value in each cell rather than any formula that happens to be inside a cell. Usually, that's what you want to have happen. But in some cases, rather than a printout of the formula's results, you want a record of the calculations used to generate the results.

Excel gives you a view setting so you can get this record. Just choose Formulas → Formula Auditing → Show Formulas. Now, Excel displays the formula's contents instead of its results—but on the current worksheet only. Excel also widens the columns so they can show more information (as formulas tend to be longer than their results). Repeat this process, and then uncheck the setting to return to normal life.

The Formulas Tab

The ribbon is stocked with a few buttons that make formula writing easier. To take a look, click the Formulas tab.

The most important part of the Formulas tab is the Function Library section at the left. It includes the indispensable Insert Function button, which you'll take for a spin in the next section. It also includes many more buttons that arrange Excel's vast catalog of functions into related categories for easier access. Figure 7-7 show how it works.

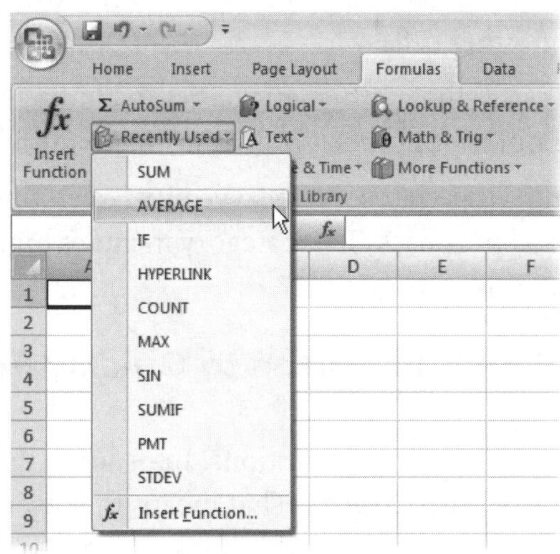

Figure 7-7. Each button in the Function Library section (other than Insert Function) pops up a mini menu of function choices. Choose one, and Excel inserts that function into the current formula. You can use this technique to find functions that you've used recently, or to browse the main function categories.

The Function Library divides its functions into the following categories:

- **AutoSum** has a few shortcuts that let you quickly add, average, or otherwise deal with a list of numbers.
- **Recently Used** has exactly what you'd expect—functions that you've recently chosen from the Function Library. If you're just starting out with functions, you see that Excel fills the Recently Used list with a small set of commonly used functions, like SUM( ).

- **Financial** functions let you track your car loan payments and calculate how many more years until you can retire rich.
- **Logical** functions let you create conditional logic for even smarter spreadsheets that make calculation decisions.
- **Text** functions manipulate words, sentences, and other non-numeric information.
- **Date & Time** functions perform calendar math and can help you sort out ages, due dates, and more.
- **Lookup & Reference** functions perform the slightly mind-bending feat of searching for information in other cells.
- **Math & Trig** functions are the mathematic basics, including sums, rounding, and all the other high-school trigonometry you're trying to forget.
- **More Functions** groups together some heavy-duty Excel functions that are intended for specialized purposes. This category includes high-powered statistical and engineering functions.

Using the Insert Function Button to Quickly Find and Insert Functions

Excel provides more than 300 built-in functions. In order to use a function, however, you need to type its name in *exactly*. That means that every time you want to employ a function, you'll need to refer to this book, call on your own incredible powers of recollection, or click over to the convenient Insert Function button.

To use the Insert Function feature, choose Formulas → Function Library → Insert Function. However, formula pros skip straight to the action by clicking the *fx* button that appears just to the left of the formula bar. (Or, they press the Shift+F3 shortcut key.)

No matter which approach you use, Excel displays the Insert Function dialog box (shown in Figure 7-8), which offers three ways to search for and insert any of Excel's functions.

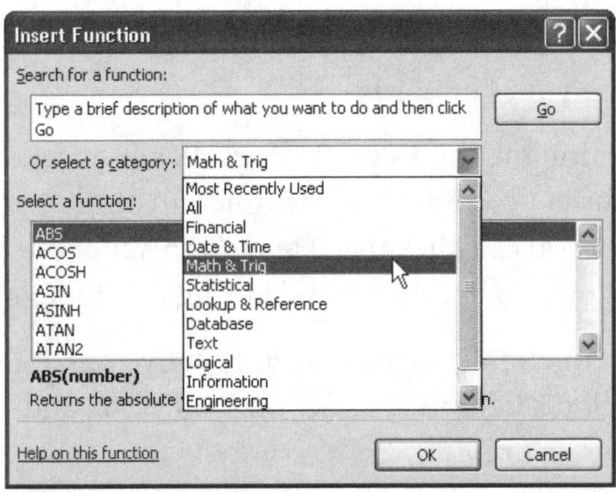

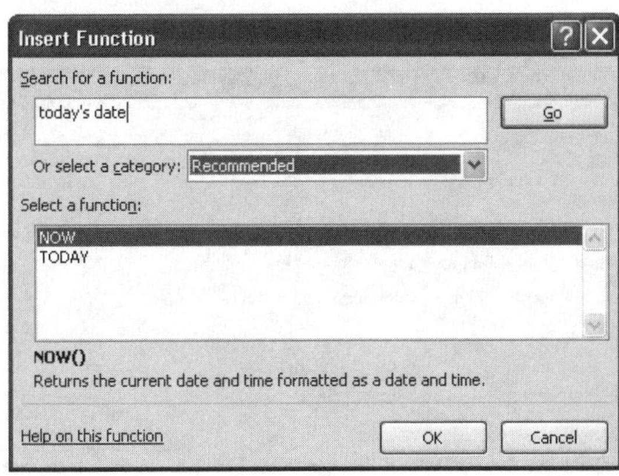

Figure 7-8. Top: The Insert Function dialog box lets you quickly find the function you need. You can choose a category that seems likely to have the functions you're interested in.

Bottom: You can also try to search by entering keywords in the "Search for a function" box. Either way, when you click one of the functions in the list, Excel presents you with a description of the function at the bottom of the window.

- If you're looking for a function, the easiest way to find one is to choose a category from the "Or select a category" drop-down list. For example, when you select the Math & Trig category, you see a list of functions with names like SIN( ) and COS( ), which perform basic trigonometric calculations.
- If you choose the Most Recently Used category, you'll see a list of functions you've recently picked from the ribbon or the Insert Function dialog box.

- If you're really ambitious, you can type a couple of keywords into the "Search for a function" text box. Next, click Go to perform the search. Excel gives you a list of functions that match your keywords.

When you spot a function that looks promising, click it once to highlight its name. Excel then displays a brief description of the function at the bottom of the window. For more information, you can click the "Help on this function" link in the bottom-left corner of the window. To build a formula using this function, click OK.

Excel then inserts the function into the currently active cell, followed by a set of parentheses. Next, it closes the Insert Function dialog box and opens the Function Arguments dialog box (Figure 7-9).

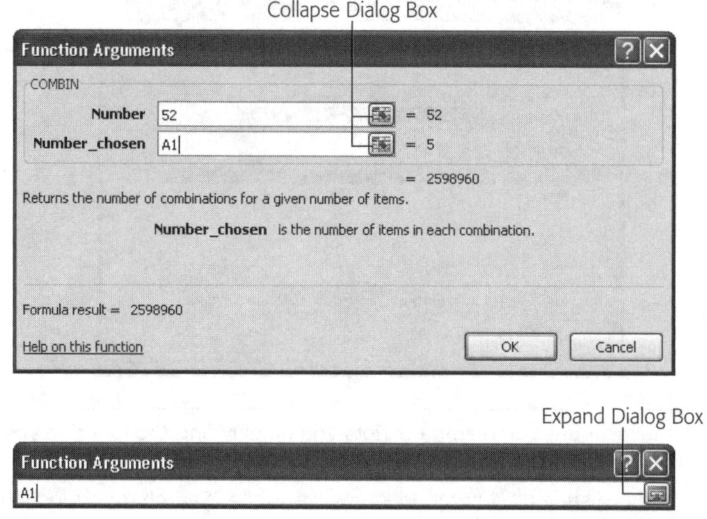

Figure 7-9. Top: Here, the COMBIN( ) function has just been inserted via the Insert Function dialog box. Because the COMBIN( ) function requires two arguments (Number and Number_chosen), the Function Arguments dialog box shows two text boxes. The first argument uses a literal value (52), while the second argument uses a cell reference (A1). As you enter the arguments, Excel updates the formula in the worksheet's active cell, and displays the result of the calculation at the bottom of the Function Arguments dialog box.

Bottom: If you need more room to see the worksheet and select cells, you can click the Collapse Dialog Box icon to reduce the window to a single text box. Clicking the Expand Dialog Box icon restores the window to its normal size.

NOTE

Depending on the function you're using, Excel may make a (somewhat wild) guess about which arguments you want to supply. For example, if you use the Insert Function window to add a SUM( ) function, then you'll see that Excel picks a nearby range of cells. If this isn't what you want, just replace the range with the correct values.

Now you can finish creating your formula by using the Function Arguments dialog box, which includes a text box for every argument in the function. It also includes a help link for detailed information about the function, as shown in Figure 7-10.

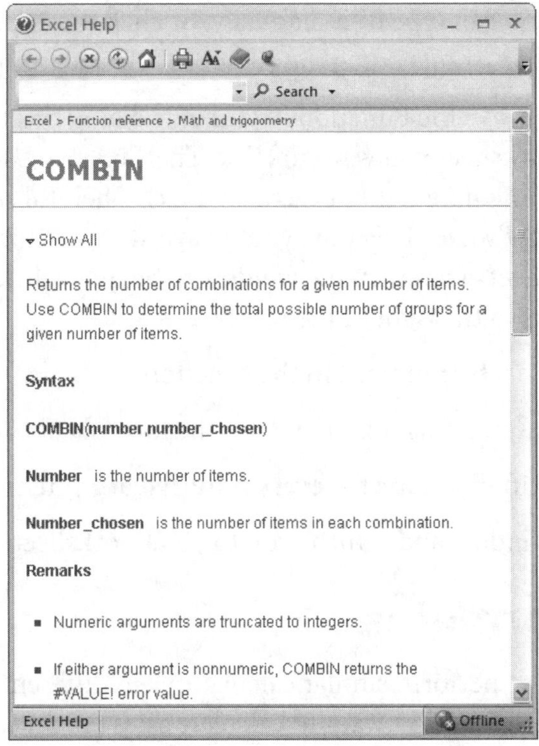

Figure 7-10. Both the Insert Function and Function Arguments dialog boxes make it easy to get detailed reference information about any function by clicking the "Help on this function" link at the bottom left of the window. The help page shown here shows the reference for the COMBIN( ) function.

To complete your formula, follow these steps:

1. **Click the text box for the first argument.**

   A brief sentence describing the argument appears in the Function Arguments dialog box.

   Some functions don't require any arguments. In this case, you don't see any text boxes, although you still see some basic information about the function. Skip directly to step 4.

2. **Enter the value for the argument.**

   If you want to enter a literal value (like the number 52), type it in now. To enter a cell reference, you can type it in manually, or click the appropriate cell on the worksheet. To enter a range, drag the cursor to select a group of cells.

   You may need to move the Function Arguments dialog box to the side to expose the part of the worksheet you want to click. The Collapse Dialog Box icon (located to the immediate right of each text box) is helpful since clicking it shrinks the window's size. This way, you'll have an easier time selecting cells from your worksheet. To return the window to normal, click the Expand Dialog Box icon, which is to the right of the text box.

3. **Repeat step 2 for each argument in the function.**

   As you enter the arguments, Excel updates the formula automatically.

4. **Once you've specified a value for every required argument, click OK.**

   Excel closes the window and returns you to your worksheet.

Copying Formulas

Sometimes you need to perform similar calculations in different cells throughout a worksheet. For example, say you want to calculate sales tax on each item in a product catalog, the monthly sales in each store of a company, or the final grade for each student in a class. In this section, you'll learn how Excel makes it easy with *relative cell references*. Relative cell references are cell references that Excel updates automatically when you copy them from one cell into another. They're the standard kind of references that Excel uses (as opposed to absolute cell references, which are covered in the next section). In fact, all the references you've used so far have been relative references, but you haven't yet seen how they work with copy-and-paste operations.

Consider the worksheet shown in Figure 7-11, which contains a teacher's grade book. In this example, each student has three grades: two tests and one assignment. A student's final grade is based on the following percentages: 25 percent for each of the two tests, and 50 percent for the assignment.

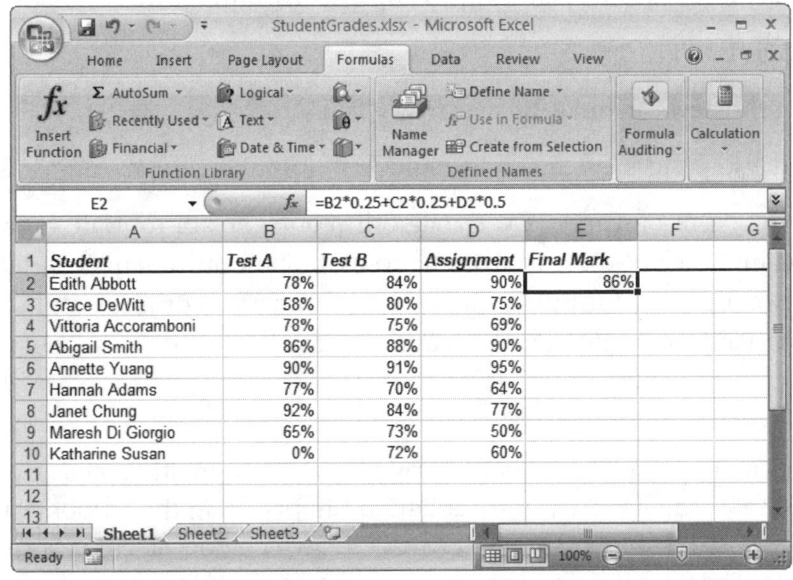

Figure 7-11. This worksheet shows a list of students in a class, and calculates the final grade for each student using two test scores and an assignment score. So far, the only formula that's been added is for the first student (in cell E2).

The following formula calculates the final grade for the first student (Edith Abbott):

```
=B2*25% + C2*25% + D2*50%
```

The formula that calculates the final mark for the second student (Grace DeWitt) is almost identical. The only change is that all the cell references are offset by one row, so that B2 becomes B3, C2 becomes C3, and D2 becomes D3:

```
=B3*25% + C3*25% + D3*50%
```

You may get fed up entering all these formulas by hand. A far easier approach is to copy the formula from one cell to another. Here's how:

1. **Move to the cell containing the formula you want to copy.**

   In this example, you'd move to cell E2.

2. **Copy the formula to the clipboard by pressing Ctrl+C.**

   You can also copy the formula by choosing Home → Clipboard → Copy.

3. **Select the range of cells you want to copy the formula into.**

   Select cells E3 to E10.

4. **Paste in the new formulas by pressing Ctrl+V.**

   You can also paste the formula by choosing Home → Clipboard → Paste.

   When you paste a formula, Excel magically copies an appropriate version of the formula into each of the cells from E3 to E10. These automatic formula adjustments occur for any formula, whether it uses functions or just simple operators. Excel then automatically calculates and displays the results, as shown in Figure 7-12.

TIP

There's an even quicker way to copy a formula to multiple cells by using the AutoFill feature introduced in Chapter 2. In the student grade example, you'd start by moving to cell E2, which contains the original formula. Then, you'd click the small square at the bottom-right corner of the cell outline, and drag the outline down until it covers all cells from E3 to E10. When you release the mouse button, Excel inserts the formula copies in the AutoFill region.

Absolute Cell References

Relative references are a true convenience since they let you create formula copies that don't need the slightest bit of editing. But you've probably already realized that relative references don't always work. For example, what if you have a value in a specific cell that you want to use in multiple calculations? You may have a currency conversion ratio that you want to use in a list of expenses. Each item in the list needs

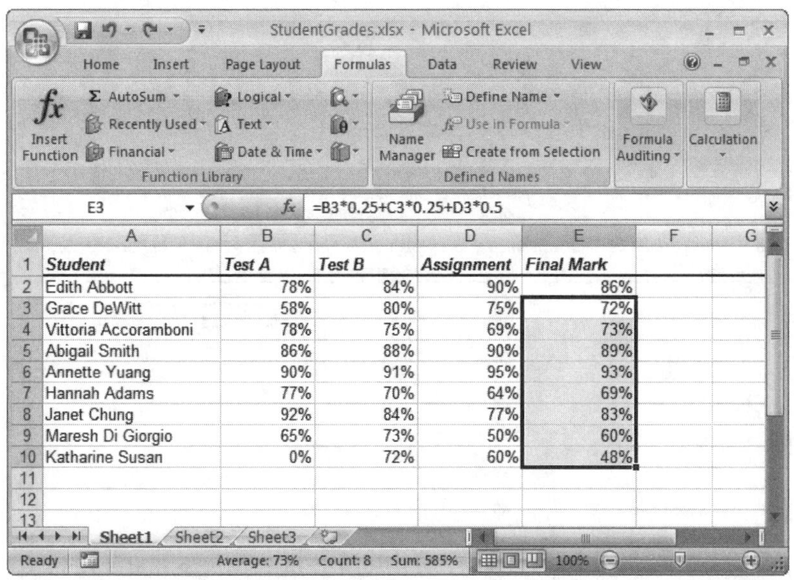

	A	B	C	D	E
1	*Student*	*Test A*	*Test B*	*Assignment*	*Final Mark*
2	Edith Abbott	78%	84%	90%	86%
3	Grace DeWitt	58%	80%	75%	72%
4	Vittoria Accoramboni	78%	75%	69%	73%
5	Abigail Smith	86%	88%	90%	89%
6	Annette Yuang	90%	91%	95%	93%
7	Hannah Adams	77%	70%	64%	69%
8	Janet Chung	92%	84%	77%	83%
9	Maresh Di Giorgio	65%	73%	50%	60%
10	Katharine Susan	0%	72%	60%	48%

Figure 7-12. When you paste the formula into one or more new cells, each Final Grade formula operates on the data in its own row. This means that you don't have to tweak the formula for each student. The formula bar shows the formula contained in cell E3.

to use the same cell to perform the conversion correctly. But if you make copies of the formula using relative cell references, then you'll find that Excel adjusts this reference automatically and the formula ends up referring to the wrong cell (and therefore the wrong conversion value).

Figure 7-13 illustrates the problem with the worksheet of student grades. In this example, the test and assignment scores aren't all graded out of 100 possible points; each item has a different total score available (listed in row 12). In order to calculate the percentage a student earned on a test, you need to divide the test score by the total score available. This formula, for example, calculates the percentage for Edith Abbott's performance on Test B:

```
=B2/B12*100%
```

To calculate Edith's final grade for the class, you'd use the following formula:

```
=B2/B12*25% + C2/C12*25% + D2/D12*50%
```

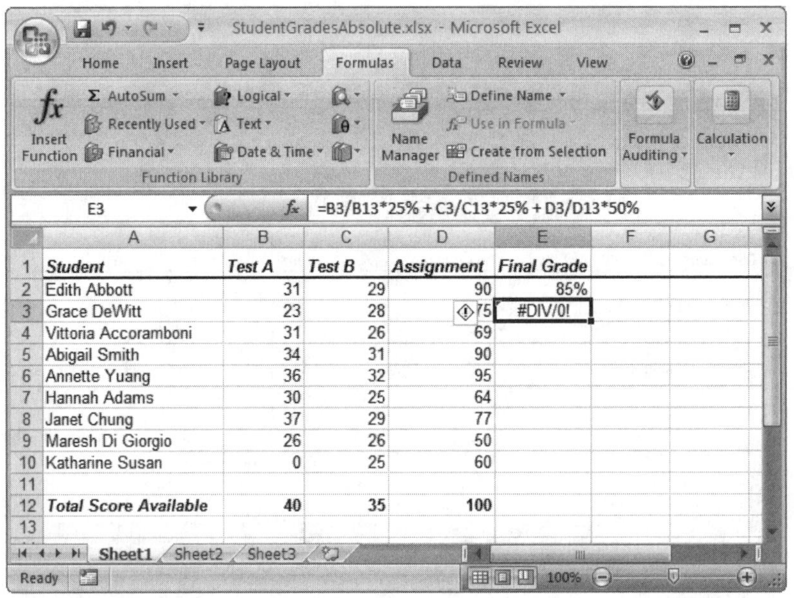

Figure 7-13. In this version of the student grade book, both the tests and the assignment are graded on different scales (as listed in row 12). When you copy the Final Grade formula from the first row (cell E2) to the rows below it, Excel offsets the formula to use B13, C13, and D13—none of which provide any information. Thus a problem occurs—shown here as a divide-by-zero error. To fix this, you need to use absolute cell references.

Like many formulas, this one contains a mix of cells that should be relative (the individual scores in cells B2, C2, and D2) and those that should be absolute (the possible totals in cell B12, C12, and D12). As you copy this formula to subsequent rows, Excel incorrectly changes all the cell references, causing a calculation error.

Fortunately, Excel provides a perfect solution. It lets you use *absolute cell references*—cell references that always refer to the same cell. When you create a copy of a formula that contains an absolute cell reference, Excel doesn't change the reference (as it does when you use *relative* cell references; see the previous section). To indicate that a cell reference is absolute, use the dollar sign ($) character. For example, to change B12 into an absolute reference, you would add the $ character twice, once in front of the column and once in front of the row, which changes it to $B$12.

Here's the corrected class grade formula (for Edith) using absolute cell references:

```
=B2/$B$12*25% + C2/$C$12*25% + D2/$D$12*50%
```

This formula still produces the same result for the first student. However, you can now copy it correctly for use with the other students. To copy this formula into all the cells in column E, use the same procedure described in the previous section on relative cell references.

UP TO SPEED

Creating an Exact Formula Copy

There's another way to copy a formula that prevents Excel from automatically changing the formula's cell references. The trick's to copy the formula itself rather than copy the whole cell (which is what you do when performing a basic copy-and-paste operation on a formula).

The process takes a few more steps, and it lets you paste only one copy at a time, but it can still come in handy if you don't want Excel to use relative references. Here's how it works:

1. First, move to the cell that contains the formula you want to copy.
2. Place this cell in edit mode by double-clicking it or pressing F2.
3. Select all the text in the cell. You can use the mouse, or you can use the arrow keys (just hold down Shift as you scroll from the beginning to the end of the cell).
4. Once you've selected the complete formula, press Ctrl+C to copy it.
5. Press Enter to leave edit mode once you're finished.
6. Move to the new cell, and press Ctrl+V to paste it.

Keep in mind that when you use this approach, you create an exact copy of the formula. That means this technique doesn't help in situations where some cell references need to be absolute, and others need to be relative.

Partially Fixed References

You might wonder why you need to use the $ character twice in an absolute reference (before the column letter *and* the row number). The reason is that Excel lets you create *partially* fixed references. To understand partially fixed references, it helps to remember that every cell reference consists of a column letter and a row number. With a partial fixed reference, Excel updates one component (say, the column part) but not the other (the row) when you copy the formula. If this sounds complex (or a little bizarre), consider a few examples:

- You have a loan rate in cell A1, and you want all loans on an entire worksheet to use that rate in calculations. If you refer to the cell as $A$1, then its column and row always stay the same when you copy the formula to another cell.
- You have several rows of loan information. The first column of a row always contains the loan rate for all loans on that row. In your formula cell, if you refer to cell $A1, then when you copy the formula across columns and rows, the row changes (2, 3, 4, etc.) but the column doesn't (A2, A3, A4, etc.).
- You have a table of loan rates organized by the length of the loan (10-year, 15-year, 20-year, etc.) along the top of a worksheet. Loans in each column are calculated using the rate specified at the top of that column. If you refer to the rate cell as A$1 in your first column's formula, then the row stays constant (1), but the column changes (B1, C1, D1, etc.) as you copy the formula across columns and down rows.

TIP

You can quickly change formula references into absolute or partially fixed references. Just put the cell into edit mode (by double-clicking it or pressing F2). Then, move through the formula until you've highlighted the appropriate cell reference. Now, press F4 to change the cell reference. Each time you press F4, the reference changes. If the reference is A1, for instance, it becomes $A$1, then A$1, then $A1, and then A1 again.

FREQUENTLY ASKED QUESTION

How Changing the Location of Cells Affects Formulas

OK, I know how Excel adjusts a formula when I copy it to another location. But what happens if I move cells around after I've created a formula?

No worries. It turns out that Excel is surprisingly intelligent. Consider the following simple formula:

```
=B1+A2
```

If you cut and paste the contents of A2 to A3, Excel automatically updates your formula to point to the new cell, without complaining once. It also performs the same automatic cleanup if you drag the contents of a cell to another location (although if you simply make a duplicate copy of the cell, Excel won't change your formula). Excel is also on the ball when you insert and delete rows and columns.

If at any time Excel can't find your cells, the formula changes to show the error code #REF! You can then take a closer look at the formula to find out what really went wrong. For example, if you delete column B from your spreadsheet (by selecting the column and using the Home → Cells → Delete command), the formula changes to this:

```
=#REF!+A2
```

Even though there's still a B1 cell in your worksheet (it's the cell that was formerly named C1), Excel modifies the formula to make it clear that you've lost your original data.

8

TABLES: LIST MANAGEMENT MADE EASY

- The Basics of Tables
- Sorting and Filtering a Table

Excel's grid-like main window gives you lots of freedom to organize your information. As you've seen in the chapters so far, tables of data can assume a variety of shapes and sizes—from complex worksheets that track expenses, to a simple list of dishes your guests are bringing to a potluck dinner.

Some tables are quite sophisticated, with multiple levels, subtotals, and summary information. But in many cases, your table consists of nothing more than a long list of data, with a single row at the top that provides descriptive column headings. These types of tables are so common that Excel provides a set of features designed exclusively for managing them. These tools let you control your tables in style—sorting, searching, and filtering your information with just a couple of mouse clicks. But before you can use any of these tools, you have to convert your garden-variety table into a *structured table*.

In this chapter, you'll learn more about what, exactly, a structured table is, how to create one, and how to make use of all its features and frills.

Note

In previous versions of Excel, the tables feature was called *lists*. It's still the same feature, but Microsoft developers were so pleased with the improvements they added in Excel 2007 that they decided it deserved a whole new name.

The Basics of Tables

An Excel table is really nothing more than a way to store a bunch of information about a group of items. Each item occupies a separate row, and different kinds of information about the item reside side by side in adjacent columns. In database terminology, the rows are *records*, and the columns of information are *fields*. For example, the records could represent customers, and the fields could contain things like name, address, purchase history, and so on.

Excel tables have a number of advantages over ordinary worksheet data:

- **They grow and shrink dynamically.** As you fill data into adjacent rows and columns, the table grows to include the new cells. And as a table changes size, any formulas that use the table adjust themselves accordingly. In other words, if you have a formula that calculates the sum of a column in a table, the range that the SUM( ) function uses expands when you add a new record to the table.

- **They have built-in smarts.** You can quickly select rows and columns, apply a custom sort order, and search for important records.
- **They excel (ahem) at dealing with large amounts of information.** If you need to manage vast amounts of information, you may find ordinary worksheet data a little cumbersome. If you put the same information in a table, you can simply apply *custom filtering*, which means you see only the records that interest you.

Creating a Table

Creating a table is easy. Here's how:

1. **Choose the row where you want your table to start.**

   If you're creating a new table, the worksheet's first row is a good place to begin. (You can always shift the table down later by putting your cursor in the top row, and then choosing Home → Cells → Insert → Insert Sheet Rows.) This first row is where you enter any column titles you want to use, as explained in the next step.

   NOTE

   Be careful when placing content in the cells directly *beneath* your table. If your table expands too far down, you'll run up against these filled-up cells. Although you can use commands like Home → Cells → Insert → Insert Sheet Rows to add some extra space when things get crowded, it's always better to start off with plenty of breathing room.

2. **Enter the column titles for your table, one column title for each category you want to create.**

   To create the perfect table, you need to divide your data into categories. For example, if you're building a table of names and addresses, you probably want your columns to hold the standard info you see on every form ever created: First Name, Last Name, Street, City, and so on. The columns you create are the basis for all the searching, sorting, and filtering you do. For instance, if you have First Name and City columns, you can sort your contacts by first name or by city.

If you want, you can start to add entries underneath the column headings now (in the row directly below the column titles). Or just jump straight to the next step to create the table.

3. **Make sure you're currently positioned somewhere inside the table (anywhere in the column title row works well), and then choose Insert → Tables → Table.**

   Excel scans the nearby cells, and then selects all the cells that it thinks are part of your table. Once Excel determines the bounds of your table, the Create Table dialog box appears, as shown in Figure 8-1.

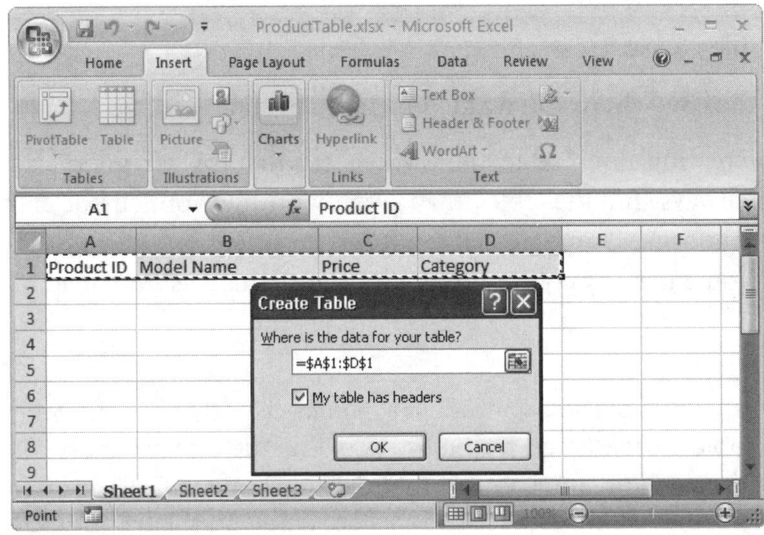

Figure 8-1. The Create Table dialog box displays the cell references for the currently selected range. In this example, the selection includes only the headings (there's no data yet). You can change the range by typing in new information or by clicking the mini worksheet icon at the right end of the cell range box, which lets you select the range by dragging on the appropriate cells in the worksheet.

4. **Make sure the "My table has headers" checkbox is turned on. This option tells Excel you're using the first row just for column headers. Then click OK.**

   Excel transforms your cells into a table, like the one shown in Figure 8-2. You can tell that your ordinary range of cells has become a genuine table by the presence of a few telltale signs. First, tables start out with automatic formatting that gives each row a shaded background (alternating between blue and gray). Second, the column headings appear in bold white letters on a dark background, and each one includes a drop-down arrow that you can use for quick filtering (a feature you'll explore on page 268).

If you create a table from a group of cells that don't include column titles, don't turn on the "My table has headers" checkbox. When you create the table, Excel adds a row of columns at the top with generic names like Column1, Column2, and so on. You can click these cells, and then edit the column titles, to be more descriptive.

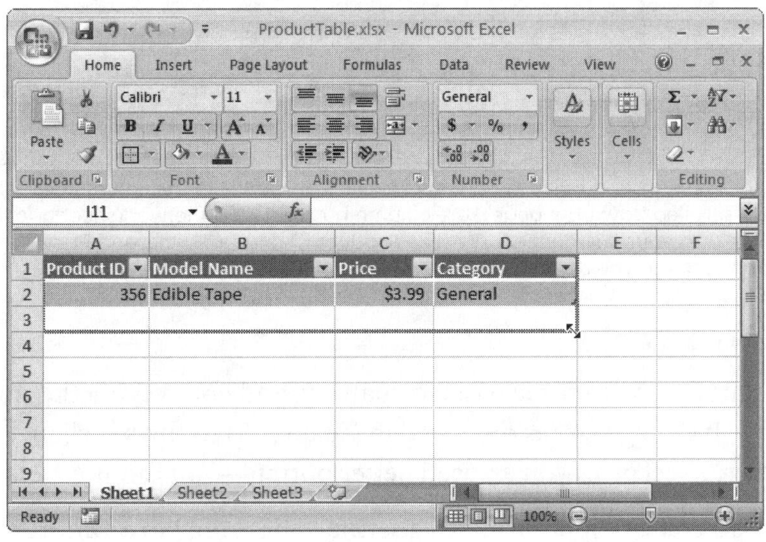

Figure 8-2. To quickly resize your table, look for the tiny triangle icon at the bottom-right corner (under the two-headed arrow in this figure), and then drag it to encompass more (or fewer) rows and columns.

Keep in mind that tables consist of exactly two elements: column headers (Figure 8-3) and rows. Tables don't support row headers (although there's no reason why you can't create a separate column and use that as a row title). Tables also have a fixed structure, which means that every row has exactly the same number of columns. You can create multiple tables on the same worksheet, but you're often better off placing them on separate worksheets so you can more easily manage them.

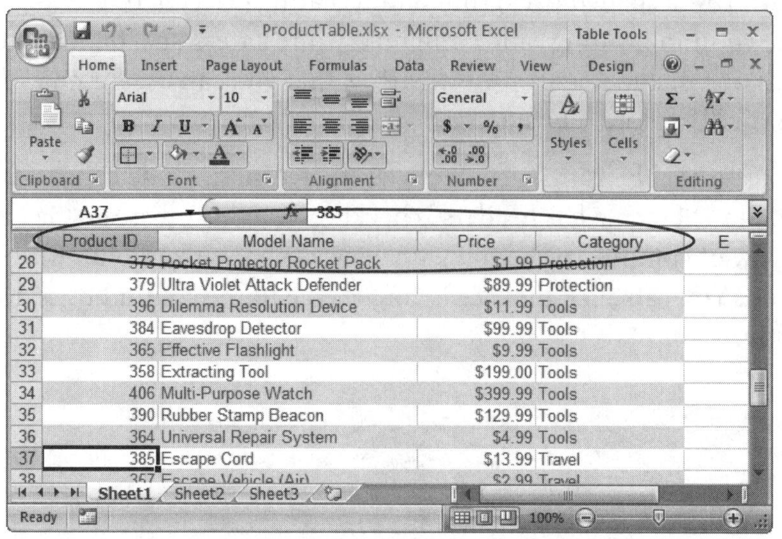

Figure 8-3. Here's one unsung frill in every table. When you can't see the column headers any longer (because you've scrolled down the page), the column buttons atop the worksheet grid change from letters (like A, B, C) to your custom headers (like Product ID, Model Name, and Price). This way, you never forget what column you're in.

Formatting a Table

Every table starts out with some basic formatting, and you can use the ribbon and the Format Cells dialog box (as discussed in Chapter 5) to further change its appearance. However, Excel gives you an even better option—you can use *table styles.*

A table style is a collection of formatting settings that apply to an entire table. The nice part about table styles is that Excel remembers your style settings. If you add new rows to a table, Excel automatically adds the right cell formatting. Or, if you delete a row, Excel adjusts the formatting of all the cells underneath to make sure the *banding* (the alternating pattern of cell shading that makes each row easier to read) stays consistent.

When you first create a table, you start out with a fairly ordinary set of colors: a gray–blue combination that makes your table stand out from the rest of the worksheet. By choosing another table style, you can apply a different set of colors and borders to your table.

NOTE

Excel's standard table styles don't change the fonts in a table. To change fonts, you can change the theme (page 170), or select some cells, and then, from the ribbon's Home → Font section, pick the font you want.

To choose a new table style, head to the ribbon's Table Tools | Design → Table Styles section. You'll see a gallery of options as shown in Figure 8-4. As you move over a table style, Excel uses its live preview feature to change the table, giving you a sneak peak at how your table would look with that style.

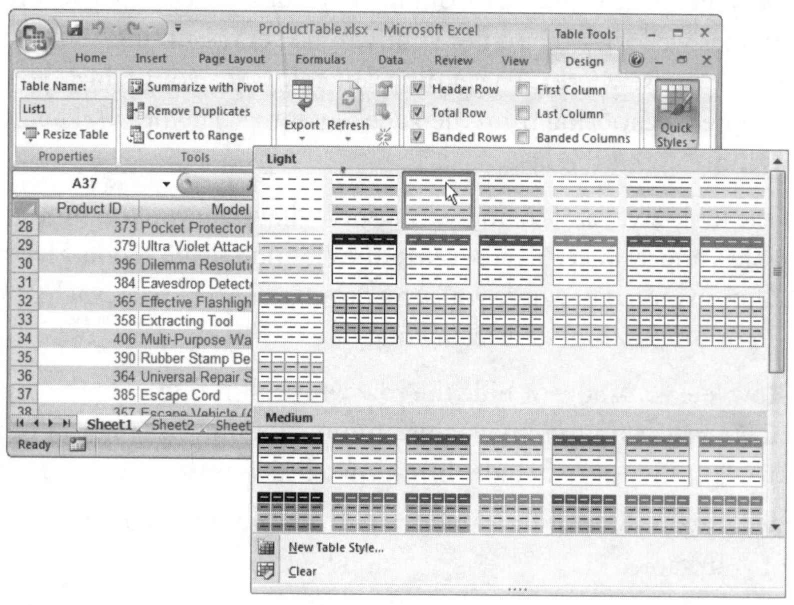

Figure 8-4. Depending on your Excel window's width, in the ribbon, you may see the table style gallery. Or, if there's not enough room available, you see a Quick Styles button that you need to click to display a drop-down style gallery (as shown here).

NOTE

Notice that some table styles use banding, while others don't.

Table styles work like cell styles, which you learned about in Chapter 5. Like cell styles, they let you standardize and reuse formatting. Table styles, however, include a whole package of settings that tell Excel how to format different portions of the table, including the headers, first and last columns, the summary row, and so on.

NOTE

You can't edit the built-in table styles. However, you can change the table styles you create. In the table gallery, just right-click a style, and then choose Modify.

You'll notice that the built-in table styles have a limited set of colors. Excel limits them because table styles use colors from the current theme, which ensures that your table meshes well with the rest of your worksheet (assuming you've been sticking to theme colors elsewhere). To get different colors for your tables, you can change the theme by choosing from the Page Layout → Themes → Themes gallery. Page 170 has more about themes.

Along with the table style and theme settings, you have a few more options to fine-tune your table's appearance. Head over to the ribbon's Table Tools | Design → Table Style Options section, where you see a group of checkboxes, each of which lets you toggle on or off different table elements:

- **Header Row** lets you show or hide the row with column titles at the top of the table. You'll rarely want to remove this option. Not only are the column headers informative, but they also include drop-down lists for quick filtering (page 268).
- **Total Row** lets you show or hide the row with summary calculations at the bottom of your table.
- **First Column** applies different formatting to the first column in your table, if it's defined in the table style.
- **Last Column** applies different formatting to the last column in your table, if it's defined in the table style.
- **Banded Rows** applies different formatting to each second row, if it's defined in the table style. Usually, the banded row appears with a background fill. Large-table lovers like to use banding because it makes it easier to scan a full row from right to left without losing your place.

- **Banded Columns** applies different formatting to each second column, if it's defined in the table style. Folks use banded columns less than banded rows, because people usually read tables from side to side (not top to bottom).

Editing a Table

Once you've created a table, there are three basic editing tasks you can perform:

- **Edit a record.** This part's easy. Just modify cell values as you would in any ordinary worksheet.
- **Delete a record.** First, go to the row you want to delete (you can be in any column). Then, choose Home → Cells → Delete → Delete Table Rows. Excel removes the row and shrinks the table automatically. For faster access that bypasses the ribbon altogether, just right-click a cell in the appropriate row, and then choose Delete → Table Rows.
- **Add a new record.** To add a record, head to the bottom of the table, and then type a new set of values just underneath the last row in the table. Once you finish typing the first value, Excel expands the table automatically, as shown in Figure 8-5. If you want to insert a row but don't want it to be at the bottom of the table, you can head to your chosen spot, and then choose Home → Cells → Insert → Insert Table Rows Above (or right-click and choose Insert → Table Rows Above). Excel inserts a new blank row immediately *above* the current row.

NOTE

Notice that when you insert or remove rows, you're inserting or removing *table* rows, not *worksheet* rows. The operation affects only the cells in that table. For example, if you have a table with three columns and you delete a row, Excel removes three cells, and then shifts up any table row underneath. Any information in the same row that exists *outside* the table is unaffected.

You may also decide to change the structure of your table by adding or removing columns. Once again, you'll find this task is like inserting or removing columns in an ordinary worksheet. (The big difference, as shown in Figure 8-6, is that any rows or columns *outside* your table remain unaffected when you add new rows or columns.)

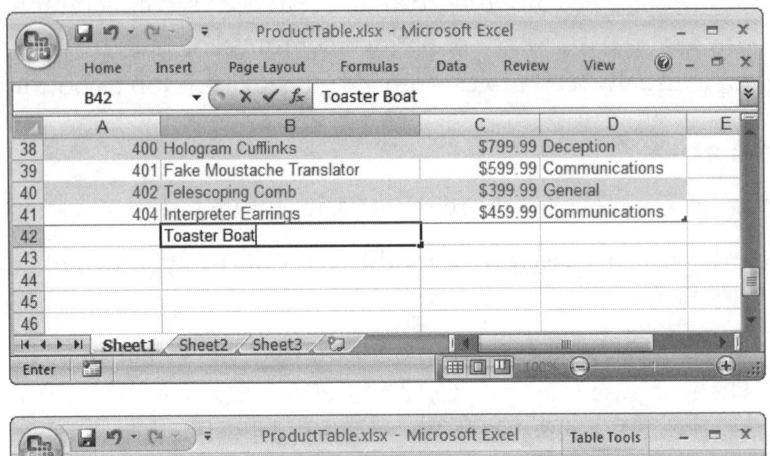

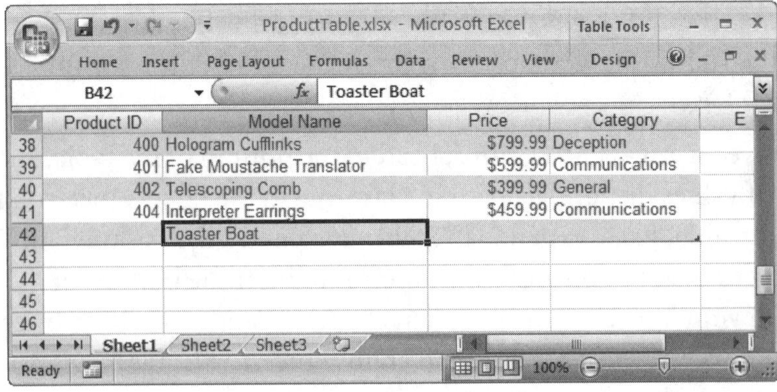

Figure 8-5. Top: Here, a new record is being added just under the current table.

Bottom: Once you enter at least one column of information and move to another cell, Excel adds the new row to the table and formats it.

To add a column to the left of a column you're currently in, select Home → Cells → Insert → Insert Table Columns to the Left. Excel automatically assigns a generic column title, like Column1, which you can then edit. If you want to add a column to the right side of the table, just start typing in the blank column immediately to the right of the table. When you've finished your entry, Excel automatically merges that column into the table, in the same way that it expands to include new rows.

To delete a column, move to one of its cells, and then choose Home → Cells → Delete → Delete Table Column.

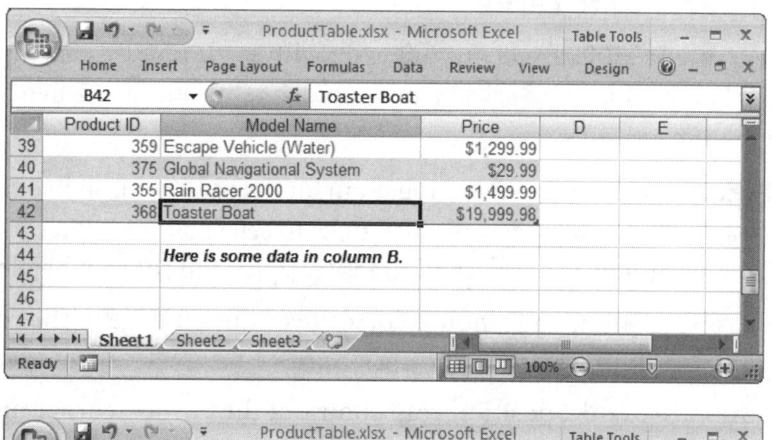

Figure 8-6. Excel makes an effort to leave the rest of your worksheet alone when you change your table's structure. For example, when expanding a table vertically or horizontally, Excel moves cells out of the way only when it absolutely needs more space. The example here demonstrates the point. Compare the before (top) and after (bottom) pictures: Even though the table in the bottom figure has a new column, it hasn't affected the data underneath the table, which still occupies the same column. The same holds true when deleting columns.

Finally, you can always convert your snazzy table back to an ordinary collection of cells. Just click anywhere in the table, and then choose Table Tools | Design → Tools → Convert to Range. But then, of course, you don't get to play with your table toys anymore.

Selecting Parts of a Table

Once you've created a table, Excel provides you with some nice timesaving tools. For example, Excel makes it easy to select a portion of a table, like an individual row or column. Here's how it works:

- **To select a column**, position your mouse cursor over the column header. When it changes to a down-pointing arrow, click once to select all the values in the column. Click a second time to select all the values plus the column header.
- **To select a row**, position your mouse cursor over the left edge of the row until it turns to a right-pointing arrow; then click once.
- **To select the entire table**, position your mouse at the top-left corner until it turns into an arrow that points down and to the right. Click once to select all the values in the table, and click twice to select all the values plus the column headers.

Figure 8-7 shows an example.

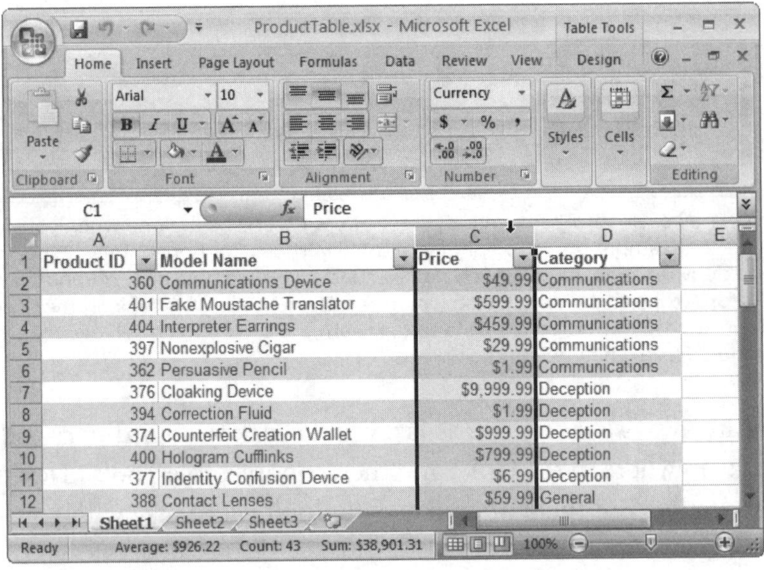

Product ID	Model Name	Price	Category
360	Communications Device	$49.99	Communications
401	Fake Moustache Translator	$599.99	Communications
404	Interpreter Earrings	$459.99	Communications
397	Nonexplosive Cigar	$29.99	Communications
362	Persuasive Pencil	$1.99	Communications
376	Cloaking Device	$9,999.99	Deception
394	Correction Fluid	$1.99	Deception
374	Counterfeit Creation Wallet	$999.99	Deception
400	Hologram Cufflinks	$799.99	Deception
377	Indentity Confusion Device	$6.99	Deception
388	Contact Lenses	$59.99	General

Figure 8-7. You can easily select an entire column in a table. Just position the mouse as shown here, and click once.

Once you've selected a row, column, or the entire table, you can apply extra formatting or create a chart (Chapter 9). However, changing a part of a table isn't exactly like changing a bunch of cells. For example, if you give 10 cells a hot-pink background fill, that's all you get—10 hot-pink cells. But if you give a column a hot-pink background fill, your formatting change may initially affect 10 cells, but every time you add a new value in that column, it also gets the hot-pink background. This behavior, in which Excel recognizes that you're changing parts of a table, and applies your change to new rows and columns automatically, is called *stickiness*.

Sorting and Filtering a Table

As you've seen, Excel tables make it easier to enter, edit, and manage large collections of information. Now it's time to meet two of the most useful table features:

- **Sorting** lets you order the items in your table alphabetically or numerically according to the information in a column. By using the correct criteria, you can make sure the information you're interested in appears at the top of the column, and you can make it easier to find an item anywhere in your table.
- **Filtering** lets you display only certain records in your table based on specific criteria you enter. Filtering lets you work with part of your data and temporarily hide the information you aren't interested in.

You can quickly apply sorting and filtering using the drop-down column headers that Excel adds to every table.

Note

Don't see a drop-down list at the top of your columns? A wrong ribbon click can inadvertently hide them. If you just see ordinary column headings (and you know you have a bona fide table), choose Data → Sort & Filter → Filter to get the drop-down lists back.

Applying a Simple Sort Order

Before you can sort your data, you need to choose a *sorting key*—the piece of information Excel uses to order your records. For example, if you want to sort a table of products so the cheapest (or most expensive) products appear at the top of the table, the Price column would be the sorting key to use.

In addition to choosing a sorting key, you also need to decide whether you want to use ascending or descending order. Ascending order, which is most common, organizes numbers from smallest to largest, dates from oldest to most recent, and text in alphabetical order. (If you have more than one type of data in the same column—which is rarely a good idea—text appears first, followed by numbers and dates, then true or false values, and finally error values.) In descending order, the order is reversed.

To apply a new sort order, choose the column you want to use for your sort key. Click the drop-down box at the right side of the column header, and then choose one of the menu commands that starts with the word "Sort." The exact wording depends on the type of data in the column, as follows:

- **If your column contains numbers**, you see "Sort Smallest to Largest" and "Sort Largest to Smallest".
- **If your column contains text**, you see "Sort A to Z" and "Sort Z to A" (see Figure 8-8).
- **If your column contains dates**, you see "Sort Oldest to Newest" and "Sort Newest to Oldest".

When you choose an option, Excel immediately reorders the records, and then places a tiny arrow in the column header to indicate that you used this column for your sort. However, Excel doesn't keep re-sorting your data when you make changes or add new records (after all, it would be pretty distracting to have your records jump around unexpectedly). If you make some changes and want to reapply the sort, just go to the column header menu and choose the same sort option again.

If you click a second column, and then choose Sort Ascending or Sort Descending, the new sort order replaces your previous sort order. In other words, the column headers let you sort your records quickly, but you can't sort by more than one column at a time.

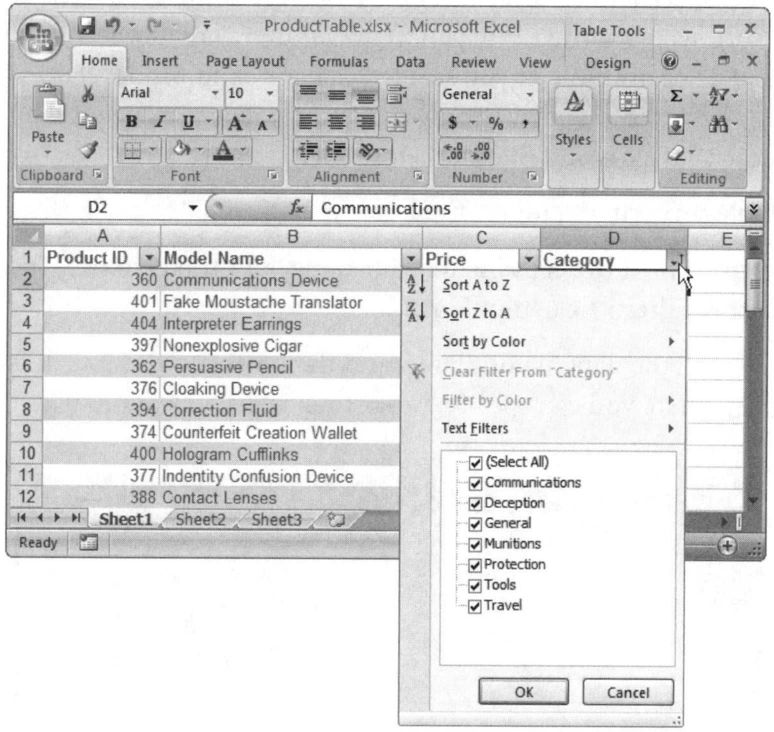

Figure 8-8. A single click is all it takes to order records in ascending order by their category names. You don't need to take any action to create these handy drop-down lists—Excel automatically provides them for every table.

Sorting with Multiple Criteria

Simple table sorting runs into trouble when you have duplicate values. Take the product table sorted by category in Figure 8-8, for example. All the products in the Communications category appear first, followed by products in the Deception category, and so on. However, Excel doesn't make any effort to sort products that are in the *same* category. For example, if you have a bunch of products in the Communications category, then they appear in whatever order they were in on your worksheet, which may not be what you want. In this case, you're better off using *multiple sort criteria*.

With multiple sort criteria, Excel orders the table using more than one sorting key. The second sorting key springs into action only if there are duplicate values in the first sorting key. For example, if you sort by Category and Model Name, Excel first separates the records into alphabetically ordered category groups. It then sorts the products in each category in order of their model name.

To use multiple sort criteria, follow these steps:

1. **Move to any one of the cells inside your table, and then choose Home → Editing → Sort & Filter → Custom Sort.**

   Excel selects all the data in your table, and then displays the Sort dialog box (see Figure 8-9) where you can specify the sorting keys you want to use.

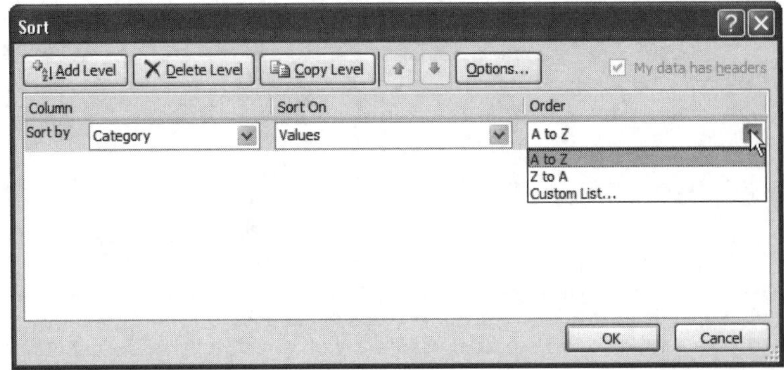

Figure 8-9. To define a sorting key, you need to fill in the column you want to use (in this example, Category). Next, pick the information you want to use from that column, which is almost always the actual cell values (Values). Finally, choose the order for arranging values, which depends on the type of data. For text values, as in this example, you can pick A to Z, Z to A, or Custom List (page 76).

NOTE

You can use the Home → Editing → Sort & Filter → Custom Sort command with any row-based data, including information that's not in a table. When you use it with non-table data, Excel automatically selects the range of cells it believes constitutes your table.

2. **Fill in the information for the first sort key in the Column, Sort On, and Order columns.**

   Figure 8-9 shows how it works.

3. **If you want to add another level of sorting, click Add Level, and then follow the instructions in step 2 to configure it.**

   You can repeat this step to add as many sorting levels as you want (Figure 8-10). Remember, it makes sense to add more levels of sorting only if there's a possibility of duplicate value in the levels you've added so far. For example, if you've sorted a bunch of names by last name, you want to sort by first name, because some people may share the same last name. However, it's probably not worth it to add a third sort on the middle initial, because very few people share the same first and last name.

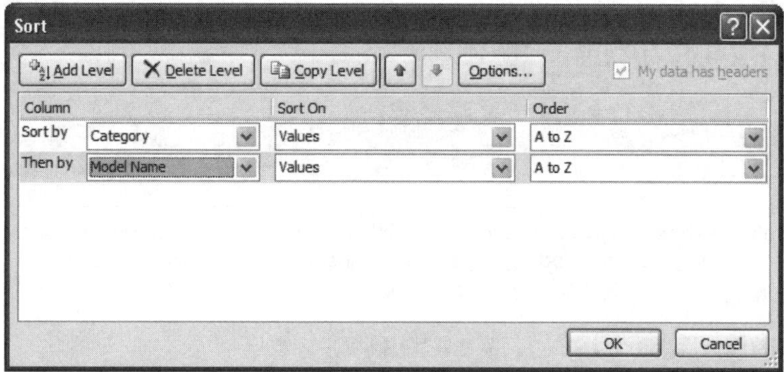

Figure 8-10. This example shows two sorting keys: the Category column and the Model Name column. The Category column may contain duplicate entries, which Excel sorts in turn according to the text in the Model Name column. When you're adding multiple sort keys, make sure they're in the right order. If you need to rearrange your sorting, select a sort key, and then click the arrow buttons to move it up the list (so it's applied first) or down the list (so it's applied later).

4. **Optionally, click the Options button to configure a few finer points about how your data is sorted.**

   For example, you can turn on case-sensitive sorting, which is ordinarily switched off. If you switch it on, *travel* appears before *Travel.*

5. **Click OK.**

   Excel sorts your entire table based on the criteria you've so carefully specified (Figure 8-11).

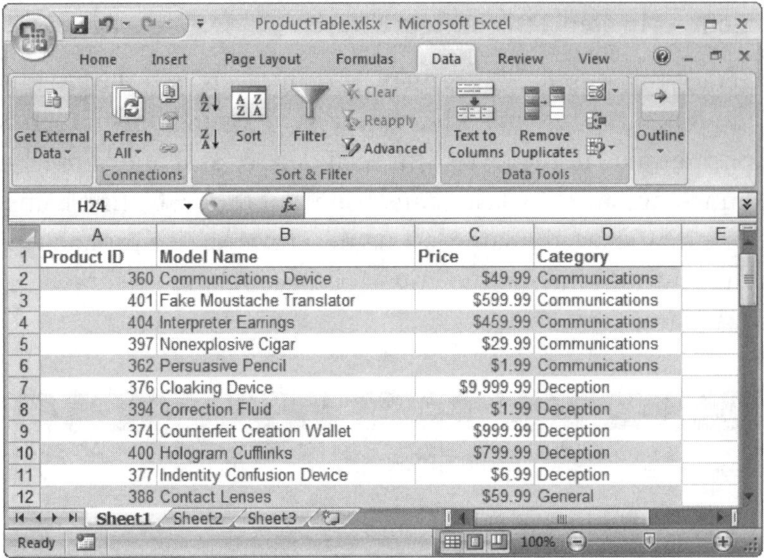

	A	B	C	D	E
1	Product ID	Model Name	Price	Category	
2	360	Communications Device	$49.99	Communications	
3	401	Fake Moustache Translator	$599.99	Communications	
4	404	Interpreter Earrings	$459.99	Communications	
5	397	Nonexplosive Cigar	$29.99	Communications	
6	362	Persuasive Pencil	$1.99	Communications	
7	376	Cloaking Device	$9,999.99	Deception	
8	394	Correction Fluid	$1.99	Deception	
9	374	Counterfeit Creation Wallet	$999.99	Deception	
10	400	Hologram Cufflinks	$799.99	Deception	
11	377	Indentity Confusion Device	$6.99	Deception	
12	388	Contact Lenses	$59.99	General	

Figure 8-11. The worksheet shows the following sort's result: alphabetically ordered categories, each of which contains a subgroup of products that are themselves in alphabetical order.

Filtering with the List of Values

Sorting is great for ordering your data, but it may not be enough to tame large piles of data. You can try another useful technique, *filtering*, which lets you limit the table so it displays only the data that you want to see. Filtering may seem like a small convenience, but if your table contains hundreds or thousands of rows, filtering is vital for your day-to-day worksheet sanity. Here are some situations where filtering becomes especially useful:

- To pluck out important information, like the number of accounts that currently have a balance due. Filtering lets you see just the information you need, saving you hours of headaches.
- To print a report that shows only the customers who live in a specific city.
- To calculate information like sums and averages for products in a specific group.

POWER USERS' CLINIC

Sorting with a Custom List

Most of the time, you'll want to stick with the standard sorting orders. For example, you'll put numbers in numeric order, dates in chronological order, and text in alphabetical order. But not always. For example, you may have good reason to arrange the categories in Figure 8-11 in a different order that puts more important categories at the top of the table. Or, you may have text values that have special meaning and are almost always used in a specific non-alphabetical order, like the days of the week (Sunday, Monday, Tuesday, and so on) or calendar months (January, February, March, April, and so on).

You can deal with these scenarios with a custom list that specifies your sort order. In the Order column, choose Custom List. This choice opens the Custom List dialog box, where you can choose an existing list or create a new one by selecting NEW LIST and typing in your values. (Page 76 has more on creating specialized lists.) Figure 8-12 shows an example.

Custom list sorting works best when you have a relatively small number of values that never change. If you have dozens of different values, it's probably too tedious to type them all into a custom list.

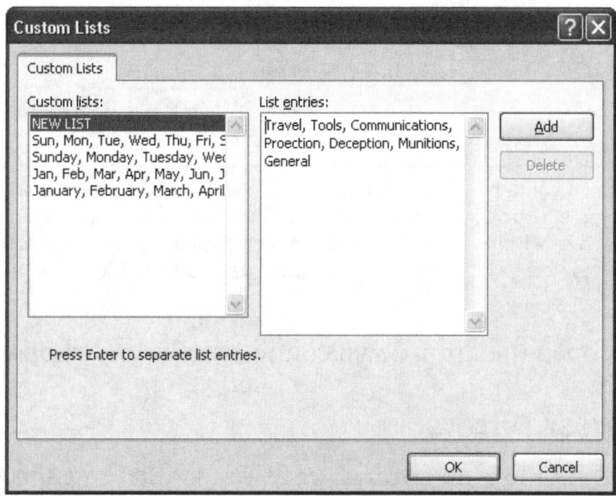

Figure 8-12. Using a custom list for your sort order, you can arrange your categories so that Travel always appears at the top, as shown here. Once you've finished entering a custom list, click Add to store the list for future use.

Automatic filtering, like sorting, uses the drop-down column headings. When you click the drop-down arrow, Excel shows a list of all the distinct values in that column. Figures 8-13 and 8-14 show how filtering works on the Category column.

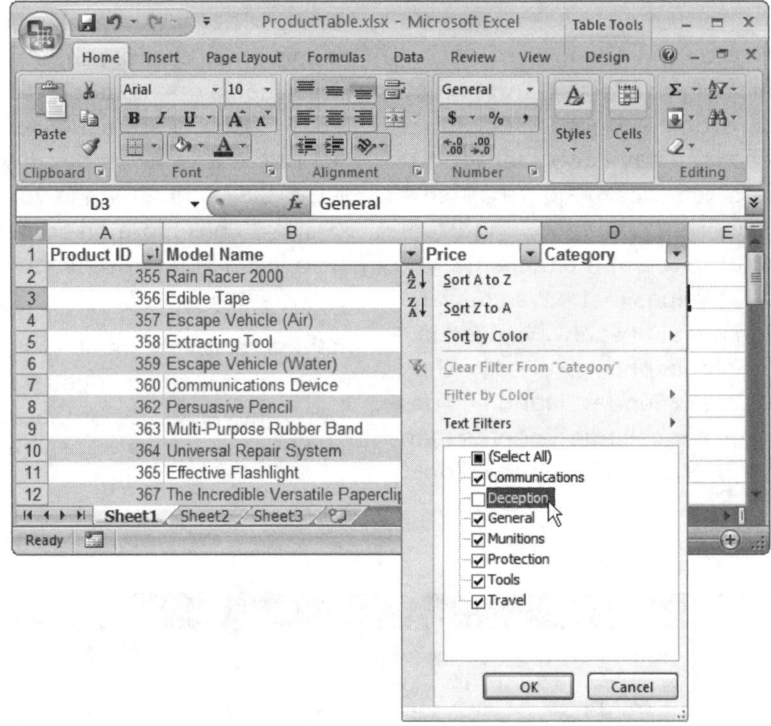

Figure 8-13. Initially, each value has a checkmark next to it. Clear the checkmark to hide rows with that value. (In this example, products in the Deception category won't appear in the table.) Or, if you want to home in on just a few items, clear the Select All checkmark to remove all the checkmarks, and then choose just the ones you want to see in your table, as shown in Figure 8-14.

To remove a filter, open the drop-down column menu, and choose Clear Filter.

Creating Smarter Filters

The drop-down column lists give you an easy way to filter out specific rows. However, in many situations you'll want a little more intelligence in your filtering. For example, imagine you're filtering a list of products to focus on all those that top $100. You could scroll through the list of values, and remove the checkmark next to every price that's lower than $100. What a pain in the neck that would be.

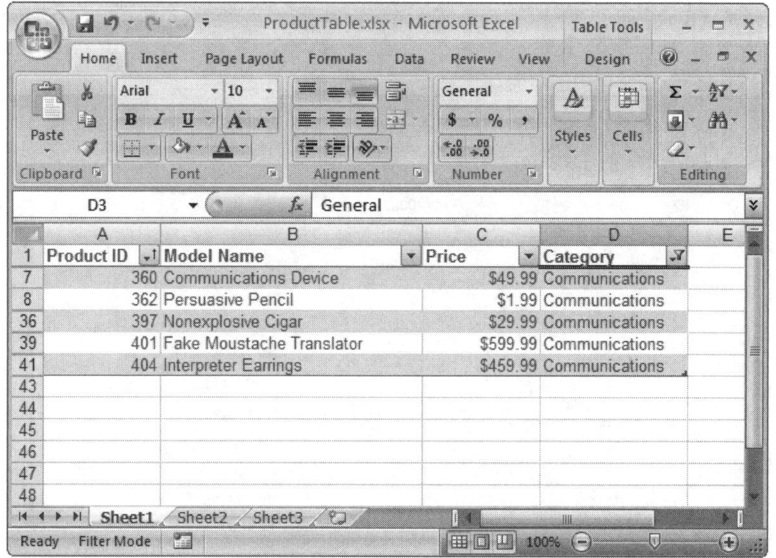

Figure 8-14. If you select Communications and nothing else from the Category list in the product table example, the table displays only the five products in the Communications category.

Thankfully, Excel has more filtering features that can really help you out here. Based on the type of data in your column (text, a number, or date values), Excel adds a wide range of useful filter options to the drop-down column lists. You'll see how this all works in the following sections.

Filtering dates

You can filter dates that fall before or after another date, or you can use preset periods like last week, last month, next month, year-to-date, and so on.

To use date filtering, open the drop-down column list, and choose Date Filters. Figure 8-15 shows what you see.

Filtering numbers

For numbers, you can filter values that match exactly, numbers that are smaller or larger than a specified number, or numbers that are above or below average.

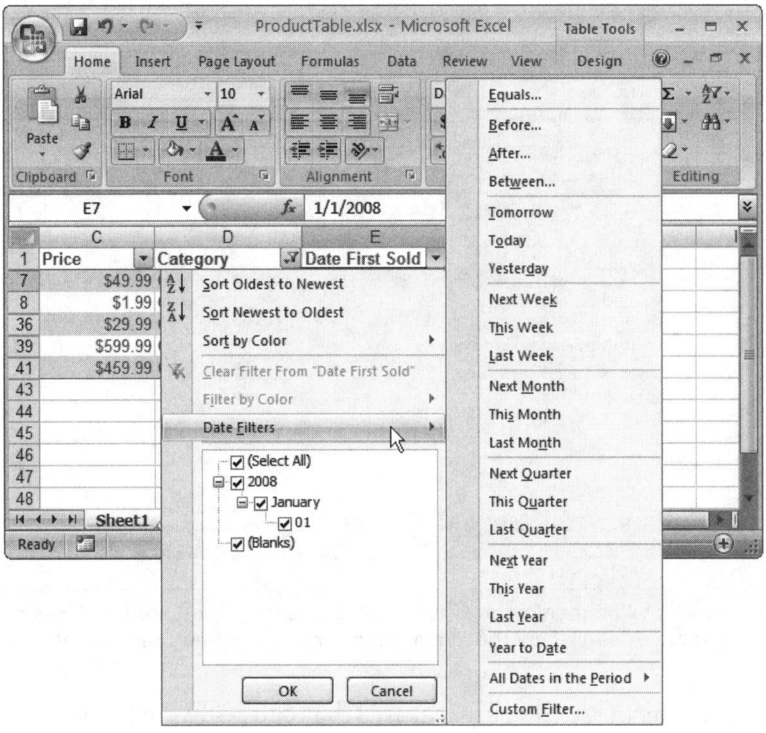

Figure 8-15. Shown here is the mind-boggling array of ready-made date filtering options you can apply to a column that contains dates. For example, choose Last Week to see just those dates that fall in the period Sunday to Saturday in the previous week.

To use number filtering, open the drop-down column list, choose Number Filters, and then pick one of the filter options. For example, imagine you're trying to limit the product list to show expensive products. You can accomplish this quite quickly with a number filter. Just open the drop-down column list for the Price column, and then choose Number Filters → Greater Than Or Equal To. A dialog box appears where you can supply the $100 minimum (Figure 8-16).

Filtering text

For text, you can filter values that match exactly, or values that contain a piece of text. To apply text filtering, open the drop-down column list, and then choose Text Filters.

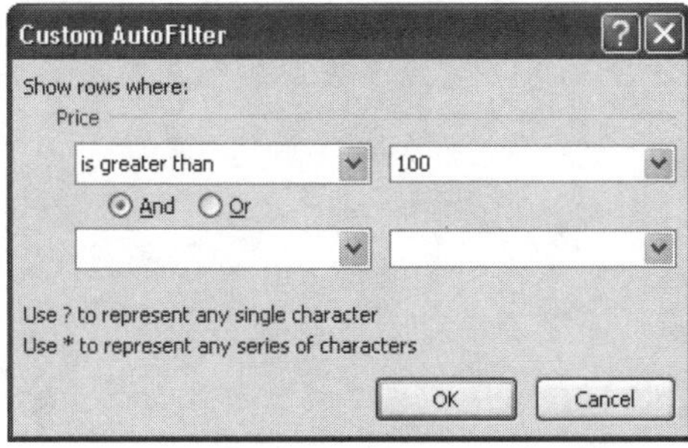

Figure 8-16. This dialog box lets you complete the Greater Than Or Equal To filter. It matches all products that are $100 or more. You can use the bottom portion of the window (left blank in this example) to supply a second filter condition that either further restricts (choose And) or supplements your matches (choose Or).

WORKAROUND WORKSHOP

The Disappearing Cells

Table filtering's got one quirk. When you filter a table, Excel hides the rows that contain the filtered records. In fact, all Excel really does is shrink each of these rows to have a height of 0 so they're neatly out of sight. The problem? When Excel hides a row, it hides all the data in that row, *even if the data is not a part of the table*.

That property means that if you place a formula in one of the cells to the right of the table, then this formula may disappear from your worksheet temporarily when you filter the table! This behavior is quite a bit different from what happens if you delete a row, in which case cells outside the table aren't affected.

If you frequently use filtering, you may want to circumvent this problem by putting your formulas underneath or above the table. Generally, putting the formulas above the table is the most convenient choice because the cells don't move as the table expands or contracts.

If you're performing filtering with text fields, you can gain even more precise control using wildcards. The asterisk (*) matches any series of characters, while the question mark (?) matches a single character. So the filter expression *Category equals T** matches any category that starts with the letter T. The filter expression *Category equals T????* matches any five-letter category that starts with T.

CREATING BASIC CHARTS

9

- Charting 101
- Basic Tasks with Charts
- Practical Charting
- Chart Types

As you become more skilled with Excel, you'll realize that entering numbers, organizing your layout, and formatting cells aren't the most important parts of spreadsheet creation. Instead, the real work lies in *analyzing* your data—in other words, figuring out a way to tell the story that lies *behind* your numbers. Excel's charting tools may be just what you need.

Charts depict data visually, so you can quickly spot overall trends. They're a fabulous way to help you find the meaning hidden in large amounts of data. You can create many different types of charts in Excel, including pie charts that present polling results, line charts that plot rising or declining assets over time, and three-dimensional area charts that show relationships between environmental conditions in a scientific experiment.

Excel's charting tools are enormously flexible: You can generate a simple chart with standard options in a couple of mouse clicks, or you can painstakingly customize every aspect of your chart's appearance (including colors, scale, titles, and even 3-D perspective). This chapter takes the first approach and explains how to generate straightforward charts.

Note

All charts are *not* created equal. Depending on the chart type you use, the scale you choose, and the data you include, your chart may suggest different conclusions. The true chart artist knows how to craft a chart to draw out the most important information. As you become more skilled with charts, you'll acquire these instincts, too.

Charting 101

Excel provides a dizzying number of different chart types, but they all share a few things. In this section, you'll learn about basic Excel charting concepts that apply to almost all types of charts; you'll also create a few basic charts. At the end of this chapter, you'll take a tour of Excel's most useful chart types.

To create a chart, Excel needs to translate your numbers into a graphical representation. The process of drawing numbers on a graph is called *plotting*. Before you plot your information on a chart, you should make sure your data's laid out properly. Here are some tips:

- Structure your data in a simple grid of rows and columns.
- Don't include blank cells between rows or columns.
- Include titles, if you'd like them to appear in your chart. You can use category titles for each column of data (placed in the first row, atop each column) and an overall chart title (placed just above the category-title row).

TIP

You can also label each row by placing titles in the far-left column, if it makes sense. If you're comparing the sales numbers for different products, list the name of each product in the first column on the left, with the sales figures in the following columns.

If you follow these guidelines, you can expect to create the sort of chart shown in Figure 9-1.

To create the chart shown in Figure 9-1, Excel performs a few straightforward steps (you'll learn the specifics of how to actually create this chart in the next section). First, it extracts the text for the chart title from cell A1. Next, it examines the range of data (from $14,000 to $64,000) and uses it to set the value—or Y-axis—scale. You'll notice that the scale starts at $0, and stretches up to $80,000 in order to give your data a little room to breathe. (You could configure these numbers manually, but Excel automatically makes common-sense guesses like these by looking at the data you're asking it to chart.) After setting the vertical scale, Excel adds the labels along the bottom axis (also known as the X-axis or category axis), and draws the columns of appropriate height.

Embedded and Standalone Charts

The chart in Figure 9-1 is an *embedded* chart. Embedded charts appear in a worksheet, in a floating box alongside your data. You can move the chart by dragging the box around your worksheet, although depending on where you put it, you may obscure some of your data.

Your other option is to create a *standalone* chart, which looks the same but occupies an entire worksheet. That means that your chart data and your chart are placed on separate worksheets.

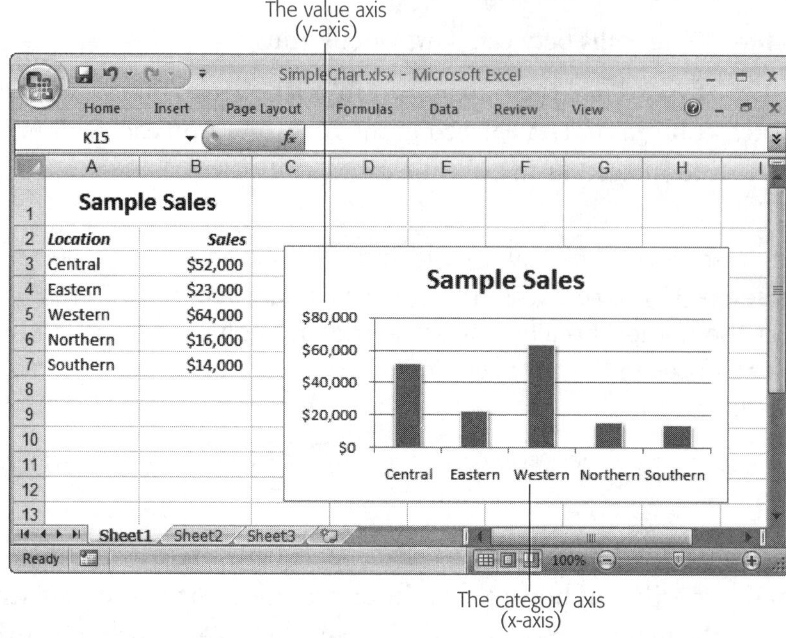

Figure 9-1. This worksheet shows a table of data and a simple column chart based on Excel's standard chart settings. Nothing fancy, but it gets the job done.

Usually, you'll use an embedded chart if you want to create printouts that combine both your worksheet data and one or more charts. On the other hand, if you want to print the charts separately, it's more convenient to use standalone charts. That way, you can print an entire workbook at once and have the charts and the data on separate pages.

TIP

If you use embedded charts, you still have the option of printing just the chart, sized so that it fills a full sheet of paper. Simply select the chart and then choose Office button → Print.

NOSTALGIA CORNER

Charts Get a Facelift

If you've worked with charts in a previous version of Excel, you'll notice that Excel 2007 adds some serious eye candy. Overall, the types of charts you can create and the options to plot your data are the same as in previous versions. However, the *rendering engine*, the system that turns your data into lines and shapes, is completely new.

Along with the new rendering engine, Excel 2007 also changes the way you create your charts. Gone is the frumpy Chart Wizard. Now, the ribbon provides quick chart creation and easy-access options for changing every aspect of a chart, from its gridlines to its legend.

Creating a Chart with the Ribbon

So how do you create a chart like the one shown in Figure 9-1? Easy—all it takes is a couple of clicks in the ribbon. Here's how it works:

1. **Select the range of cells that includes the data you want to chart, including the column and row headings and any chart title.**

   If you were using the data shown in Figure 9-1, you'd select cells A1 to B7.

   For speedier chart building, just position your cursor somewhere inside the data you want to chart. Excel then automatically selects the range of cells that it thinks you want. Of course, it never hurts to remove the possibility for error by explicitly selecting what you want to use before you get started.

TIP

And for even *easier* charting, start by creating an Excel table (Chapter 8) to hold the data you want to chart. Then, if you position yourself somewhere inside the table and create a new chart, Excel automatically selects all the data. It also automatically updates the chart if you add new rows or remove existing data.

2. **Head to the ribbon's Insert → Charts section. You'll see a separate button for each type of chart (including column charts, line charts, pie charts, and so on). Click the type you want.**

   When you choose a chart type, you get a drop-down list of subtypes (Figure 9-2).

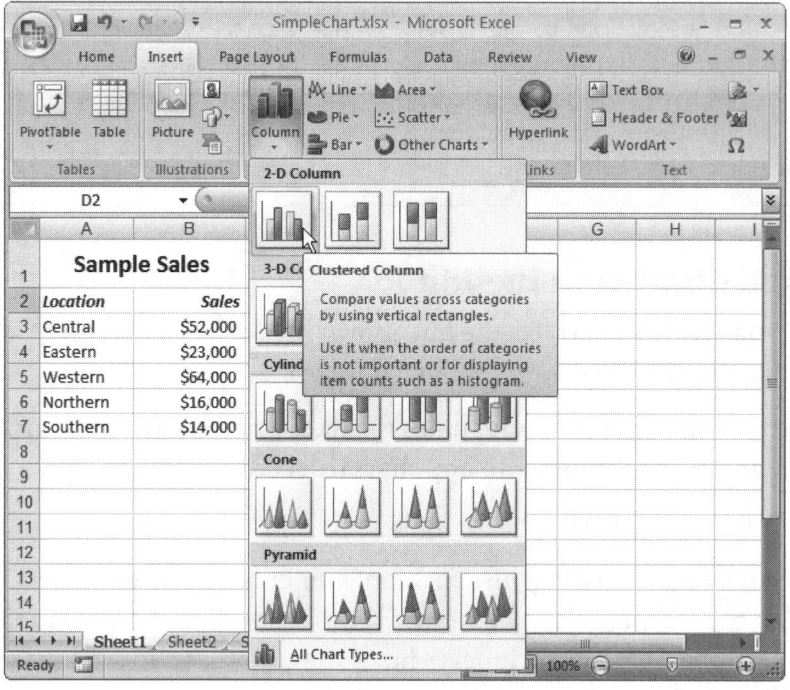

Figure 9-2. Under each chart choice are yet more subtypes, which add to the fun. If you select the Column type (shown here), you'll get subtypes for two- and three-dimensional column charts, and variants that use cone and pyramid shapes. If you hover over one of these subtypes, a box appears with a brief description of the chart.

The different chart types are explained in more detail later in this chapter. For now, it's best to stick to some of the more easily understood choices, like Bar, Column, or Pie. Remember, the chart choices are just the starting point, as you'll still be able to configure a wide range of details that control things like the titles, colors, and overall organization of your chart.

3. **Click the subtype you want.**

   Excel inserts a new embedded chart alongside your data, using the standard options (which you can fine-tune later).

NOTE

If you don't want to make *any* choices, you can actually build a chart with one key press. Just highlight your data and press F11. This step creates a column chart on a new worksheet. Although you can't undo this operation, you can always delete the new chart worksheet and start over.

The Chart Tools Ribbon Tabs

When you select a chart, Excel adds three new tabs to the ribbon under the Chart Tools heading. These tabs let you control the details of your charts:

- **Design.** This tab lets you change the chart type and the linked data that the chart uses.
- **Layout.** This tab lets you configure individual parts of the chart. You can add shapes, pictures, and text labels, and you can configure the chart's gridlines, axes, and background.
- **Format.** This tab lets you format individual chart elements, so you can transform ordinary items into eye candy. You can adjust the font, fill, and borders uses for chart titles and shapes, among other things.

In this chapter, you'll spend most of your time using the Chart Tools | Design tab.

Basic Tasks with Charts

Unlike the orderly rows of numbers and labels that fill most worksheets, charts float *above* your data, locked inside special box-like containers. To take advantage of these chart boxes, you need to understand a little more about how they work.

POWER USERS' CLINIC

Browsing Excel's Chart Gallery

Excel pros sometimes find that the ribbon approach is a bit awkward when you're trying to find a less commonly used chart type. In this situation, you may prefer to look at the full list of chart types and subtypes. To do so, head to the ribbon's Insert → Charts section, and then click the dialog launcher (the square-with-an-arrow icon in the bottom-right corner). You see the Insert Chart dialog box (Figure 9-3).

The Insert Chart dialog box doesn't just let you create charts. You can also designate the default chart type (the one that's used if you select some cells, and then press F11 to create a chart in a single bound). To designate a default chart, select it, and then click "Set as Default Chart".

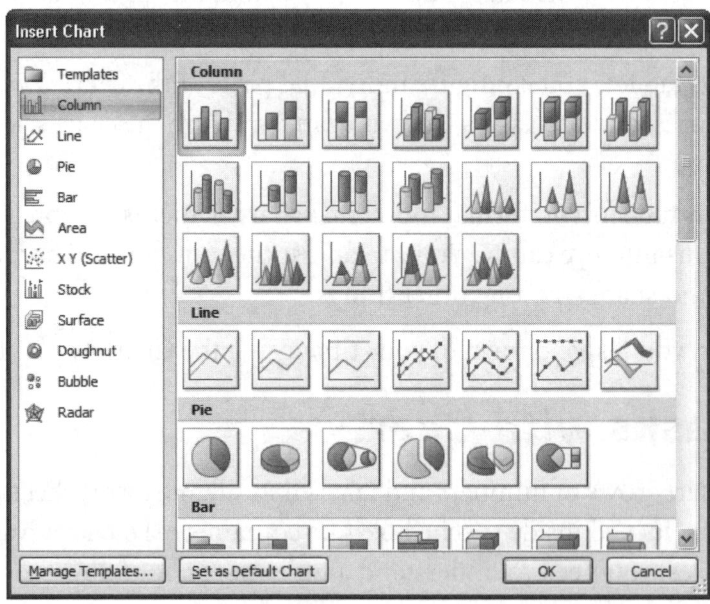

Figure 9-3. The gallery on the Insert Chart dialog box's right side has a thumbnail of every chart subtype, grouped by type. You can scroll through them all, or you can choose a type from the list on the left to jump straight to a specific section. When you find what you want, click OK to create it.

Moving and Resizing a Chart

When you insert a chart into an existing worksheet, it becomes a floating object, hovering above your worksheet. Depending on where Excel puts it, it may temporarily obscure your data. The chart box doesn't damage your data in any way, but it can end up hiding your worksheet's numbers and text (both onscreen and in your printouts).

You have to learn to grab hold of these floating boxes and place them where you really want them. The process is pretty straightforward:

1. **Click once on the chart to select it.**

   You'll notice that when you select a chart, Excel highlights the worksheet data the chart uses. At the same time, three new tabs appear in the ribbon, under the Chart Tools heading (Figure 9-4).

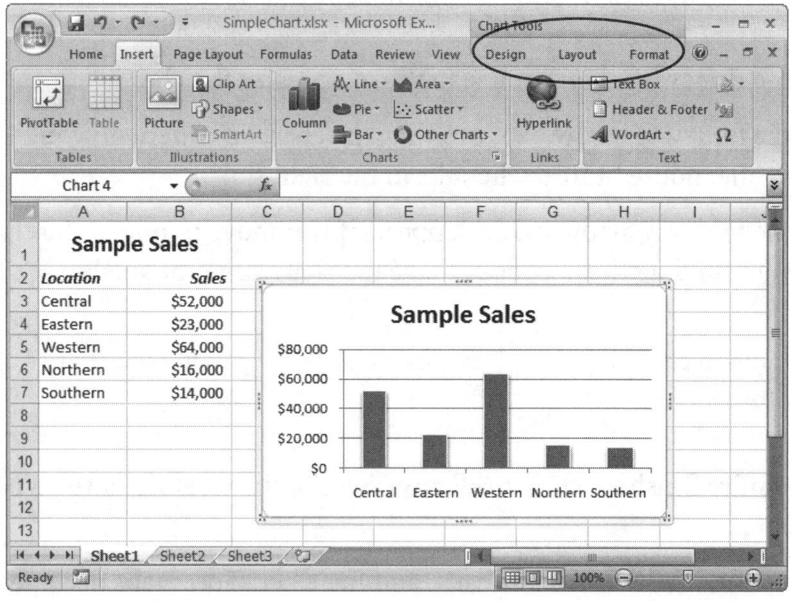

Figure 9-4. You'll know you've selected the chart when three new charting tabs appear in the ribbon under the Chart Tools heading.

2. **Hover over the chart border until the mouse pointer changes to a four-way arrow.**

   Figure 9-5 shows what you're looking for.

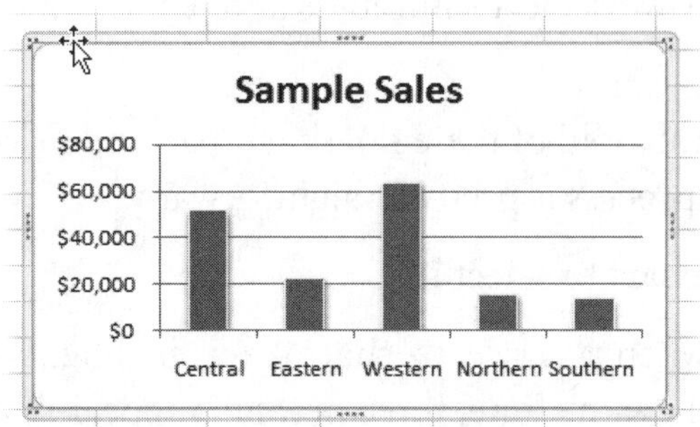

Figure 9-5. The four-way arrow is a signal that you can click here to move the chart. If you move to one of the corners, you'll see an angled two-way arrow, which lets you resize the chart.

3. **Click and drag with your mouse to move or resize the chart.**

   Using the four-way arrow, you can drag the chart anywhere on your worksheet, releasing the mouse button when it's in the right spot.

   Using the two-way arrow (which appears if you move to one of the chart's corners), you can drag the border to make the chart larger or smaller.

TIP

To remove a chart in one fell swoop, just select it with the mouse, and then press Delete.

4. **When you're finished, click a cell anywhere in the worksheet to go back to your data.**

   At this point, life returns to normal, and the Chart Tools tabs disappear.

NOTE

You can resize a chart in another, slightly more circuitous way. You can set the Height and Width boxes in the Chart Tools | Format → Size section of the ribbon. Although this isn't as quick as dragging the chart edge, it lets you set the size exactly, which is indispensable if you have several charts on the same worksheet and you need to make sure they're all the same size.

UNDER THE HOOD

How Excel Anchors Charts

Although charts appear to float above the worksheet, they're actually anchored to the cells underneath. Each corner of the chart is anchored to one cell (these anchor points change, of course, if you move the chart around). This fact becomes important if you decide to insert or delete rows or columns anywhere in your worksheet.

For example, consider the chart shown in Figure 9-1. Its top edge is bound to row 2, and its bottom edge is bound to row 12. Similarly, its left edge is bound to column C, and its right edge to column I. That means if you insert a new row above row 2, the whole chart shifts down one row. If you insert a column to the left of column C, the whole chart shifts one column to the right.

Even more interesting is what happens if you insert rows or columns in the area that the chart overlaps. For example, if you insert a new row between the current row 10 and row 11, the chart stretches, becoming one row taller. Similarly, if you delete column D, the chart compresses, becoming one column thinner.

If it bugs you, you can change this sizing behavior. First, select the chart and head to the ribbon's Chart Tools | Format → Size section. Then, click the dialog launcher (the square-with-an-arrow icon in the bottom-right corner). When the Size and Properties dialog box appears, choose the Properties tab. You'll see three "Object positioning" options. The standard behavior is "Move and size with cells", but you can also create a chart that moves around the worksheet but never resizes itself ("Move but don't size with cells") and a chart that's completely fixed in size and position ("Don't move or size with cells").

Creating a Standalone Chart

Even without your input, Excel usually makes common-sense choices, so you can often build a chart without needing to tweak any of these options.

You have two options for placing charts in a workbook. You can create an embedded chart, which appears in an existing worksheet (usually next to the appropriate data), or you can create a standalone chart, which appears in a new worksheet of its own (Figure 9-6).

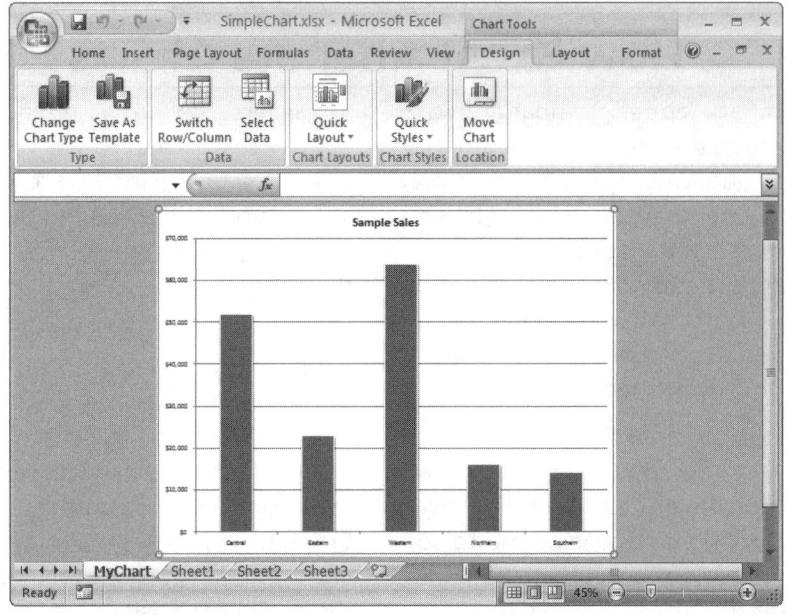

Figure 9-6. A standalone chart lives in a separate worksheet that doesn't have any other data and doesn't include the familiar grid of cells.

Ordinarily, when you pick a chart type from the ribbon, Excel creates an embedded chart. However, you can easily switch your chart over to a new worksheet if you're running out of room—just follow these steps:

1. **Right-click the chart, and then choose Move Chart (or, select the chart, and then choose Chart Tools | Design → Location → Move Chart).**

   The Move Chart dialog box appears (Figure 9-7).

2. **Choose "New sheet", and then enter the name for the new worksheet.**

3. **Click OK.**

   Excel creates the new worksheet and places the chart on it. The new worksheet goes in front of the worksheet that contains the chart data. (You can always move the worksheet to a new position in your workbook by dragging the worksheet tab.)

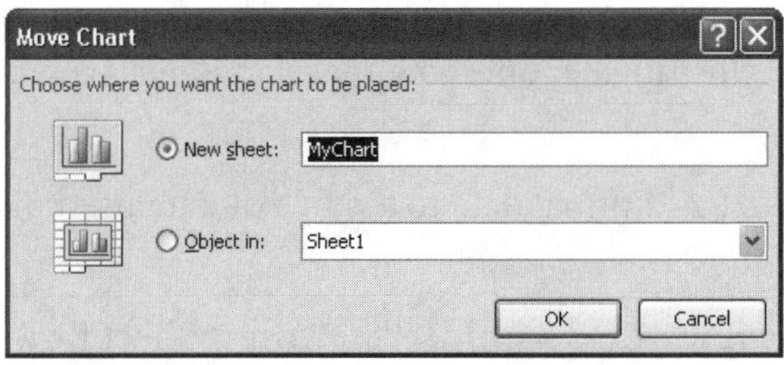

Figure 9-7. Using the Move Chart dialog box, you can transfer the chart to a standalone worksheet (as shown here) or shuffle it over to another worksheet and keep it as an embedded worksheet. (If you want the latter option, it's just as easy to select the chart and use a cut-and-paste operation to move it to a new worksheet.)

NOTE

You can move or resize only embedded charts—the ones that appear in floating boxes inside other worksheets. If you've created a standalone chart, you can't move or resize it. Instead, it automatically shrinks or enlarges itself to match the Excel window's display area.

Editing and Adding to Chart Data

Every chart remains linked to the source data you used to create it. When you alter the data in your worksheet, Excel refreshes the chart with the new information automatically.

NOTE

Excel's got no restriction on linking multiple charts to the same data. So, you can create two different types of charts (like a pie and a column chart) that show the same data. You can even create one chart that plots all the data and another chart that just uses a portion of the same information.

However, there's one tricky point. Any range you define for use in a chart is *static*, which means it doesn't grow as your data grows. That means that if you add a new row at the bottom of the range, it doesn't appear on the chart because it's outside of the chart range.

If you do want to insert additional data to a range of data used in a chart, you have a couple of options:

- **You can use the Home → Cells → Insert → Insert Sheet Rows command.** If you do, Excel notices the change, and automatically expands the range to include the newly inserted row. However, this command works only if you add a row into the middle of your data. If you try to tack a row onto the end, Excel still ignores it, and you'll need to use the solution described in the next bullet point.
- **After you insert new rows, you can modify the chart range to include the new data.** This approach is the most common, and it's quite painless. First, select your chart by clicking the edge of the chart box, or a blank space in the chart. Excel highlights the linked worksheet data with a colored border. Click this colored border, and drag it until it includes all the new data you want. When you release the mouse button, Excel refreshes the chart with the new information. See the box on page 289 for more information.

Excel is smart enough to adjust your chart range in some situations. If you drag your chart data to a new place on your worksheet, Excel updates the chart to match automatically.

Changing the Chart Type

When you create a chart, you choose a specific chart type. However, in many situations you may want to try several different chart types with the same data to see which visualization tells your story better. Excel makes this sort of experimentation easy. All you need to do is click your chart to select it, and then make a different choice from the ribbon's Insert → Charts section. You can use this technique to transform a column chart into a pie chart.

You can also choose Chart Tools | Design → Type → Change Chart Type to make a choice from the Change Chart Type dialog box, which looks just like the Insert Chart dialog box shown in Figure 9-3.

POWER USERS' CLINIC

Charting a Table

You can use the Excel table feature (discussed in Chapter 8) with charts. Tables and charts make a perfect match. Tables grow and shrink dynamically in size as you add or delete records. If a chart's bound to a table, the chart updates itself as you add new information or remove old data.

You've already learned how to build a new chart using an existing table. (Just move inside the table, and then make a selection from the ribbon's Insert → Charts section). But even if you've already created the chart with an ordinary range of cells, you can still use a table—all you need to do is convert the linked range to a table.

In the sales report example shown in Figure 9-1, here's what you'd need to do:

1. Select the range of cells that contain all the data, not including the chart's title (cells A2 to B7).
2. Select Insert → Tables → Table.

Now, as you add new items to the table, Excel adds them to the chart immediately.

When you chart a table, you also gain the ability to use other features, like easier sorting and filtering. You can use sorting to determine the order that items appear within a chart (which is occasionally useful), and you can use filtering to hide rows and to chart only a portion of the data (which is often indispensable). If you apply a filter condition that shows only the three best performing regions, the chart updates itself so that it shows only this data. You'll find this technique particularly handy when you're creating charts that use multiple series, as described later in this chapter.

For more information about filtering and the ever-impressive table feature, flip back to Chapter 8.

Printing Charts

How you print a chart depends on the type of chart you've created. You can print embedded charts either with worksheet data or on their own. Standalone charts, which occupy separate worksheets, always print on separate pages.

Embedded charts

You can print embedded charts in two ways. The first approach is to print your worksheet exactly as it appears on the screen, with a mix of data and floating charts. In this case, you'll need to take special care to make sure your charts aren't positioned over any data you need to read in the printout. To double-check, use Page Layout view (choose View → Workbook Views → Page Layout View).

You could also print out the embedded chart on a separate page, which is surprisingly easy. Just click the chart to select it, and then choose Office Button → Print (or Office Button → Print → Print Preview to see what it'll look like). When you do so, Excel's standard choice is to print your chart using landscape orientation, so that the long edge of the page is along the bottom, and the chart's wider than it is tall. Landscape is usually the best way to align a chart, especially if it holds a large amount of data, so Excel automatically uses landscape orientation no matter what page orientation you've configured for your worksheet. If you want to change the chart orientation, select the chart, then choose Page Layout → Page Setup → Orientation → Portrait. Now your chart uses upright alignment, just as you may see in a portrait-style painting.

NOTE

If you select an orientation from the Page Layout → Page Setup → Orientation list while your chart is selected, you *don't* end up configuring the orientation for the worksheet itself. Instead you configure the embedded chart's orientation when you print it out on a separate page. If you want to configure the orientation for the whole worksheet, make sure nothing else is selected when you choose an orientation.

Excel also includes some page setup options that are specific to charts. To see these options, head to the Page Layout → Page Setup section, click the dialog launcher in the bottom-right corner to show the Page Setup dialog box, and then choose the

Chart tab (which appears only when you've got a chart currently selected). You'll see an option to print a chart using lower print quality ("Draft quality"), and in black and white instead of color ("Print in black and white").

Standalone charts

If you're using a standalone chart, your chart always prints out on a separate page, sized to fit the whole page. To print out just the chart page alone (rather than the whole workbook), switch to the chart's worksheet, and then choose Office Button → Print. To print out the entire workbook—which prints your data worksheet and chart worksheet on different pages—look in the "Print what" section and select the "Entire workbook" option.

Excel automatically sets all chart worksheets to Landscape orientation, which orients the page so that the long edge runs horizontally across the bottom. If this layout isn't what you want, before you print the chart, choose Page Layout → Page Setup → Orientation → Portrait. Remember, if you're still not sure how your printout will look, you can always use the handy Page Layout View to see a sneak preview. For more information about printing Excel files, see Chapter 6.

Practical Charting

Figure 9-1 showed you how to chart a list that contains two columns you want to graph—one with text labels and one with numeric data. But, in real life, you'll probably need to deal with many different types of data that occupy many different configurations on your worksheet.

Consider all the possible variations on the simple sales chart shown in Figure 9-1. You may need to compare the sales figures but, rather than showing region-to-region comparisons, you want to show how well (or poorly) each of your firm's products sold. Or perhaps you want to chart the quarterly performance of different stores over a five-year period, or determine the relationship between sales and profitability. All these charts require a slightly different arrangement of data. In the next section, you'll get a quick introduction to all these possibilities, using just the simple column chart and line chart.

UP TO SPEED

Data in Different Scales

Remember when your mother told you not to compare apples and oranges? The same rule applies with charts. When you add multiple series, each series should use the same *scale*. In other words, the points for each series should be plotted (placed on the chart) using the same measurement system.

The worksheet in Figure 9-8 works perfectly well because the different series of sales figures all use the same unit—dollars. But if one series recorded sales totals in dollars and another recorded them in Euros (or, even worse, recorded totally different data like the number of units sold), the chart would be inconsistent.

Excel doesn't complain if your series use different scales—in fact, it has no way of noticing that anything's amiss. And if you don't notice either, you'll create a misleading chart.

Your chart may imply a comparison that isn't accurate or, if the scale is radically different, the chart can get so stretched that it starts to lose detail. If you have sales figures from $50,000 to $100,000 and units sold from 1 to 100, the scale stretches from 1 to 100,000, and the differences in sales totals or units sold are too small to show up at all.

What's the solution? Don't mix different scales. Ideally, convert values to the same scale (in this case, use the currency exchange rate to turn Euros into U.S. dollars before you create the chart). Or just create two charts, one for each data series.

Charts with Multiple Series of Numbers

A *series* is the sequence of numbers that you plot on a graph. In the simple chart example (Figure 9-1), there's one series of numbers, which represents the sales figures for a company's different regions. Of course, a real chart usually adds extra layers of detail. You may want to compare the sales figures from several different years. In this case, you'd add a separate column to your worksheet data for each year. Then you'd add each column to your chart as a separate series.

It doesn't take any extra expertise to create a chart that uses multiple series—you just select the right range of cells and pick a chart option from the ribbon, just as you would for a chart that has a single series. Different types of charts handle multiple series in different ways. The clustered column chart creates a separate bar for each value in a row, as shown in Figure 9-8. A line chart, on the other hand, shows a separate line for each series (as demonstrated in the next section). For more possibilities, take a look at the "Chart Types" section on page 300.

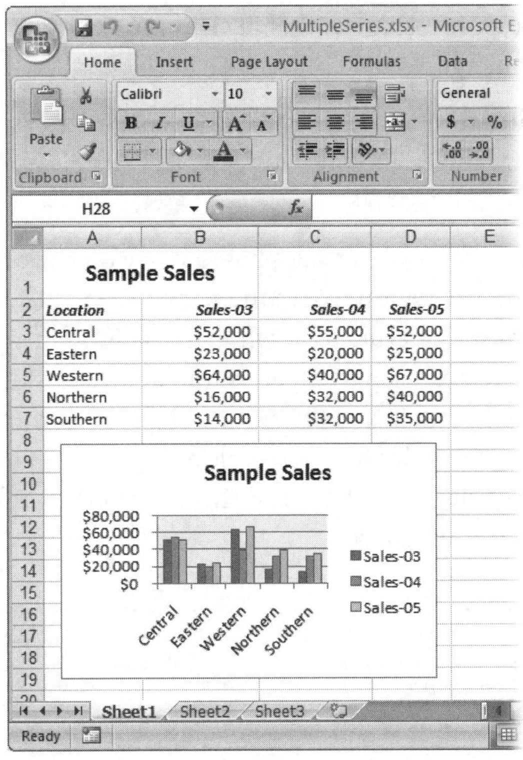

Figure 9-8. This chart has three series of sales figures (one for each year) and five sets of columns (one for each region). Each of the five sets has three bars, one for each data series. The regions are labeled on the category axis, but you'll need to consult the legend to determine which year each column represents.

TIP

You can add multiple series to an existing chart without starting over from scratch. First, select the chart so that the linked data becomes highlighted. Then, click the rightmost edge, and drag it to the right to expand the range so that it includes the new columns (which, of course, you've already added to your worksheet).

Controlling the Data Excel Plots on the X-Axis

Excel's charting tool has a dirty little secret. You may not realize it right away, but sooner or later, whether it's your first chart or your fortieth, you'll stumble onto the fact that Excel makes a fairly important decision for you about what data shows up in your chart's X-axis. Unfortunately, this decision may not be what you want. Fortunately, you can change it.

But what causes the situation in the first place? Excel creates your charts according to the way the data's organized in your worksheet. A simple example shows you the effect.

The worksheet in Figure 9-9 looks at sales based on two factors: the year when the sales were recorded, and the region where the sales were made. In technical charting terms, the regions form the *category axis*, while the sales figures form the *value axis*. In other words, Excel creates a separate series for each year. But it makes just as much sense to organize the table in a different way, by making the year the category axis and creating a separate series for each region! Figure 9-9 contrasts these two different ways of looking at the same data, and shows how they affect the way Excel groups your data in a column chart.

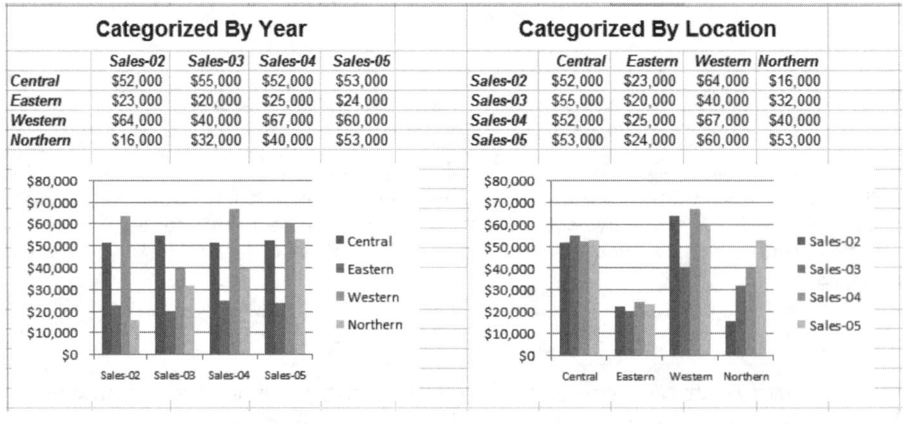

Categorized By Year

	Sales-02	Sales-03	Sales-04	Sales-05
Central	$52,000	$55,000	$52,000	$53,000
Eastern	$23,000	$20,000	$25,000	$24,000
Western	$64,000	$40,000	$67,000	$60,000
Northern	$16,000	$32,000	$40,000	$53,000

Categorized By Location

	Central	Eastern	Western	Northern
Sales-02	$52,000	$23,000	$64,000	$16,000
Sales-03	$55,000	$20,000	$40,000	$32,000
Sales-04	$52,000	$25,000	$67,000	$40,000
Sales-05	$53,000	$24,000	$60,000	$53,000

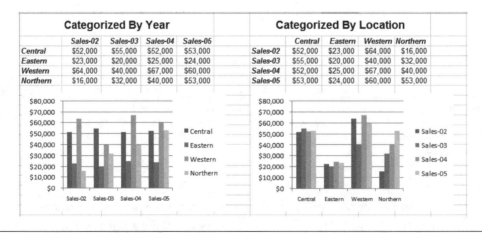

Figure 9-9. This worksheet shows the same data charted in two different ways. In the first table (left), the category axis lists the sales years, which are used to group the regions. In the second table (right), the category axis lists the regions, which are used to group the years.

The column chart example is fairly innocent. Although you may prefer one way of looking at the data over the other, they're relatively similar. However, most Excel charts aren't as forgiving. The line chart's a classic example.

In a line chart, each line represents a different series. If you list the sales years on the category axis (as shown on the left side of Figure 9-10), you end up with a separate line for each region that shows how the region has performed over time. But if you invert the table (shown on the right side), you end up with a chart that doesn't make much sense at all: a series of lines that connect different regions in each year. Figure 9-10 illustrates the problem.

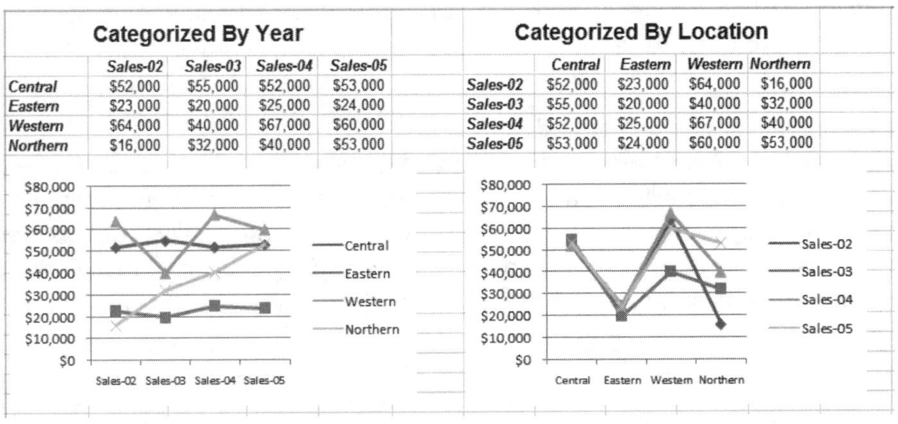

Categorized By Year

	Sales-02	Sales-03	Sales-04	Sales-05
Central	$52,000	$55,000	$52,000	$53,000
Eastern	$23,000	$20,000	$25,000	$24,000
Western	$64,000	$40,000	$67,000	$60,000
Northern	$16,000	$32,000	$40,000	$53,000

Categorized By Location

	Central	Eastern	Western	Northern
Sales-02	$52,000	$23,000	$64,000	$16,000
Sales-03	$55,000	$20,000	$40,000	$32,000
Sales-04	$52,000	$25,000	$67,000	$40,000
Sales-05	$53,000	$24,000	$60,000	$53,000

Figure 9-10. The chart on the left is pretty straightforward. The chart on the right shows a line for each year, which makes sense if you concentrate on what's being depicted, but mainly illustrates the way people can use computers to complicate things.

Clearly, when you create a line chart, you need to make sure the chart ends up using the data in a way that makes the most sense. So, how does Excel decide how to plot the data? Essentially, Excel makes a best guess about your data. If you have more rows than columns, Excel assumes that the first column represents the category axis. If you have more columns than rows (or if you have the same number of rows and columns), Excel assumes that the first *row* represents the category axis, as in Figure 9-10.

Fortunately, you have the power to override Excel's choice if you need to. Just select your chart, and then choose Chart Tools | Design → Data → Switch Row/Column.

UP TO SPEED

The Difference Between a Column and a Line

With simple column charts, life is easy. It doesn't matter too much what data you choose to use for your category axis because your choice simply changes the way data's grouped. Other chart types that follow the same principle include pie charts (which only allow one series), bar charts (like column charts, but oriented horizontally instead of vertically), and donut charts (where each series is a separate ring).

The same isn't true for line charts and most other types of Excel charts. The category axis you use for a line chart is important because the values in each series are connected (in this case, with a line). This line suggests some sort of "movement" or transition as values move from one category to another. That means it makes sense to use a line to connect different dates in a region (showing how sales have changed over time), but it probably doesn't make sense to use a line to connect different regions for each date. Technically, this latter scenario (shown on the right side of Figure 9-10) should show how yearly sales vary as you move from region to region, but it's just too counterintuitive for anyone to interpret it properly.

As a general rule of thumb, use time or date values for the category axis. You should do this *especially* for chart types like line and area, which usually show how things change over time.

Non-Contiguous Chart Ranges

So far, all the chart examples have assumed the data you want to chart is placed in a single, tightly packed table. But what if your information is actually scattered across your worksheet? This scenario may seem unlikely, but it actually occurs quite often when you need to chart only *part* of the data in a table. Say you want to create a chart using two or three columns, and these columns aren't next to each other. In this case, you need to take a few extra steps when you create your chart.

Imagine you have a table that records the monthly sales of 10 different regional offices. However, you want to create a chart that compares only two of these offices. Your chart will use the category information in column A (which contains the month in which the sales were recorded), along with the values in column C and column D (which contain the total amount of sales for the two regions in which you're interested).

The easiest way to create this chart is to start by selecting the non-contiguous range that contains your data. Here's what you need to do:

1. **First, use the mouse to select the data in column A.**

   Excel surrounds the data with a marquee. Don't click anywhere else yet.

2. **Then, hold down the Ctrl key while you move the mouse over and select the data in columns C and D.**

   Because you're holding down the Ctrl key, column A remains selected (see Figure 9-11).

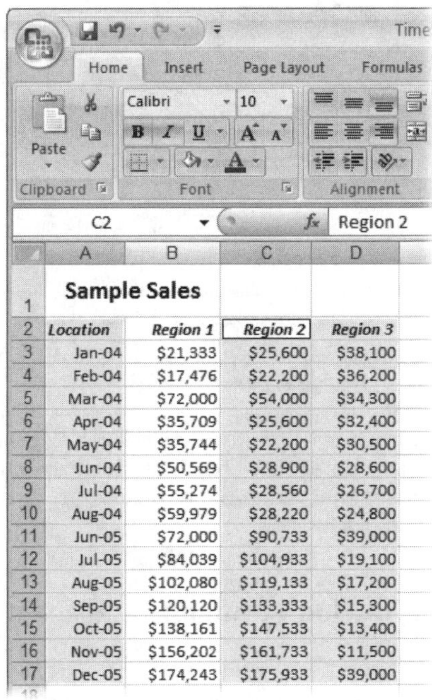

	A	B	C	D
1	Sample Sales			
2	Location	Region 1	Region 2	Region 3
3	Jan-04	$21,333	$25,600	$38,100
4	Feb-04	$17,476	$22,200	$36,200
5	Mar-04	$72,000	$54,000	$34,300
6	Apr-04	$35,709	$25,600	$32,400
7	May-04	$35,744	$22,200	$30,500
8	Jun-04	$50,569	$28,900	$28,600
9	Jul-04	$55,274	$28,560	$26,700
10	Aug-04	$59,979	$28,220	$24,800
11	Jun-05	$72,000	$90,733	$39,000
12	Jul-05	$84,039	$104,933	$19,100
13	Aug-05	$102,080	$119,133	$17,200
14	Sep-05	$120,120	$133,333	$15,300
15	Oct-05	$138,161	$147,533	$13,400
16	Nov-05	$156,202	$161,733	$11,500
17	Dec-05	$174,243	$175,933	$39,000

Figure 9-11. This worksheet shows a non-contiguous selection that ignores the numbers from region 1. When you create the chart, Excel includes only two series in the chart: one for region 2, and one for region 3.

3. **Now choose Insert → Charts, and then pick the appropriate chart type.**

   Excel creates the chart as usual, but uses only the data you selected in steps 1 and 2, leaving out all other columns.

This approach works most of the time. However, if you have trouble, or if the columns you want to select are spaced *really* far apart, then you can explicitly configure the range of cells for any chart. To do so, follow these steps:

1. **Create a chart normally, by selecting part of the data, and then, from the Insert → Chart section of the ribbon, choosing a chart type.**
2. **Select the chart, and then choose Chart Tools | Design → Data → Select Data.**

   The Select Data Source dialog box appears (Figure 9-12).

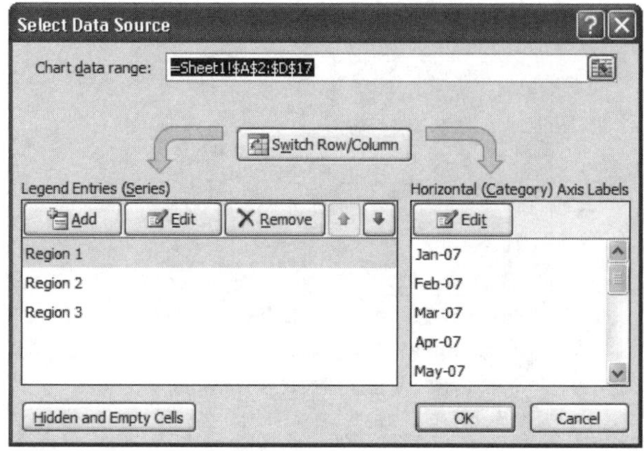

Figure 9-12. This dialog box demonstrates a handy secret about Excel charting. Excel not only records the whole range of cells that contain the chart data (as shown in the "Chart data range" text box), it also lets you see how it breaks that data up into a category axis and one or more series (as shown in the Legend Entries (Series) list).

3. **Remove any data series you don't want and add any new data series you do want.**

   To remove a series, select it in the Legend Entries (Series) list, and then click Remove.

   To add a new series, click Add, and then specify the appropriate cell references for the series name and the series values.

You can also click Switch Row/Column to change the data Excel uses as the category axis (page 278) and you can adjust some more advanced settings, like the way Excel deals with blank values, and the order in which it plots series (as explained in the following sections).

Changing the Order of Your Data Series

If your table has more than one series, Excel charts it in the order it appears on your worksheet (from left to right if your series are arranged in columns, or from top to bottom if they're arranged in rows). In a basic line chart, it doesn't matter which series Excel charts first—the end result is still the same. But in some charts, it *does* make a difference. One example is a stacked chart (Figure 9-14), in which Excel plots each new series on top of the previous one. Another example is a 3-D chart, where Excel plots each data series behind the previous one.

You can easily change your data series' order. Select your chart, and then choose Chart Tools | Design → Data → Select Data. Now select one of the series in the Legend Entries (Series) list, and then click the up or down arrow buttons to move it. Excel plots the series from top to bottom.

Changing the Way Excel Plots Blank Values

When Excel creates a chart, its standard operating procedure is to *ignore* all empty cells. The value of 0 doesn't count as an empty cell and neither does text (Excel plots any cells that contains text as a 0).

So what's the difference between an ignored cell and a cell that contains the number 0? In some types of charts, there's no difference. In a bar or pie chart, the result is the same—you don't see a bar or a pie slice for that data. However, in some charts, there *is* a difference. In a line chart a 0 value is plotted on the chart, but an empty cell causes a break in the line. In other words, the line stops just before the missing data, and then starts at the next point. This broken line indicates missing information.

If you don't like this behavior (perhaps because your empty cells really do represent 0 values), you can change it. Select your chart, and then choose Chart Tools | Design → Data → Select Data to get to the Select Data Source dialog box. Then, click the Hidden and Empty Cells button, which pops open a dialog box with three choices:

- **Gaps.** Excel leaves a gap where the information should be. In a line chart, this breaks the line (making it segmented). This option is the standard choice.
- **Zero.** Excel treats all blank cells as though they contain the number 0.
- **Span with line.** Excel treats all blank cells as missing information and tries to guess what should go in between. If a line chart goes from 10 to 20 with a blank cell in between, Excel interpolates the data point 15 and plots it.

You can also switch on or off the "Show data in hidden rows and columns" setting to tell Excel whether it should include cells that are hidden when creating a chart. This setting determines how Excel deals with data when you use filtering in a table, or when you explicitly hide rows or columns using the Home → Cells → Format → Hide & Unhide menu. Ordinarily, Excel treats these missing values just like blank values, and ignores them.

Chart Types

Although there's a lot to be said for simple column charts—they can illuminate trends in almost any spreadsheet—there are a few other basic chart types worth getting to know.

Column

By now, column charts probably seem like old hat. But column charts actually come in several different variations (technically known as *subtypes*). The main difference between the basic column chart and these subtypes is how they deal with data tables that have multiple series. The quickest way to understand the difference is to look at Figure 9-13, which shows a sample table of data, and Figure 9-14, which charts it using several different types of column charts.

NOTE

In order to learn about a chart subtype, you need to know its name. The name appears when you hover over the subtype thumbnail, either in the Insert → Charts list (Figure 9-2) or the Insert Chart dialog box (Figure 9-3).

Number of Students in Each Room		
	Male	Female
Cafeteria	42	24
Lounge	13	16
Games Room	73	40
Lecture Hall	31	40
Library	19	18

Figure 9-13. This simple table of data records the number of female and male students in several rooms at a university. The category is the room name, and there are two data series: the numbers of male students, and the numbers of female students. This data is perfect for a column chart, but different subtypes emphasize different aspects of the data, as you can see in Figure 9-14.

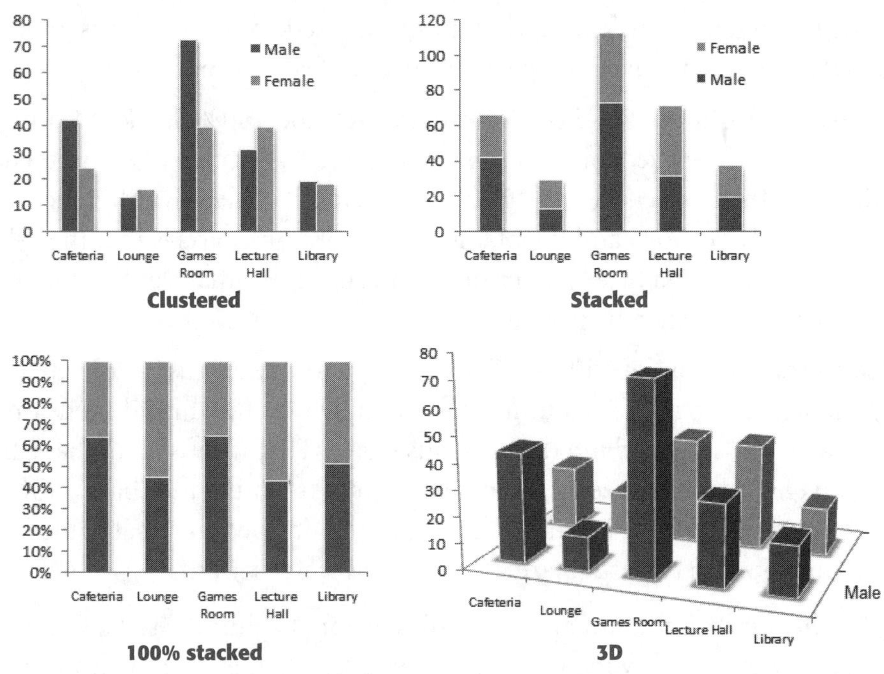

Figure 9-14. The Clustered Column makes it easy to compare the gender of students in each room, but makes it somewhat more difficult to compare different rooms. The Stacked Column is an elegant way to compress the data, and it lets you compare the total number of students in each room without losing the gender information. The 100% Stacked Column makes each column the same height, so it's useless for comparing total student numbers but perfect for comparing how the gender breakup varies depending on the room. (Notice the scale also changes to reflect that you're comparing percentage values.) Finally, the 3-D chart shows you all the data at once by placing the male student counts in front of the female student counts.

Here's a quick summary of your column chart choices:

- **Clustered Column.** In a clustered column, each value is shown in its own separate column. To form a cluster, the columns are grouped together according to category.
- **Stacked Column.** In a stacked column, each category has only one column. To create this column, Excel adds together the values from every series for each category. However, the column is subdivided (and color-coded), so you can see the contribution each series makes.
- **100% Stacked Column.** The 100% stacked column is like a stacked column in that it uses a single bar for each category, and subdivides that bar to show the proportion from each series. The difference is that a stacked column always stretches to fill the full height of the chart. That means stacked columns are designed to focus exclusively on the percentage distribution of results, not the total numbers.
- **3-D Clustered Column**, **Stacked Column in 3-D**, and **100% Stacked Column in 3-D.** Excel's got a 3-D version for each of the three basic types of column charts, including clustered, stacked, and 100 percent stacked. The only difference between the 3-D versions and the plain-vanilla column charts is that the 3-D charts are drawn with a three-dimensional special effect, that's either cool or distracting, depending on your perspective.
- **3-D Column.** While all the other 3-D column charts simply use a 3-D effect for added pizzazz, this *true* 3-D column chart actually uses the third dimension by placing each new series *behind* the previous series. That means if you have three series, you end up with three layers in your chart. Assuming the chart is tilted just right, you can see all these layers at once, although it's possible that some bars may become obscured, particularly if you have several series.

Along with the familiar column and three-dimensional column charts, Excel also provides a few more exotic versions that use cylinders, cones, and pyramids instead of ordinary rectangles. Other than their different shapes, these chart types work just like regular column charts. As with column and bar charts, you can specify how cylinder, cone, and pyramid charts should deal with multiple series. Your options include clustering, stacking, 100% stacking, and layering (true 3-D). See Figure 9-15 for an example.

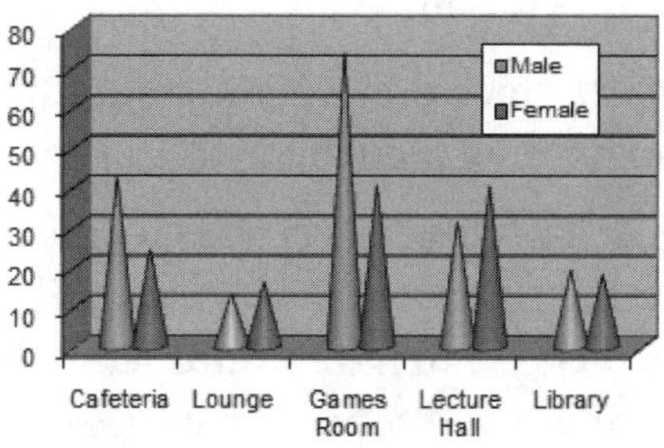

Figure 9-15. Though a cone chart looks a little different, it's really just a column chart in disguise.

Bar

The venerable bar chart is the oldest form of data presentation. Invented sometime in the 1700s, it predated the column and pie chart. Bar charts look and behave almost exactly the same as column charts—the only difference being that their bars stretch horizontally from left to right, unlike columns, which rise from bottom to top.

Excel provides almost the same set of subtypes for bar charts as it does for column charts. The only difference is that there's no true three-dimensional (or layered) bar chart, although there are clustered, stacked, and 100% stacked bar charts with a three-dimensional effect. Some bar charts also use cylinder, cone, and pyramid shapes.

TIP

Many people use bar charts because they leave more room for category labels. If you have too many columns in a column chart, Excel has a hard time fitting all the column labels into the available space.

Line

People almost always use line charts to show changes over time. Line charts emphasize trends by connecting each point in a series with a line. The category axis represents a time scale or a set of regularly spaced labels.

Excel provides several subtypes for line charts:

- **Line.** The classic line chart, which draws a line connecting all the points in the series. The individual points aren't highlighted.
- **Stacked Line.** In a stacked line chart, Excel displays the first series just as it would in the normal line chart, but the second line consists of the values of the first and second series added together. If you have a third series, it displays the total values of the first three series, and so on. People sometimes use stacked line charts to track things like a company's cumulative sales (across several different departments or product lines), as Figure 9-16, bottom, demonstrates. (Stacked area charts are another alternative.) Stacked line charts aren't as common as stacked bar and column charts.

NOTE

Lines can never cross in a stacked line chart because each series is added to the one (or ones) before it. You can change which line is stacked at the top by changing the order of the series. To do this, rearrange your table of data on the worksheet (Excel places the rightmost column on top).

- **100% Stacked Line.** A 100% stacked line chart works the same as a stacked line chart in that it adds the value of each series to the values of all the preceding series. The difference is that the last series always becomes a straight line across the top, and the other lines are scaled accordingly so that they show percentages. The 100% stacked line chart is rarely useful, but if you do use it, you'll probably want to put totals in the last series.
- **Line with Markers, Stacked Line with Markers, and 100% Stacked Line with Markers.** These subtypes are the same as the three previous line chart subtypes, except they add markers (squares, triangles, and so on) to highlight each data point in the series.
- **3-D Line.** This option draws ordinary lines without markers but adds a little thickness to each line with a 3-D effect.

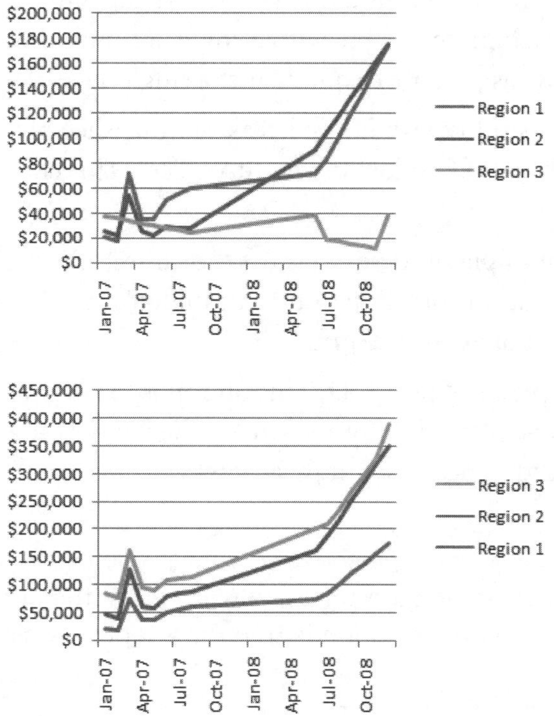

Figure 9-16. Here are two different line chart variations—both of which show the same information, although you'd never be able to tell that from looking at them quickly.

Top: This chart is a regular line chart that compares the sales for three different regions over time.

Bottom: This chart is a stacked line chart, which plots each subsequent line by adding the numbers from the earlier lines. That makes the stacked line chart a great vehicle for illustrating cumulative totals.

Pie

Pie charts show the breakdown of a series proportionally, using "slices" of a circle. Pie charts are one of the simplest types of charts, and one of the most recognizable.

Here are the pie chart subtypes you can choose from:

- **Pie.** The basic pie chart everyone knows and loves, which shows the breakup of a single series of data.

- **Exploded Pie.** The name sounds like a Vaudeville gag, but the exploded pie chart simply separates each piece of a pie with a small amount of white space. Usually, Excel charting mavens prefer to explode just a single slice of a pie for emphasis.
- **Pie of Pie.** With this subtype, you can break out one slice of a pie into its own, smaller pie (which is itself broken down into slices). This chart is great for emphasizing specific data.
- **Bar of Pie.** The bar of pie subtype is almost the same as the pie of pie subtype. The only difference is that the breakup of the combined slice is shown in a separate stacked bar, instead of a separate pie.
- **Pie in 3-D** and **Exploded Pie in 3-D.** This option is the pie and exploded pie types in three dimensions, tilted slightly away from the viewer for a more dramatic appearance. The differences are purely cosmetic.

NOTE

Pie charts can show only one series of data. If you create a pie chart for a table that has multiple data series, you'll see just the information from the first series. The best solution is to create separate pie charts for each series.

Area

An area chart is very similar to a line chart. The difference is that the space between the line and the bottom (category) axis is completely filled in. Because of this difference, the area chart tends to emphasize the sheer magnitude of values rather than their change over time. Figure 9-17 demonstrates.

Area charts exist in all the same flavors as line charts, including stacked and 100% stacked. You can also use subtypes that have a 3-D effect, or you can create a true 3-D chart that layers the series behind one another.

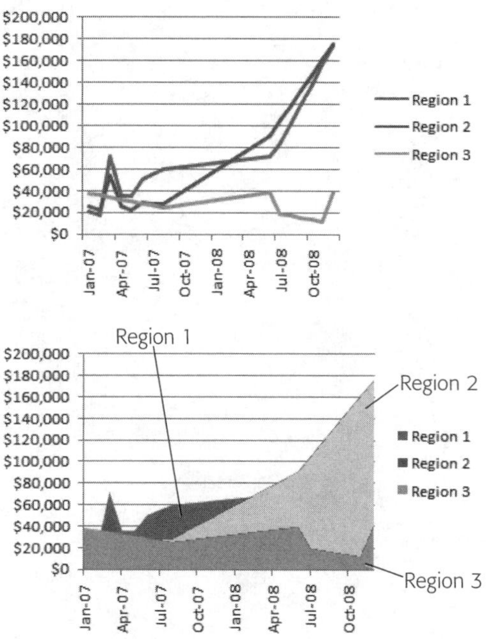

Figure 9-17. This example compares a traditional line chart (top) against the area chart (bottom). As you can see, the area chart makes a more dramatic point about the rising sales in region 2. However, it also obscures the results in region 1.

TIP

Stacked area charts make a lot of sense. In fact, they're easier to interpret than stacked line charts because you can easily get a feeling for how much contribution each series makes to the total by judging the thickness of the area.

CUSTOMIZING THE QUICK ACCESS TOOLBAR

A

- The Quick Access Toolbar

EXCEL, IN PREVIOUS VERSIONS, let its fans move toolbars, rearrange buttons, and even scramble the order of items in the main menu. Reckless customizers could transform Excel so completely that no one else would be able to use their computers, and the instructions in books like this one would be useless.

Excel 2007 clamps down on customization. Unless you're willing to get your hands dirty with a serious programming language, the ribbon is off limits. Instead, Excel lets you customize one tiny portion of screen real estate—the Quick Access toolbar.

This limitation might sound like a major one, but it's actually a reasonable compromise. People who love to tweak and refine their workplaces (you know who you are) get to add all the timesaving shortcuts they need. Everyone else can relax. No matter what computer you're working on, the ribbon is always there, with its comforting sameness and carefully organized tabs.

The Quick Access Toolbar

You've already seen the Quick Access toolbar (known to Excel nerds as the QAT). It's the micro-size toolbar that sits above the ribbon. The Quick Access toolbar has only icons, but you can hover over a button to get the full command text.

When you first start out with Excel, the Quick Access toolbar is a lonely place, with buttons for quickly saving your workbook and undoing or redoing the last action. However, Excel gives you complete control over this space, including the ability to add new buttons. You can most quickly add stuff by clicking the down-pointing arrow at the far right side. Figure A-1 shows how it works.

NOTE

If you don't like Quick Access toolbar's placement, Excel gives you one other option. Click the drop-down arrow, and then choose "Show Below the Ribbon" to move your toolbar under the ribbon so your mouse has less distance to travel.

You might add buttons to the Quick Access toolbar for two reasons:

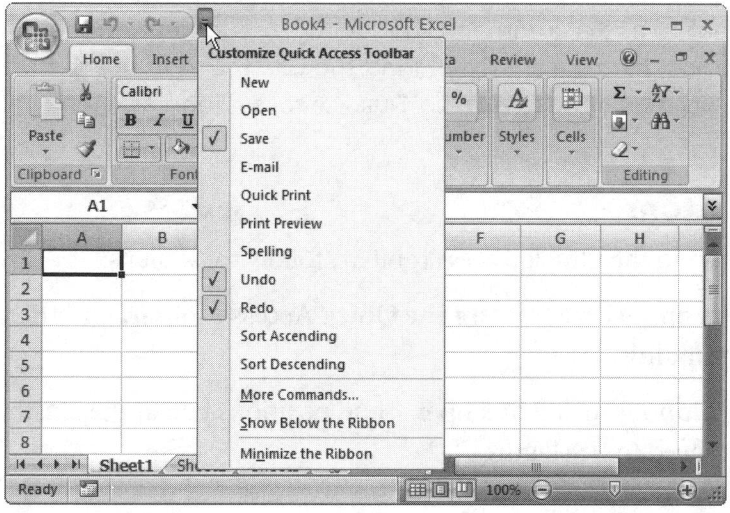

Figure A-1. When you click the drop-down arrow on the Quick Access toolbar, Excel shows a list of often-used commands that you can add just by clicking them. These commands include some for creating a new workbook, opening an existing workbook, emailing your current workbook, sending it to the printer with no questions asked, and firing up the spell checker. But to see all your possibilities, you need to choose More Commands.

- **To make it easier to get to a command you use frequently.** If it's in the Quick Access toolbar, you don't need to memorize a keyboard shortcut or change the current ribbon tab.
- **To get to a command that the ribbon doesn't provide.** Excel has a small set of unpopular commands that it lets you use, but that it doesn't keep in the ribbon. Many of these commands are holdovers from previous versions of Excel. If you have a long-lost favorite Excel feature that's missing, it just might be available via the Quick Access toolbar's extra buttons.

Keyboard lovers can also trigger the commands in the Quick Access toolbar with lightning speed thanks to Excel's KeyTips feature (page 7). When you press the Alt key, Excel displays a number superimposed over every command in the Quick Access toolbar (starting at 1 and going up from there). You can then press the number to trigger the command. So in the Quick Access toolbar shown in Figure A-1, Alt+1 saves the workbook, Alt+2 opens the Undo list, and so on.

Tip

If you want to add a command that duplicates something that's already in the ribbon, here's a shortcut. Find the command in the ribbon, right-click it, and then choose Add to Quick Access Toolbar.

Adding Buttons

To add a button to the Quick Access toolbar, follow these steps:

1. **Click the drop-down arrow on the Quick Access toolbar, and then choose More Commands.**

   The Excel Options dialog box opens, and positions you at the Customize section where you need to be (Figure A-2).

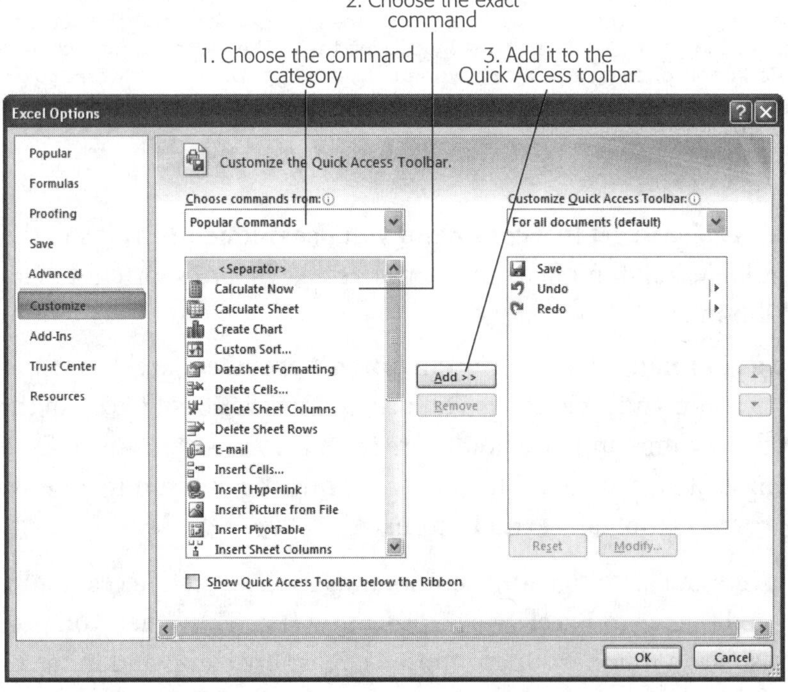

Figure A-2. The Customize section of the Excel Options window has two areas. The list on the left lets you choose the command you want to add. The list on the right shows the commands that currently appear in the Quick Access toolbar.

2. **Choose a category from the "Choose commands from" list.**

   The library of commands that you can add to the Quick Access toolbar is enormous. To make it easier to find what you want, it makes sense to choose a specific category. Many of the categories overlap—Excel simply provides them to make finding what you want easier. Here are the top choices:

   - **Popular Commands** gives you a short list of commands that Excel jockeys love. If you're trying to get quick access to a commonly used feature, you just might find it here.
   - **Commands Not in the Ribbon** provides all the leftovers—commands that Microsoft didn't consider useful enough to include in the ribbon. This list holds some commands that are superseded or partially duplicated by other commands, commands that are included in other dialog boxes, and commands that were used in previous versions of Excel and put out to pasture in this release.
   - **All Commands** includes the full list of choices. As with the other categories, it's ordered alphabetically.

   Under these categories are several additional categories that correspond to the Office menu and various tabs in the ribbon. For example, you can choose the Insert tab to see all the commands that appear in the ribbon's Insert tab.

3. **Once you've chosen the category you want, pick the command from the list below, and then click Add.**

   The command moves from the list on the left to the list on the right, placing it on the Quick Access toolbar (Figure A-3).

4. **You can repeat this process (starting at step 2) to add more commands.**

   Optionally, you can rearrange the order of items in the Quick Access toolbar. Just pick a command, and then use the up and down arrow buttons to move it. The topmost commands in the list are displayed to the left on the Quick Access toolbar.

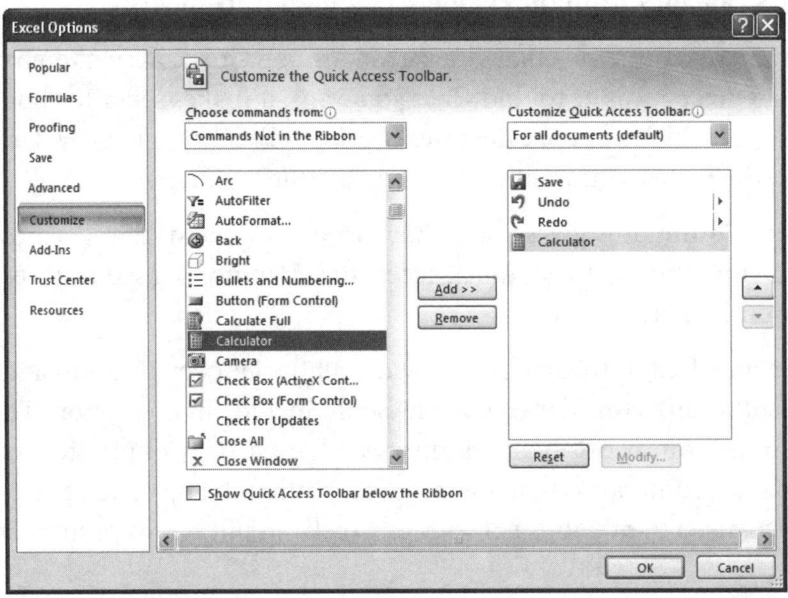

Figure A-3. In this example, the Calculator command is being added to the Quick Access toolbar, so you can pop open the handy Windows calculator whenever you need it, without leaving Excel.

Tip

If you've customized the heck out of your Quick Access toolbar and want to go back to a simpler way of life, then click the Reset button.

5. **When you're finished, click OK to return to Excel with the revamped Quick Access toolbar.**

   Adding a Quick Access toolbar isn't a lifetime commitment. To get rid of a command you don't want anymore, right-click it, and then choose Remove from Quick Access Toolbar.

Note

You might notice the tempting Modify button, which lets you change a command's name and picture. Unfortunately, it works only for macro commands (programmable shortcuts).

Customizing Specific Workbooks

Do you have a button or two that you're using incessantly, but just for a specific workbook? In this situation, it may not make sense to customize the Quick Access toolbar in the normal way. If you do, you'll get your extra buttons in *every* workbook you use, including those in which the extras aren't useful.

Excel has a great feature to help you out in this situation. You can customize the Quick Access toolbar for an individual workbook. That way, whenever you open that workbook, the buttons you need appear in the Quick Access toolbar. When you close it (or open another workbook in a separate window), the buttons disappear.

NOTE

Customizing individual workbooks has advantages and disadvantages. The disadvantage is that you need to perform this task separately for every workbook, which can take a lot of time. The advantage is that your customizations are recorded right in your workbook file. As a result, they stick around if you open the workbook on someone else's computer.

To customize the toolbar for a single workbook, follow the same steps that you used in the previous section. Start by clicking the Quick Access toolbar's drop-down arrow, and then choosing More Commands. However, before you add any commands, change the selection in the "Customize Quick Access Toolbar" list, which appears just above the list of commands in the Quick Access toolbar. Instead of using "For all documents (default)", choose your workbook's name (as in "For SecretSanta.xlsx"). This list starts off empty. Then, follow the normal steps to add buttons.

When Excel displays the Quick Access toolbar, it combines the standard buttons (as configured in the previous section) with any buttons you've defined for the current workbook (Figure A-4).

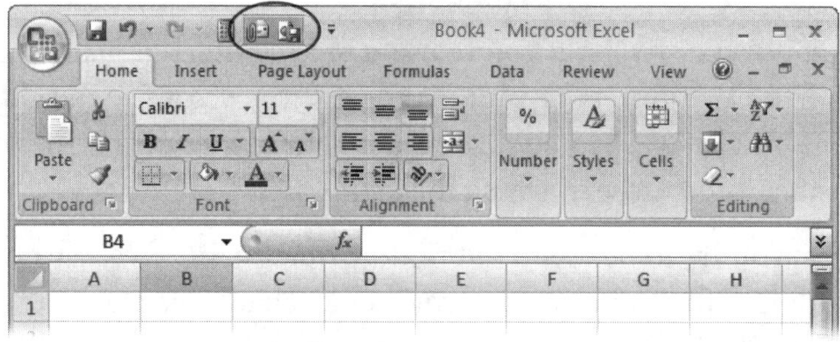

Figure A-4. The workbook-specific buttons (circled) always appear after the standard buttons and have a slightly different appearance (a darker background). You can define the same button as a standard button and a workbook-specific button, in which case it appears twice.

NOSTALGIA CORNER

What Happens to My Custom Toolbars?

Using the customization features in previous versions of Excel, you might have designed your own specialized toolbars (which you could then attach to a workbook file). The bad news is that Excel no longer provides this feature, so you can't enhance or modify your existing toolbars. The good news is that you can still access your custom toolbar, just in a slightly different way.

All the buttons from custom toolbars and custom menus end up on a separate tab, named Add-Ins. This tab appears only if there's a custom toolbar or menu in the workbook. When it appears, it ends up at the every end of the series of tabs. This arrangement may not be the prettiest, but it makes sure that the solutions Excel gurus have already created will keep working in Excel 2007.

If you want to keep your custom commands closer at hand, you can add them to the Quick Access toolbar. There are three items you need to look for (in the All Commands list): Custom Toolbars, Menu Commands, and Toolbar Commands. When you add these to the Quick Access toolbar, they appear as drop-down menus that, when clicked, show all the custom commands in your current workbook.

INDEX

Symbols

Numbers

A

B

C

D

E

F

G

H

I

J

K

L

M

N

O

P

Q

R

S

T

U

V

W

X

Y

Z

COLOPHON

Marlowe Shaeffer was the production editor for *Excel 2007 for Starters: The Missing Manual*. Sanders Kleinfeld and Adam Witwer provided quality control. Dawn Mann wrote the index.

The cover of this book is based on a series design originally created by David Freedman and modified by Mike Kohnke, Karen Montgomery, and Fitch (*www.fitch.com*). Back cover design, dog illustration, and color selection by Fitch.

Tom Ingalls designed the interior layout, which was modified by Ron Bilodeau. Robert Romano and Jessamyn Read produced the illustrations.

Related Titles from O'Reilly

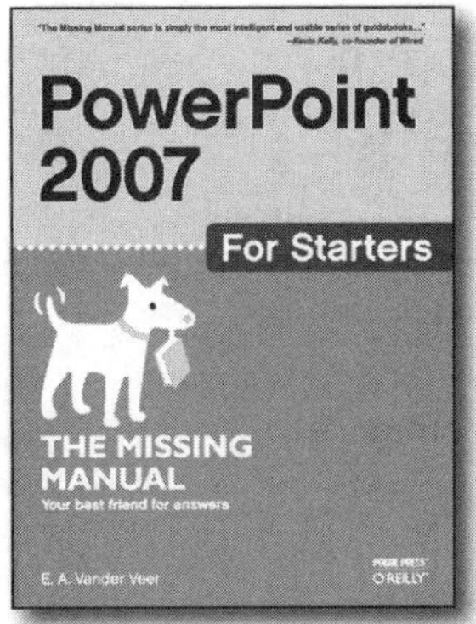

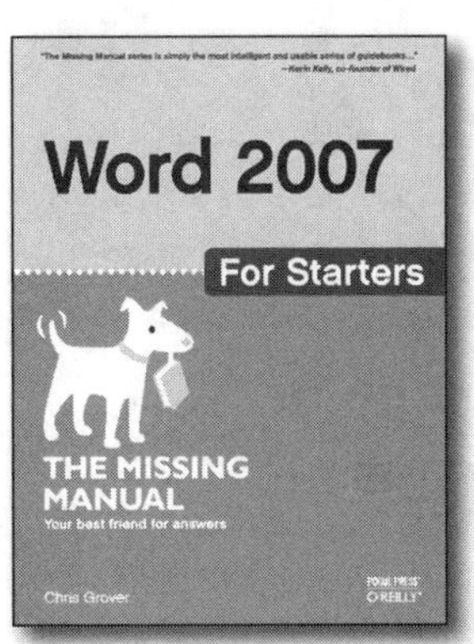

Missing Manuals

Access 2003 for Starters: The Missing Manual

Access 2007 for Starters: The Missing Manual

Access 2007: The Missing Manual

AppleScript: The Missing Manual

AppleWorks 6: The Missing Manual

CSS: The Missing Manual

Creating Web Sites: The Missing Manual

Digital Photography: The Missing Manual

Dreamweaver 8: The Missing Manual

eBay: The Missing Manual

Excel 2003 for Starters: The Missing Manual

Excel 2007: The Missing Manual

FileMaker Pro 8: The Missing Manual

Flash 8: The Missing Manual

FrontPage 2003: The Missing Manual

GarageBand 2: The Missing Manual

Google: The Missing Manual, 2nd Edition

Home Networking: The Missing Manual

iMovie HD 6: The Missing Manual

iPhoto 6: The Missing Manual

iPod: The Missing Manual, 5th Edition

Mac OS X: The Missing Manual, Tiger Edition

Office 2004 for Macintosh: The Missing Manual

PCs: The Missing Manual

Photoshop Elements 5: The Missing Manual

PowerPoint 2007 for Starters: The Missing Manual

PowerPoint 2007: The Missing Manual

QuickBooks 2006: The Missing Manual

Quicken 2006 for Starters: The Missing Manual

Switching to the Mac: The Missing Manual, Tiger Edition

The Internet: The Missing Manual

Windows 2000 Pro: The Missing Manual

Windows XP for Starters: The Missing Manual

Windows XP Home Edition: The Missing Manual, 2nd Edition

Windows XP Pro: The Missing Manual, 2nd Edition

Windows Vista: The Missing Manual

Windows Vista for Starters: The Missing Manual

Word 2007 for Starters: The Missing Manual

Word 2007: The Missing Manual

Other O'Reilly Titles

Excel 2007 Pocket Reference

Writing Excel Macros with VBA, 2nd edition

Excel Hacks

Analyzing Business Data with Excel

Excel Scientific and Engineering Cookbook

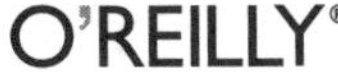

Our books are available at most retail and online bookstores.
To order direct: 1-800-998-9938 • *order@oreilly.com* • *www.oreilly.com*
Online editions of most O'Reilly titles are available by subscription at *safari.oreilly.com*

The O'Reilly Advantage

Stay Current and Save Money

Order books online:
www.oreilly.com/order_new

Questions about our products or your order:
order@oreilly.com

Join our email lists: Sign up to get topic specific email announcements or new books, conferences, special offers and technology news
elists@oreilly.com

For book content technical questions:
booktech@oreilly.com

To submit new book proposals to our editors:
proposals@oreilly.com

Contact us:
O'Reilly Media, Inc.
1005 Gravenstein Highway N.
Sebastopol, CA U.S.A. 95472
707-827-7000 or
800-998-9938
www.oreilly.com

Did you know that if you register your O'Reilly books, you'll get automatic notification and upgrade discounts on new editions?

And that's not all! Once you've registered your books you can:

» Win free books, T-shirts and O'Reilly Gear

» Get special offers available only to registered O'Reilly customers

» Get free catalogs announcing all our new titles (US and UK Only)

Registering is easy! Just go to www.oreilly.com/go/register

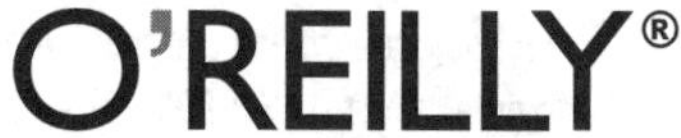

Better than e-books

Buy *Excel 2007 for Starters: The Missing Manual* and access the digital edition FREE on Safari for 45 days.

Go to www.oreilly.com/go/safarienabled
and type in coupon code FCQPCFH

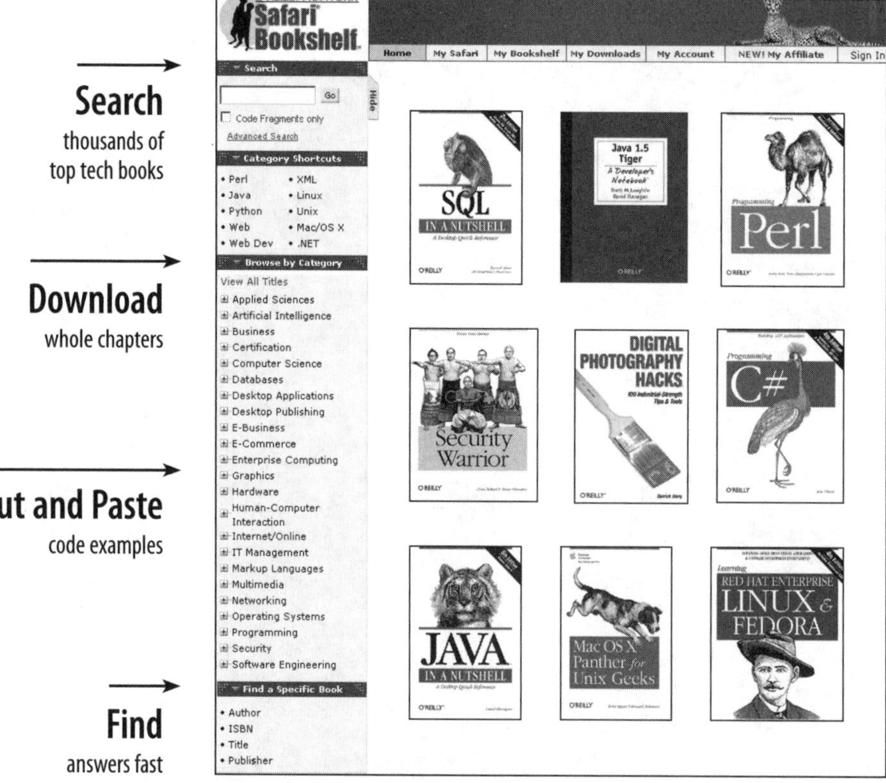

Search Safari! The premier electronic reference library for programmers and IT professionals.

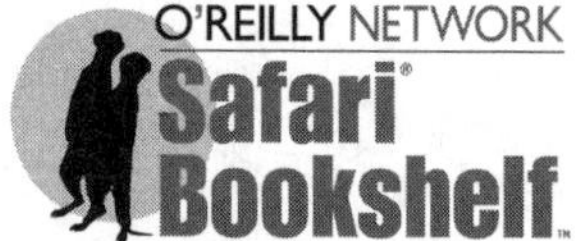

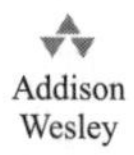

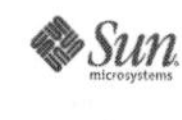

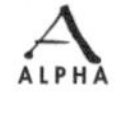

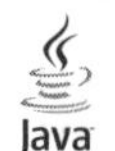

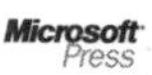

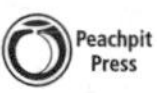

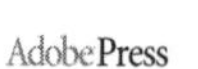

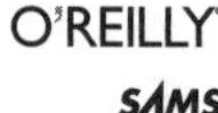

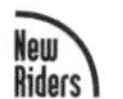

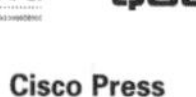

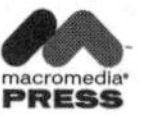

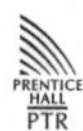